Barefoot to Wings

Albert V. Malone

Copyright © 2007 by Albert V. Malone

ISBN 0-7414-3784-8

Published by:

INFI∞ITY
PUBLISHING.COM

1094 New DeHaven Street, Suite 100
West Conshohocken, PA 19428-2713
Info@buybooksontheweb.com
www.buybooksontheweb.com
Toll-free (877) BUY BOOK
Local Phone (610) 941-9999
Fax (610) 941-9959

Printed in the United States of America

Printed on Recycled Paper

Published February 2007

CONTENTS

"Barefoot to Wings" Photo Captions by Chapter & Number

2nd row down, L. to R.; Dewey Burleson Clyde Burleson, Lily (Pidcock) Burleson, FlossieBurleson, Lee Burleson, Alf Patterson. Mattie (Burleson) Patterson, Claude Hobson, Nora Burleson, Rebecca (Burleson) Hobson.
3rd row, seated L. to R.; Reverend Brown, Mary (Burleson) DeNoon, Bill DeNoon, Baby Hugh DeNoon, Mary, a.k.a. Molly (Norvel) Burleson, baby Norma Burleson, John W. Burleson and Mrs. Mary Pidcock
4th row, L. to R; Viola Burleson, Sam Burleson and Lee DeNoon.

13 Grandparents, Amanda (Ketchum) and Marion F. Malone.

13b Bert & Nora Malone (left) and Raymond & Viola Malone on right—circa 1920.

16 14 Author in "beanie" and green suspenders as a freshman at MSM.

15 Bill of tuition and fees at MSM in 1942.

18 16 Ab, Wib and Gib—furlough, Christmas, 1943.

17 Ab and Wib, March, 1944.

22 18 Left to right: Copilot Laws, Bombardier Beno, Pilot Bergman and Navigator Malone in front of quarters at Hethel Air base in England.

19 Author with cigar at Hethel.

20 B-24 Liberator bomber R+, "Delectable-Doris."

21 "Delectable Doris"

22 Bombs away from a 389th Bomb Group

FOREWORD

I was moved to write this book because I wanted my daughters, son and granddaughters to have a basic knowledge of their genealogy on the paternal side and to endow them with a kinship to living and growing up during an era when conditions could be considered primitive relative to contemporary standards.

While our children were growing up I would regale them at times with stories of my childhood, but memories dim and I would find they had forgotten. And why wouldn't they forget? —No lights to turn on with switches, no refrigerators, no water from faucets, only two dresses or two pairs of trousers (one for Sunday and one for the other days), no hot showers or bathrooms, washing clothes on a scrub board, and the list can go on and on. Most kids have never seen milk emerging from anything other than a plastic or boxed container. Even when school classes are taken for tours of modern dairies they see milk only after it has been removed from long lines or carousels of cows via mechanical connections and gathering systems. Few will ever experience the joy of squeezing a stream of milk from a cow's teat into the face and mouth of a barnyard cat standing upright on hind legs.

I am concerned that schools do not appear to be teaching history as it happened. I cannot remember my kids while in grade or high school asking me about my involvement in World War II. They have inquired but little about memorabilia. I'm hopeful that these memoirs will not only help my children know their father better, but will foster a readiness to challenge some of the politically motivated distortions of American war history. Maybe they will be prompted to request some military insignia, medals or other mementoes.

As I penned these memoirs and wrote many of the inimitable and engaging tales and expressions of our Ozark neighbors I became convinced that this compendium would be of general interest—both to those reading for pleasure and to those interested in Ozark and military history.

I have written from my heart and as I would talk with you. Just as I am I come. Some writers and editors would modify my language, text and style, but they would change me too, and I decline their well-meant intentions.

This book is dedicated to my children but I hope there will be many other readers who will enjoy and vicariously experience some Ozarkian and military history.

Albert V. Malone

PREFACE

The author was born in December 1923, and grew up in a small rural community named Seaton Missouri. The population of Seaton consisted of the author, his parents and siblings. Seaton gained its status as a city by virtue of the post office located there within the confines of a general store operated by the father who was also the postmaster. Seaton is located in south central Missouri in a region generally classified as the Ozark Plateau Country. It is almost equidistant from the cities of Rolla, Salem and St. James though actual distances and routes of travel were contingent on whether the creeks were up or not or if spring thaws didn't render the dirt roads impassable except by horseback.

There is no residence at the Seaton site anymore. The replacement store building constructed in 1956 remains but not in use. The post office was closed in 1965. The site is located on state route JJ but Seaton road signs at the site were removed by thieves and have not been replaced by the Missouri Highway Department. Seaton is no longer identified on Missouri highway maps. However it is identified on United States Geological Survey maps and also can be located on other map sites on the Internet.

The economy of the area was based on hardscrabble farming and employment in the timber industries. It was an era of living without rural electric power and all the amenities associated with its applications. Most farming operations were dependent on horsepower on the hoof.

The author describes country life as he lived it from birth through schooling and into the World War II era. He takes you through the tribulations of the droughts, torna-does and the great depression and describes the life of the community as the people endured and survived by toil, amid tears, love, laughter and compassion for their neighbors. Comparisons to contemporary living are drawn and should be of interest to students of generational history.

The author's experiences during the World War II era are delineated, beginning with training in the Army Air Forces and culminating with combat flying in the European theatre of operations. Thirty combat missions as a navigator of B-24 Liberator bombers are chronicled and detailed. The history buffs of World War II flying will find much in these stories to enhance their history of the strategic bombing wars waged against Germany.

Transition from war to peace did not come easily to the young warrior, but a return to the relative tranquility of the Ozarks was beneficial to the reconciliation of mind and soul with the ultimate decision to return to college and preparation for campaigns and battles of more benign nature.

ACKNOWLEDGMENTS

I thank my dear wife, LauraBelle, for her encouragement and assistance with editing and compilation. Also, for her patience as I complained about my travails with her typewriter and its eccentricities. My thanks, too, to daughters Teddi, Terrell and Penette for their editing of the draft manuscript and insightful advice.

I am especially grateful to Mrs. Cora Jeffrey for providing a copy of the log of her husband Howard, who compiled and wrote "Logge of Ye Old Static Chaser", his recording of flying combat missions as radio operator of B-24 Liberators with the 389th Bomb Group of the Eighth Air Force. His log provided much valuable information, which was not recorded in my navigational logs and charts. "Jeff" or "Bink" and I were crewmates during the period when I flew my last fifteen combat missions. "Jeff" indeed was one of the finest airmen whose competence and calmness under fire was a comforting and stabilizing influence on the rest of the crew--a true gentleman and kind friend. "Jeff" passed away at his home in Norwich, N.Y. on 18th July 1996.

At the completion of my first draft of this manuscript, both my older brother Wilbert and sister Kathleen were living. Wilbert died on April 21, 1998 after an extended illness caused by complications from a stroke. Kathleen died on March 2, 1999 after a two-year battle with cancer. After his stroke Wilbert could not speak effectively but his mind was sharp as a tack and his memory excellent until a short while before he passed away.

I informed Wilbert and Kathleen that this manuscript was in preparation for publishing, and they would be included in some of my stories about growing up in

Seaton. Both approved of my efforts and looked forward to seeing my writings in print.

Wib was a sounding board and counselor as I related some of my stories and plied him with questions while we visited during his illness. In some instances his memory was better than mine, and by a nod or shake of his head he confirmed or agreed with my presentations. His grins of approval and attempts at laughter are cherished memories.

Family and friends miss my brother and sister, and I hope this book will be a welcome reference for reminiscing and remembering them.

The photo of the B-24 Liberator bomber on my cover page shows "Delectable Doris" in a combat zone during World War II operations. I tell about our flying "Doris" on several missions and then relate the story of her demise in the Epilogue of this book.

This photo was taken by Army Air Force photographic services and was given to me along with other related aircraft photos after completing my missions with the Second Division of the Eighth Air Force.

1/　　　　　Early Dew

The morning of 29th December 1923 dawned on a cold and snowy landscape at Seaton, Missouri. The winds of the northwesterner continued with sweeping snow flurries during the day and by nightfall the country roads were becoming difficult to navigate with a Model-T Ford.

The weather does not acknowledge the incoming or departure of the inhabitants of this world. And it was so on this late December day when the birthing pains of Nora V. Malone became intense and frequent.

Late in the evening Bert Malone, husband of Nora, was nervously watching the clock and knew it was time to go for Doc Dillon who resided at Winkler about four miles away. Earlier, Bert had managed to crank the engine of his Model-T into life and had parked it in a location near the house where it would be more sheltered from the wind and swirling snow. He had blanketed the hood and radiator to keep out the snow and retain heat to keep the engine cooling water from freezing.

Bessie Happel, wife of Ed Happel and the recognized midwife of the Seaton community, had arrived in the afternoon and would hold down the fort until Doc Dillon arrived.

The T's engine roared to life again after a few hefty cranks and Bert headed out into the night on the snow-filled roads. The side curtains were loose and torn in places and the wind whistled through and around the driver.

Doc Dillon maintained a snappy horse and buggy rig for traveling but with the advent of more autos in the area he preferred that someone drive and fetch him in an auto.

Bert made it through to Winkler and after Doc had gathered up his medical bag, put on earmuffs and a long coat they headed for Seaton. By this time the storm had relented and with less wind they could follow the car tracks left from the outgoing trip. The T's lights operated off the magneto-generator and provided poor illumination at best and would dim with diminishing speed.

Motorists had to slow to maneuver the ford at Norman creek and when coming out would immediately have to climb a steep hill on the west side.

Without momentum Bert spun in the snow and threw rocks on the first hill out of the creek but kept on digging and after reaching the top of the hill got a better run at the remaining Cooper hills to get up and over for the final leg to Seaton.

Doc claimed he made it just in time to make the delivery but my mother said she had her doubts. Anyway, I, Albert Vernon Malone arrived in this earthly veil of tears and through the grace and goodness of God have survived to the time of this writing.

My parents moved to Seaton in late 1922 and I have the distinction of being the first natural born citizen of Seaton.

When Doc Dillon filled out the papers of birth certification he spelled my last name as Melone. I had kicked around the United States and overseas with the armed forces of the United States without ever needing a birth certificate and was unaware of Dillon's mistake until I needed birth certification to apply for a passport and got a copy of my birth certificate from the Missouri Bureau of Vital Statistics.

I was then living in the Syracuse, New York area and did not have time to go through the process of obtaining a corrected copy. I took my problem to a very nice and accommodating lady at the Syracuse passport office and with copies of military records and my military picture I.D. card she filed for my passport. My passport was issued promptly and in time to obtain my required visas.

With due respect to Doc Dillon he was acquainted with some persons on our genealogical tree who had been using Melone as their surname and that may have been on his mind when he wrote out my birth record.

Purportedly, I was a skinny and colicky baby, exhibiting at an early age an obstreperous and cantankerous nature.

There is no picture proof of such contentions but it might be said that there is more truth than poetry in that observation since some may argue that my character and nature have not changed much since those early days.

As I grew up I developed a good ball-pitching arm and it was fair at pitching hay too. Development must have begun early as they told me later that I handily pitched my food and food containers from the table as I was learning to consume foods other than breast milk.

My parents purchased a special and extra heavy crockery type baby bowl for presentation of my food and which I could not lift to unceremoniously and indiscriminately dump my food or throw the bowl from the table.

This bowl is now in my possession and is one of my few cherished antiques. I wonder if I could bust it today. Occasionally, my loving wife says she would be willing to test it on my head, but she really likes the bowl and it occupies a special place on one of her kitchen display shelves. It is in good condition with only craze marks in the glaze and some faded lettering.

I became uninhibited early it seems and before my age of recall—I drank "coal oil" (kerosene) one day while following my Dad around the storage area at his store and warehouse. Incidentally, I was in high school before I learned a "wirehouse" as pronounced by us was a warehouse—actually we enunciated it more like "warrhouse". Well, they say I survived the swigging of coal oil without any serious consequences though even today I wonder. Could it have affected the left lobe of my brain? I have always been excessively right-handed and hardly able to scratch with my left hand. Or is it the other way around—the right brain lobe controlling the motor functions? I never can keep that straight along with other miscellaneous trivia.

In the same era I strayed into the nearby woods and was traveling away from home when my parents found me at dusk—they said the red coat I was wearing was shining through the gathering darkness and our old dog "Shep" was pacing alongside. Possibly we were headed for the Garrison place because Mrs. Garrison sort of catered to me. Once I was making a big fuss in the store for one of the little cast iron toy cars on sale (already had one) and Dad resisted with a firm no. Mrs. Garrison, who happened to be present, picked me up, carried me around and behind the store counter, got a car off the shelf and gave it to me. She had no inclination whatsoever to pay for it. Dad didn't make a whimper. In later years I realized that Mrs. Garrison, a rather rambunctious and homely woman had him buffaloed with her aggressiveness. She also was a good customer.

My earliest recall goes back to about the age of five. It was in this era that my mother lost twin boys at birth in our home. They were premature but appeared perfectly normal. It's likely that under proper medical care they would have survived. Even today, when visiting Morrison cemetery in Dent County I wonder what the twins would have been like if they had lived.

My sister was sixteen months younger than I and I was always teasing her and trying to lead her into mischief. Of course, when we got into trouble I had someone to share the blame and Dad was always easier on her when disciplining came into play.

We lived only about a quarter mile from the Highland ("Blackjack"). schoolhouse. The schoolhouse foundation consisted of columns of stones used for footings and supports of perimeter and structural cross members and at such spacing and heights as to allow easy access for small folks underneath the floor. One spring day I talked my sister into going with me to the schoolhouse. I was five then (no kindergarten in those halcyon days). School was in session. We took up large sticks then crawled under the schoolhouse and started beating on the underside of the floor with our cudgels. I would have loved to have seen the faces of the students when the racket began and we soon did see the face of Austin Bell, the teacher, as he came roaring out the door. We fled for home through the woods and without looking back as Austin's growls followed us as we tore into the woods.

4

It seems I tried to tag along with Dad wherever he went and without hat or coat no matter the inclemency of the weather. It is no wonder that I have been plagued with sinus troubles most of my life.

I remember well the hot spring day when I was riding with Dad in the topless open Model-T Ford headed for Clinton Bank, about three miles from our place at Seaton. In those days Clinton Bank was a thriving place with a schoolhouse, a general store operated by my uncle Elmer Malone, a seasonal canning factory and rail yards for handling incoming freight and shipments from a large prop and railroad tie purchasing operation that was conducted by Elmer and my grandfather Malone.

The rail service came by a spur line from Bangert and ended at Decamp to the north about six miles away. The line was sometimes described as the Winkler branch and Winkler was the next station just a mile north from Clinton Bank. A station between Winkler and Decamp was named Vilean. The main St.Louis & San Francisco rail line ran from Salem through Bangert to Cuba and thence to St.Louis. The railroad tracks ran right in front of the Clinton Bank store and within a few feet of the store's front porch. I was always thrilled to see the huffing engine stop and chug through.

Clinton Bank got its name because of iron ore mining. From 1900 and into the World War I era the hematite iron ore deposits of the area were extensively mined. Open type mining locations were often called banks (banks of ore deposits) and significant banks of iron ore were found at the Clinton Bank site. There is no official history of the Clinton naming but it is thought that a Mr.Clinton was a mining engineer or a high-ranking official of the mining company that explored and first opened the Clinton bank or "cut".

Several mines were located in the Clinton Bank area including shaft type operations. Mines were located at Decamp and at sites in between Decamp and Clinton Bank. One open cut mine was situated just west of Seaton and named the Smith Mine. When hunting with my brother in the area of the Smith Mine during our early teens only a few vestiges of mining activities remained—today it would likely be difficult to define the specific mining site.

The Winkler railroad spur was constructed primarily to serve the needs of the iron ore mines. The mines required lots of timber props for shoring of shafts and runs and the railroads required rail ties—therefore sponsoring a large business in the cutting and hewing of such timbers. My Dad described his employment during his teen years in both the mines and the tie-making businesses. Most of the ties were hand hewn using a broad ax and adz. My grandfather Malone was a grader and buyer of ties and shipped props and ties to mines and railroads in several states. These businesses were well supported by a vast supply of timber in the contiguous areas. However, by the end of World War I much of the forests with the choice stands of oaks had been severely depleted.

At the store location Uncle Elmer also operated a canning factory for a short while. Tomatoes were purchased from local farmer-growers and processed using wood-fueled pit furnaces to cook the fruit for peeling and canning. Ladies from the surrounding communities were employed to do much of the hand labor required in the process of preparation, canning, labeling and packaging. Tinned cans were used for containers and sealed in a manner pretty much as that of today but without an automated mechanization system. A poor growing season combined with the onset of the Great Depression caused this enterprise to be terminated.

The Clinton Bank mines and other mines in the Winkler rail branch territory closed soon after the end of World War I because they were not able to compete with better grades of ores and more extensive deposits in other locations such as the Mesabi Range in Minnesota.

With the onset of the Great Depression the expansion of the railroads ceased and the tie business declined to virtually nothing at Clinton Bank. Some mining props business continued for a while but also petered out as the depression deepened. At the same time most other businesses at Clinton

Bank and at other locations along the Winkler branch such as Vilean and Decamp also severely declined or petered out.

The Clinton Bank store was closed for some time and then reopened a couple of different times by members of my grandfather's family. The store was not really successful again and burned to the ground in 1939.

The original Clinton Bank schoolhouse survived into the 1950's until the consolidation of rural schools ended its services. The building was converted to a combination residence-general store and today is used as a residence only.

The Winkler railroad spur ceased operations as the depression continued and never officially operated again. During World War II the rails were taken up and used for scrap steel in vital war defense manufacturing plants. The roadbed was abandoned after ties were removed. Later some of the roadbed was developed into county roads. Vestiges of the roadbed are yet visible in many places.

To return to our trip to Clinton Bank when I was about five years old. We were traveling on our Seaton road and at a point only about a quarter mile before junction with the Salem-to-St.James road on which Clinton Bank was located. We were just a half-mile from Clinton Bank when a flock of wild turkeys crossed the road in front of us and ran into the woods. Dad stopped the Model-T (hardly on a dime), jumped out, grabbed his ubiquitous 12-gauge single barrel shotgun and took after them. After about 15 minutes he came back huffing and puffing but empty handed except for the shotgun and a handful of cartridges.

Our "T" didn't sport a starter and had to be hand cranked. Dad cranked and cranked and cranked some more while my vocabulary became broader with each crank, but to no avail. Red-faced with blistered hands and exhausted he ceased cranking. Probably the "T" engine was too hot for the magneto to function properly or maybe the trouble was vapor lock. Anyway, after waiting about 30 minutes the old jalopy cranked okay and we clattered on to Clinton Bank, but we had missed the arrival and departure of the train. Dad's mood improved some as the day wore on. Nonetheless, I warily kept on good behavior.

The nature of the Model T continued to be irascible and unpredictable. It was still hard to start at times so it was parked uphill about 100 yards from the county road to allow us to push it off to gain enough momentum to induce the engine to start. This procedure worked well until one day uncle Fred Castleman got in to drive it off and for once in my life I must have been psychic and didn't climb in while the rig was up on the hill. My brother Wib got in with Fred after giving the "T" a push to start it rolling. Half way down the hill Fred hit a bump while working on the bands and spark controls and bounced into a big hickory tree in the yard—almost head on. Fred came off with some scratches. Wib thought his nose was broken but it turned out to be a major nosebleed.

Dad worked on the old "T" a lot, repairing and installing new parts but it finally played out and we didn't get another car for nearly a year. The car's top and side curtains had been worn out long before and we had traveled in the fresh air summer and winter. The depression was raging but more about that later.

Eating bowl used by author as a baby

2/   Every Thing I Needed To Know

Kindergartners were non-existent during my days in our neck of the woods. I was four months shy of age six when entering first grade at "Blackjack", a one-room country school with few amenities. The door and windows were bereft of screens. The walls and ceiling had not been insulated and the heating system was a sheet metal wood-fueled stove stoked by hand. The air-conditioning system consisted of windows controlled up or down by the physical exertions of students at the command of the teacher—and like today's highly developed mechanical and electrical sytems not everyone could be pleased with the control settings.

Our water supply was a cistern filled by runoff from the roof as collected by eaves troughs when there was enough rain. During drought periods the supply might have to be replenished by hauling in containers of water to be poured into the cistern or to be used directly from the container. At the time we thought we were quite modern with a chain-and-cups hand cranked pump for retrieving the water.

Electricity was not available until after the end of World War II. School sessions were conducted during daylight hours. On dark gloomy days if you were not seated near a window you just squinted more than normal. When community meetings and events were held in the schoolhouse at night lighting was provided by kerosene lamps mounted on special hangers along the wall.

"Blackjack" sanitary disposal facilities were outstandingly primitive. Girls went into the northwest contiguous forest and the boys used the nearby east woods to relieve themselves. It was incumbent of each individual to provide personal sanitary accessories and woe to the neophyte who was not educated to the hazards of the attractive and soft green leaves of the poison ivy plant. After the economic throes of the depression eased somewhat the school board of directors managed somehow to scratch up enough money for materials and labor to build two outdoor privies on school ground near the northwest grove of trees. Then our facilities could be described as modern primitive. Now, the boys could better appreciate the reaction of occupants when they threw stones against the girl's privy—previously they were limited to enjoying the screeches and threats emitted as they hurled stones into the northwest woods—a sure fire means of establishing location. Most teachers decried these mischievous activities but rarely took disciplinary action other than remonstrating to the boys. After all to catch them red handed was not easy.

Austin Bell, a neighbor and a legendary country schools teacher for several decades and then circuit clerk and recorder of Phelps County for several years, was my first grade teacher.

Younger students were placed at desks in the front of the room so the teacher could keep a close eye on them. My desk abutted against a long bench in front that was used for groups of students called up for recitation and instruction by class and subject of study.

The fall day was quite warm and I was drowsy and fiddling with something noisily on my desk when Austin, from in front of his class on the bench, threw a piece of chalk at me. The chalk hit me in the chest and ricocheted on to my desk. Spontaneously and with no hesitation, I picked up the piece of chalk and threw it back at him. At first astonishment shown on Austin's face then quickly he strode to my desk and leaned over me growling with an inimical scowl for an interminable time (probably not over 15 seconds). Then he calmly walked back to his class and took up where he had left off. I was so scared I almost wet my pants.

Austin was famous for throwing things at napping or misbehaving students. Again the fall day was hot and all the windows were up and without screens. The flies and bees were buzzing in and out and searching for leftover lunch fragments. A girl with desk near a window was causing a disturbance and Austin threw a blackboard eraser at her. She ducked and the eraser sailed out the window. She shaped up and during recess he sent the girl to retrieve the missile.

Early on I learned a lot from Austin about negotiation, diplomacy, courtesy, patience and integrity. He was also my second grade teacher and during that school year I found a small rubber ball on the playground. Since no one had announced the loss of a ball I claimed the find as mine. Subsequently, an older boy noticed the ball in my possession and claimed it as his property. Desperately, clasping the ball to me, and in danger of being boy-handled, Austin appeared on the scene, quickly sizing up the situation. He gently led me aside and quietly explained that the other boy very well could have lost the ball. He counseled that the "losers-weepers-finders-keepers" outlook was not really representative of the most acceptable ethics. Then he said "give him the ball", while simultaneously pressing a nickel into my hand and adding, "this will buy another ball for you." It all became clear to me and I handed over the ball that at that time wouldn't sell for more than five cents. I don't remember how I spent Austin's nickel but I know it didn't go for a ball.

I was the subject of much teasing and manipulation by some of the loafers who came to Dad's store. At the second grade stage of development I was more acutely aware that girls were different than boys. The jokers and teasers took advantage of my growing knowledge, encouraging and cajoling me to hug one of the girls in my class when she entered the store. I was all primed and upon her arrival, immediately ran to her, throwing my arms around her as she cleared the door. Startled and embarrassed she ran to the other end of the store and cried. The little girl rapidly recovered her equanimity when Dad presented candy to her. He later advised me to seek counsel other than that of the local lollygaggers. Watching this little girl grow up, I knew she would never be so demure and shy again.

Several cats were in residence around our house and store, and I claimed one large gray tom that was gentle and well behaved until a store customer started bringing his large shepherd-collie mix dog with him to the store. The dog would chase my cat up a tree or off to the woods every time. Again, there was much counsel, advice and prompting from the loafers and lollygaggers at the store. Crushed glass sandwiched in a couple of biscuits would be just the medicine for the curing of the dog's ambitious nature. After the next cat chase I was prepared for Fido with a nice meal. He swallowed each biscuit with one gulp. When the customer returned to the store two weeks later his dog was not with him. Dad asked, "what happened to your dog"—not having any idea of the real circumstances because I had not told any one about my devious plotting. The man replied that the dog had died a slow death of what he didn't know. With a guilty conscience I reckon, I later confessed to my parents who were shocked. However, they chastised me only by telling me that I had chosen the wrong method to solve the problem and the dog had suffered a terrible death. The customer was attached to the animal and I think my parents believed the less said the better for fear of what the man might do if he knew the full story.

A beautiful grove of oak trees grew on the school grounds adjoining the nearby county road and in the fall we boys liked to play threshing machine under the trees. Piles of fallen leaves were constructed, then we took turns straddling the piles and flailing the leaves between our legs and out behind us emulating the discharge of chaff from a grain threshing machine. All went well when Elmer was not around. Elmer was a large boy assigned to eighth grade but with lesser grade academic ability. He would run through our leaf stacks kicking them apart before we could initiate our threshing game. Carl, my best friend, the most ingenious and mischievous of our crew, decided we should get old Elmer. When he wasn't nearby we built an extra large and tempting pile of leaves around a stump. When Elmer saw our specially prepared pile he was so eager to bust it that he backed off to put extra effort into his charge to smash the stack. Results were very gratifying to us. He came out cussing, grimacing and limping. Threatening but not daring enough to try to whomp all of us he went away glowering. Our leaf piles were not busted anymore that season.

During my grade school years an office of Superintendent of Schools was responsible for administrative oversight of Phelps County rural schools. For as long as I can remember, Ralph Marcellus filled the job of Superintendent. Annually, he visited each school at least once, and his visits were exciting events for the students. Ralph, a large and impressive man, always wore a suit, which got our attention. Always friendly but very serious, and after observation of activities for a while followed by a short speech, he departed. You could hear the teacher's massive sigh of relief—except during the tenure of Austin who was unflappable about such occurrences.

The Utters were lovely neighbors located on a farm about one and a half miles southeast of us. They came to Missouri from Colorado while in their mid-fifties, arriving as the depression was beginning, but finances did not seem to be a major problem to them as it was with everyone else in our neighborhood. They subscribed to a Denver daily newspaper and Mrs. Utter saved the Sunday comics for us. She occasionally accumulated issues until making a trip to the store, and we anxiously and eagerly awaited her arrival with this treasure of reading material. After the drought of 1936 the Henry Utters moved back to Colorado and for several years Mrs. Utter would periodically mail to us a large roll of accumulated Sunday comics.

Actually, two brother-Utters came to Missouri at about the same time and purchased farms that joined at one point. Mrs. Henry Utter as aforementioned was our comics benefactor.

Al Utter, two years younger than Henry, arrived with his wife and a daughter aged about 30. Al built two fireplaces on to the farmhouse he had acquired, believing in utilizing the vast resources of oak firewood found on his farm. Later, when Al was asked how he liked the fireplaces he ejaculated, "Go talk to the women, I'm too busy cutting wood to keep the fires going".

14

Cleve and Alfie (nee Payne) Bowen lived in our community and had five children; Albert, Irene, Grover, Hazel and Dorothy. Grover was near my age and we got along well together in school. Spelling and ciphering matches or contests were conducted on Friday afternoons before school closing. Grover and I were usually the finalists in the mathematical exercises. He was a solid competitor, often besting me in multiplication but I could overtake him in addition. We both performed well in the spelling matches. I wish my current spelling was as accomplished as then. Grover died in action in Italy during World War II, receiving posthumously the Silver Star for valor, gallantry and exceptionally meritorious service.

On Sunday, April 23, 1961, the new Army Reserve Training Center at Rolla, Missouri was dedicated and named in honor of Staff Sergeant Grover E. Bowen. The training center was officially named The Staff Sergeant Grover E. Bowen U. S. Army Reserve Training Center in a memorialization ceremony held at Buehler Park, Rolla. Many U. S. Army, government, and local dignitaries, including the immediate family of Grover were present. The event was reported and chronicled by staff of the Rolla Daily News.

3   Burn, Baby Burn

During third grade Ruth Hale was my teacher. She was a very capable teacher and a very fine young lady liked by everyone. During the school week she boarded with my parents, but their progeny gained no favoritism in school. Our house was a popular place all the school year, especially to some of my young uncles and my parent's male cousins. Ruth enjoyed outdoor activities with her students and she taught us how to make and walk on stilts. I haven't tried to walk on stilts since, hummmmm!!

The school year passed quickly and an apple cutting party at our house was one of the highlights of this period. Our old Wealthy apple trees produced a bumper crop and to preserve them my Mother decided we would peel, slice and dry them. To handle the abundance, neighbors were invited in to an apple cutting party. There was a great turnout for the affair and quite a few apples were processed for drying, yet it appeared that more deals and plans were cut than apples. I didn't see any of the young "jakes" peel an apple but I saw them visiting with Ruth.

Apple slices and pieces were spread on roof racks and other elevated surfaces and sun dried. By the time winter was over I had lost my appetite for stewed dried apples. Moreover, fears always lingered in my mind as to what might have been incorporated with the drying apples while exposed to the atmosphere.

The following school year I had been elevated to the fourth grade but was not pleased that Ruth had taken a teaching job at another school. Our new teacher would be an elderly gentleman named James (Jim) Hess who had preceded Ralph Marcellus as county school superintendent (see page 11, Chapter 2). Ralph was the son-in-law of Mr. Hess but he didn't visit our school while Mr. Hess was teaching. Jim in his rejuvenated role of teacher was not a ball of fire but was kind, patient and tolerant of some of the boys who tested his authority. He encouraged us to read and brought special books for those interested. I liked Jim and even corresponded with him later in the summer...in reflection likely thinking he might bring more books to me. Progress was great until spring when calamity struck; at least it seemed so to some pessimistic souls.

The schoolhouse served as a community meeting and gathering place for church and other activities. It was a warm Sunday spring morning, the windows were open (no screens) and the buzz of bees, insects and flies were competing with the mumblings and manifestations of the preacher. Uncle Clarence Malone was sitting in the back near a west window and suddenly he interrupted the church services with a yell, "Erse, your house is on fire". The Coppedge family was in church and their house was located about 250 yards from the schoolhouse. A strong west wind was rolling huge black clouds of smoke and debris toward us. Everyone rushed from the schoolhouse and ran to the Coppedge place that was obscured from view by a narrow belt of timber. The house was engulfed in flames by the time we reached it and there was nothing anyone could do to save the house.

The house had been roofed with successive layers of asphalt type rolled roofing material. As the heat became intense great thermal drafts carried burning pieces of this roofing high into the air and strong westerly winds carried burning pieces eastward. Then someone not mesmerized by the massive burning of the house shouted, "Hey, that stuff may reach the schoolhouse". Most of the crowd rushed back to the schoolhouse and sure enough four or five pieces had already landed on the old dry wood-shingled roof and had already fired some shingles.

Much yelling ensued as people scurried for buckets or other containers to get water from the cistern. Only one water bucket was found at the schoolhouse and other containers were limited. Also, a makeshift ladder was the only equipment available to access the roof so water could be tossed on the burning shingles, now on fire in several places. There was no time to get containers from home.

Secretly most of the students had hopes that the fire would prevail since we would get a vacation from school and we wanted a new schoolhouse. I can remember Walter "Bud" Ketchum working feverishly to douse the fires and yelling, "We have to get it out, we'll never get another one". Even the cover on the chain-cup well pump was pressed into service but to no avail. Resources to check the fires were just not adequate nor available. We watched with mixed emotions as the roaring fire consumed the structure and contents.

Many caring and industrious people lived in our school district and flying in the face of Bud's dire predictions, a committee was formed immediately to find the wherewithal to build a new schoolhouse.

The year was 1932 and we were deep in an economic depression, but nonetheless, the committee and three school board members managed to find financing, develop construction plans and through competitive bidding contract a carpenter to build the new schoolhouse. "Coody" Riley who lived a mile and a half southeast of Seaton was the successful bidder at a price of $60.00. Even at depression prices it was a low-ball bid and some questioned if he could get the job done for that sum. His bid was based on the school district furnishing most of the labor, materials and supplies. "Coody" was a nice man, a competent carpenter and a widower for many years. After his wife had died he had raised three boys to their teens and he badly needed work to continue to support his family. The boys were older than I, but my brother Wib and I hunted with them occasionally. The Riley boys gave us a pup that became one of our best squirrel dogs. We named him Laddie.

Most everyone in the community pitched in to complete the building, and accomplished the job without architects, consultants or tradesmen other then local and "jackleg" talent. The County Superintendent provided administrative guidelines and helped to make funding arrangements for the district to pay off the bonded indebtedness through district taxation.

The new building was completed and furnished with new desks and other necessary items in time to start school in late September. It is amazing what people can do when they are not encumbered by the many and various levels of governmental bureaucracy that are in effect today. This feat could not be accomplished today in twice the time or for inflation adjusted twice the cost.

Our new building was still heated by a wood fueled stove and had no electricity because none was to be had. The building was constructed with a nice vestibule entrance and a separate room for a library and storage. The original cistern continued to supply our water. Our lighting was much improved by a row of closely spaced windows along the south side of the main room.

After the old building burned down I had hoped for a vacation from school, but no way. With succinct elocution Dad spoke, "You, your brother and sister will complete the school year at Clinton Bank School", and we did. We rode our old mare "Baldy" three miles each way to and from Clinton Bank to attend school. "Baldy" was stabled in a shed near the Clinton Bank store and during lunchtime we gave her a snack of oats or other grains. Sometimes all three of us would ride but at other times my older brother or I would ride with our sister while the other walked.

We liked the Clinton Bank teacher, Dorothy Condray, who later would marry our Uncle Robey Malone.

How the fire started which destroyed the Coppedge home was never determined, but rumors were about that arson might have been the source. They lost everything to the fire but the clothes on their backs. Neighbors were generous and contributed clothes, bedding, utensils, tools and other supplies until they could get back on their feet. Erse and Eva Coppedge, daughter Marie and son Carl were good neighbors. We exchanged work in haying and purchased our riding mare, "Old Baldy", from them. They were leasing the farm and house. The lessor could not afford to replace the house so the Coppedges moved to another community.

I was in the fifth grade for the opening year of our new schoolhouse. Our new teacher was attractive, a nice young woman and an adequate instructor. However, during the school year she became much involved with a local stud. Surreptitious and discrete observers had confirmed that the teacher and lover were clandestinely trysting –during the teacher's trek to her boarding house and sometimes in the schoolhouse after school. Many parents in the district thought she was not fit to teach another term. Feelings ran high. The school board of directors consisted of only three members and Dad was a director who was outvoted two to one and the teacher was hired again for the next term.

Relations deteriorated until Dad and one director had a fight at the store. I saw the beginning of the fracas from our house as Dad shoved Frank out the door on to the porch, then followed by them struggling and rolling down the steps to the ground. While they were wrestling and battling on the ground my mother was going to end the fight by whacking Dad's opponent in the head with a hammer, but before she could get in a lick, Erse Coppedge got on the scene, stopped her arm in mid air, then separated the combatants. Dad sustained a small gash on his head where Frank had hit him while Dad was choking him. A confidant divulged that Frank was carrying a small-sharpened piece of metal riveted to a belt wrapped around his hand, apparently expecting a confrontation.

Dad refused to enroll us at "Blackjack" and we were allowed to attend school at Clinton Bank for the next term. Other students also were switched to Clinton Bank. Mom and Dad's stand for decency and morality was a far cry from the tolerance of immorality and permissiveness of our contemporary society. Tis a pity that there has been so much degeneration in the concerns and values of so many.

Our horse, Old Baldy, had died, so my sister and I walked the three miles to Clinton Bank School. Dad would transport us when possible during inclement weather and travelers with vehicles would give us a ride when headed our way.

By this time my older brother, who had started grade school a year early and also skipped a grade, was attending high school at Hawkins Bank, a two-room schoolhouse located about five miles from Seaton and south-southeast toward Salem. Grades nine and ten only were offered there.

We were glad to have Dorothy Condray again for our teacher and also made several new friends. A highlight of the term was Carl Shoemate's charge across the schoolyard hollering, "Here comes a big Jersey bull". He stumped his toe, falling to slide on his face through the dirt and gravel. Up he came with a bloody mouth full of stone and very lacerated lips and chin. Carl was chagrined but he was tough and never whimpered. Little pieces of stone worked out of his lower lip for months afterward.

A lot of fun and excitement was created when the Vaughan kids brought an old buggy chassis to school and we took turns pulling and riding. As many as possible would pile on and since the frame was absent a box bed it was difficult for some to hang on. On one occasion the buggy was particularly heavy loaded when Irene Vaughn fell off and a narrow-tired wheel ran right over her belly. We were scared she might be severely injured or killed the way she responded, but apparently the wind had been knocked out of her and the only injuries were bruises. The teacher put a quietus on buggy operations thereafter and Irene wouldn't even look at the buggy again.

Closure regulations for mining were unheard of during this era. Many mines simply had been abandoned after removal of any salvageable equipment. The teacher and our parents cautioned us to stay away from the old mining sites in the vicinity of Clinton Bank. One old pit was only about 50 yards from the boundaries of the schoolyard. Both a pit mine and an abandoned shaft mine were just yards away from the junction of our Seaton road and the Salem-St.James road. Of course, as one might suspect, my brother and I surreptitiously explored these mining sites on more than one occasion.

Norman Creek crossed our road about half way between home and Clinton Bank. No bridge of any kind existed at the fording place. Vehicles were simply driven across the creek bed from one side of the channel to the other. During flood stages when no one could ford the creek, my sister and I stayed overnight with Uncle Willie and Aunt Jennie. They lived in a large white two-story farmhouse about a half-mile east of the creek and toward Clinton Bank. Aunt Jennie liked to have us and she was a good cook. Their children had grown up and left home. Actually, Uncle Willie was Dad's uncle but he was always Uncle Willie to us too. We reveled in the stories he loved to tell as we sat in front of a large fireplace in their living room. He was a man of small stature—not a bit over five feet and six inches in height and only 135 pounds soaking wet. He liberally applied a byword, "by swanser", and once he informed me, "By swanser, as a young man, I was a right smart of a man". He favored good riding horses and had been a cattleman all his life.

Before the end of the school term the election of a new school board of directors in our "Blackjack" district resulted in the hiring of a different teacher for the next school year. Consequently, we returned to schooling in our own district and boy, what a change.

Ocal Mizell was a handsome man of large and trim stature, probably in his upper twenties with slight tinges of gray at the edges of his hair that seemed to impart an extra measure of dignity to his demeanor. He chose to board with the Goldens who lived within 250 yards of the schoolhouse and were childless. He complained once to my Dad at the store that he got cold sometimes at night and they didn't supply enough bed covers. The word must have gotten back to the Goldens through the local grapevine since Dad didn't hear any more complaints. He drove an open-top Model-T Ford and returned to his home in Safe, Missouri for the weekends.

One Monday morning in early spring Norman Creek was in flood stage. We were gathered at the school, gleefully expecting a holiday, just knowing that Ocal couldn't cross the creek. But lo-and-behold at 9 a.m., just when we were about to leave the schoolhouse, here came Ocal striding up the road. He had waded the muddy torrents and was wet to his shoulders. He didn't have a change of clothes with him because he wouldn't risk stepping on a loose stone or in an unknown hole to fall and submerge in the water with anything he might have carried over his head. Upon his arrival he immediately put school into gear and wore those clothes until the end of the school day. Dad gave him a lift to the creek that had receded to a depth that allowed them to cross to retrieve Ocal's "T"parked on the other side.

Ocal commanded a taut ship with discipline sharp and defined, an avid hair puller when recalcitrance raised its head, and soon all students were relatively docile with the exception of Carl Shoemate, my best friend, who was just too evasive and slippery to get caught in some of his shenanigans. But Ocal was as fair as he was strict. He simply was not going to discipline anyone unless he could catch them in the act and he never caught Carl. I'm convinced it was his ultimate frustration.

Ocal was a top-notch teacher and I was sorry he didn't return for the next school term. Mrs. Welsh was my teacher for eighth grade. In her fifties, she was academically sound, a good organizer but not as much a diplomat, counselor and arbiter as Austin Bell. The district allowed a small stipend for starting fires and daily cleanup of the rooms after school. Mrs. Welch hired me to handle the janitorial job and I performed the work satisfactorily for the full school year. I don't remember the pay rate but I was pleased to have the job. I was relieved when the term ended and ready for high school with great anticipation for the big time action.

During my years of rural one-room schoolhouse education we certainly were short of the amenities considered essentials today, but we were well grounded in the fundamentals of reading, writing and arithmetic—this can't be said for many of today's schools. Also, we were more knowledgeable of geography than kids now at those grade levels. We were bereft in respect to athletic facilities, but most of our teachers encouraged and assisted us with improvisations involving track and ball games. No funds were allocated for sports activities. The teachers and students scavenged for bats and balls and from the nearby forests we cut and whittled uprights and bars for jumping and pole vaulting. In the winter when there was sufficient snow we played the game "Fox and the Geese."

Sexual discrimination was not a problem in our extra-curricular activities. Our school library was quite Spartan but we were proud users of the World Book Encyclopedias that were acquired by stretching the district book budget.

Local, county and state regulations relative to truancy, discipline and corporal punishment, dress and civil codes, attendance, etc. were minimal in contrast to bureaucratic systems of today. Parents were the front line and expected to handle those matters. They were examples of responsibility that should be emulated today.

Dad always said, "If you get a whipping at school you will get another when you get home."

4/   Living It Up

Electric service was not available in our area until after World War II. The present Intercounty Electric Cooperative Association had planned to run lines to the Seaton area prior to then but the war reduced the availability of supplies and manpower. In anticipation of electrical service Dad had a deep well drilled and then used a hand pump until electrical power was available. Hand pumping water from a depth of 280 feet will introduce anyone to real work and leave one with aching arm muscles.

My entire raisin' years at Seaton were without benefit of electricity (other than batteries) or well water. Our primary drinking and cooking water supply was a cistern. During prolonged dry spells some water for washing clothes was hauled from a spring on Norman creek.

We sported a two-holer for our best go at personal sanitary disposal. In fair weather we males might go "shake a bush" since a forested area was nearby. For us, water conservation was an art form, and some of the wooly-eyed environmentalists of today could take some lessons from our experience.

Baths were a luxury during those days but not available under luxurious circumstances. When about ten years old I was taking a bath in a galvanized washtub. It was wintertime and I had placed the tub next to a sheet metal type wood stove to take advantage of the warmer air near the stove. We shelled ear corn by hand for chicken feed in the same stove heated room and the day of my bath someone had discarded some of the corncobs on the floor near the stove. Finishing my bath, I got out of the tub, stepped on a corncob, which rolled, and one of my buttocks slid against the stove with a sizzle. A patch of skin about the size of my hand was blistered. Some ointment was obtained from a doctor in Salem and the injury healed rather quickly, though I did more standing than sitting for several days. After healing with new skin growth, my rump and lower back became infested with boils. My parents theorized that too rapid healing of the wound caused the boils, but I haven't found any medical information in support of that diagnosis.

Lighting equipment consisted of coal oil (kerosene) lamps and lanterns, and flashlights for special and emergency uses. Batteries for lighting cost dear money, so we used them sparingly. Much debate was engendered by the type and sizing of the glass globe enclosures for the wicks of the kerosene lamps. Generally, using larger diameter globes dispersed more light, but they had to be shaped to the sizing of the wicks too. Under the most favorable conditions lighting was poor for reading and close-up work.

After scrimping and saving my mother accumulated enough money to purchase an Aladdin kerosene fueled lamp that utilized a woven filament mantle for the illuminating element. A glass globe, larger and taller than the conventional kerosene lamps, enclosed the mantle. It was indeed an exciting moment when the Aladdin was first fired. The candlepower was much greater than a conventional wick-fired lamp. After firing, the mantles became fragile and when moving the lamp we had to be very careful to not shake or jar the unit or the mantle would fracture—the mantles were relatively expensive for us. We cherished our Aladdin for reading and mother's needlework. However the sturdy and reliable wick fired kerosene lamps were our mainstay for many more years.

One evening my parents were late milking the cows and dusk was approaching. I was only six and before going to the barn they warned my sister and me not to try to light any of the lamps. When darkness set in and they had not returned to the house, I decided we needed some light and off came a glass globe in preparation to light the wick. I dropped the globe on the floor and it smashed to smithereens. Frightened of the consequences, I ran and hid on the back porch in a large shipping crate that normally was used as a doghouse. When our parents returned they quickly discovered the

26

debris from the broken globe and began looking for me. My sister had not hidden and didn't know where I was hiding. They searched inside and outside for an hour or more, yelling my name, but no one thought to look in the doghouse. I could sense their anxiety after all the futile searching, so finally I got up enough courage to come out and make my presence known. Luckily, they were so relieved at my appearance that my punishment was mostly verbal reprimanding. The dogs didn't seem to mind my usurpation of their bedroom.

We never used candles—I suppose their use could not justify the cost. Our only potential supply of tallow fat for candle making was our cattle but we didn't butcher beef.

Pork was our main source of meat. Dad always raised some hogs both for table meat and for sale. At the appropriate time he would choose three or four pigs for special attention in preparation for butchering. They might get better rations depending on the cost and availability of grain and other feeds. The pigs were fed and fattened until they weighed 200-250 pounds with maturity coinciding with fall weather when cooler days were desirable for safe handling and storage of meat.

Butchering made a big day—long and arduous for all. Dad endeavored to predict the weather and select a day with clear, cool, crisp and sunny conditions. Early in the morning fires were started under barrels and huge iron kettles filled with water. Grandpa Malone usually helped us because he was good with a knife and always an astute advisor. When the water was almost boiling it was time for the killing. We shot the hogs with a .22 rifle and dropped them in their tracks without further movement other than some quivering, if hit by the bullet in the right place, which was just an inch or so above the level of and between the eyes. They were not restrained for the shooting, and patience was required, waiting for an immobile head, or the knockdown shot could be missed. No one wanted the killing job. I was recruited at age nine after I had become proficient with the .22 rifles and had demonstrated my capabilities under Dad's monitoring.

My shot missed the mark only once and I was so chagrinned and disturbed by actions of the crippled hog that Dad completed the disagreeable task.

Opening its jugular vein with a designated sticking knife bled the dead hogs. Some people saved the blood for making a concoction called "blood sausage", but not us. However, the blood, hair and the squeal were about the only things we didn't salvage and use.

After drainage of blood, the hog was moved to a platform that was built so a large barrel could be retained against one side at an angle to hold enough hot water so the hog could be partially immersed and sloshed up and down until the hair was conditioned for removal by scraping. This was all hand work and very physically demanding. Two persons handled the hog, each grabbing a leg and working in unison. After the head half was sloshed, the hog was pulled from the barrel and the rear half inserted in the barrel. The handlers had to work rapidly or the water cooled so much the hair didn't readily come off when scraped with knives. Being of small stature I couldn't handle the dousing job until more muscles had developed around the age of 13-14.

Following the hair removal the hog was hung by a gambrel stick on a pole that was laid across two tree limbs or fastened by other means at a height sufficient to elevate the carcass off the ground. A gambrel stick is simply a heavy stick sharpened on both ends and long enough to spread the legs apart when the sharpened ends are inserted through slits between the leg bone and the main tendon of the hind legs. Our Ozark enunciation for the stick was "gamlin".

After hanging the carcass was eviscerated or gutted and the entrails and internal organs collected in a tub. Following gutting the carcass was placed on a cutting table made from planks placed on saw horses or other supports. Ham and bacon sections were severed from the carcass and stored in a building called the smokehouse where salt was applied for curing and preservation. Small amounts of black pepper were sometimes added.

Winter was unusually warm one year and Dad worried that the hams might spoil, so he kept laying on the salt until the hams were hardly edible unless cooked with beans or other foods that needed salt for savor.

We didn't cut out pork chops but instead stripped out the back straps and cut them into small steak size parcels for frying. Meat from the hog's head was often used in a concoction called headcheese—it was not a favorite of mine. Dad claimed to relish boiled pig hocks but I could never understand why. Pork spareribs are one of my favorite meat dishes if they are properly prepared, omitting any of the gooey sauces so prevalent in some eateries.

The remainder of the carcass meat was ground, shaped into sausage balls or patties, then cooked and canned for preservation. All grinding was accomplished with a small cast steel unit which was hand cranked. The same design can be purchased today from several sources. However, output is slow and most deer hunters like myself now use a small electric motor driven unit to increase the grinding rate— saving a lot of elbow grease and avoiding sore arm muscles. One year my mother inadvertently added an excessive amount of sage to the sausage balls and we could hardly stomach them. Even the dogs became sausage shy. She had to blend much of it into other dishes to make the balls appetizing.

Our pork supply was supplemented with wild game but more about that later.

Our farm was small but contained enough pasture and hay land to support a herd of five or six milk cows and a steer or two. We endeavored to schedule the breeding of the cows so a regular supply of fresh milk was available for drinking, cooking, baking and butter. Without your own dairy products supply system those dairy-originated foods were hard to come by, although neighbors at times bartered or exchanged milk products. Normally, the cow's calves were sold as vealers at 200 to 300 pounds so the cows could be milked regularly.

The lactation scheduling did not always go as planned and at times we came up short of desired quantities of milk, while at other times a surplus would develop and if we couldn't barter or give it away, the hogs were treated to a special meal.

In my earlier childhood, cream used for making butter was obtained by letting the milk sit in large crocks until the cream formed on top, then it was skimmed off. Later when we purchased a hand-cranked cream separator we sold any surplus cream to buying stations in town. Later yet, Dad installed a cream buying station at his store.

All of our family liked buttermilk except me and I still cannot stand it. Clabbered milk was tolerable when no options were available.

My mother and older brother raised and nurtured some of about every species of the fowl family. Laying hens, geese, ducks, guineas, turkeys and frying chickens were included in the menagerie.

Geese and ducks lost their down and fine feathers in no time flat when the nimble and fast picking fingers of my mother got hold of them. These products of the waterfowl went into fine featherbeds placed on top of straw tick mattresses—all handmade bedding by my mother. Mighty fine sleeping, especially in a cold room on a cold winter night.

Our servings of food may not have been the finest of cuisine, but we usually enjoyed a balanced diet long before anyone had heard of a nutritionist—thanks to the hard work and ingenuity of my mother and her innate sense of nutritional requirements.

We grew apple, peach and plum trees that bore fruit irregularly due to the vagaries of late frosts, insects and diseases. Horticultural advice wasn't readily available to us, and we couldn't afford equipment or pesticides needed to make regular spraying treatments. Fruits from the trees were supplemented with vine and bush berries such as blackberries, blueberries and gooseberries, which grew in the wild throughout much of the countryside. Many hazards and obstacles had to be surmounted during the picking and collecting of wild berries—briars, poison ivy, snakes, ticks, chiggers, bruises on bare feet from sticks and stones and heat stroke. I survived all of those outdoor challenges, although I was subjected to many tick and chigger bites plus a severe case of ivy poisoning.

Berries were consumed while fresh, sometimes with cream as a special treat, but most of the harvest was canned or processed into jams, jellies and preserves. Berries were cooked and canned in glass jars when the supplies were adequate, but in the processing a lot of the fresh flavors were lost that now are mostly preserved by freezing..

Dad developed a 75 foot row of Concord grapes, but after a few years began to neglect the tending and pruning that is necessary to obtain good harvests. Nevertheless, a decent crop would be grown occasionally when pests and diseases didn't prevail. The fruit was eaten fresh and converted into jams, jellies and juice, which was canned. Dad was adamant about his opposition to consumption of alcohol and would not consider making wine. Uncle Earl, my brother Wib and I put together a batch of grape juice with other ingredients and hid it for fermentation. I don't remember our recipe, but our product was not fit to drink. Poor results combined with the necessity for covert operations caused us to lose interest in further experimentation.

Red plum preserves was one of my favorite desserts but not for some people. Uncle Willie Malone was having dinner (noon meal now called lunch) with us one day when my mother said, "Pass Uncle Willie the plum preserves". Promptly and unabashedly he snapped, "No thanks, I've had a dish of plum preserves stuck under my nose all my life". I think he was right because every time I visited at his house a bowl of red plum preserves was ensconced on the table in a special red dish, even when meals were not being served. I never thought to ask Aunt Jennie but she must have liked them and probably snacked on them between meals.

My mother made mean cobblers and never worked from recipes—it was all in her head. Fresh fruit cobblers are just about the best dessert in this universe, especially one made with fresh-picked wild huckleberries.

Early in the spring I helped my mother pick greens, but I have lost knowledge of the various plants and weeds that were most edible. Anyway, wild greens made mighty fine fare before lettuce was ready in the garden. The greens were cooked in water and eaten with vinegar while adding salt and pepper to taste as they were eaten. Greens with beans and cracklins cornbread make a fabulous meal.

Dry beans were one of the few staple food products besides sugar, salt, flour and corn meal that Dad allowed us to take from his store. We grew and scrounged for most of our foodstuffs. We liked any of the varieties of beans—navy, pinto, black and great northern. Black-eyed peas also were savored. Often my mother cooked beans in a large tall black iron pot with capacity to cook enough beans to last two or three days depending on how many faces looked across the table. I preferred my beans cooked to enough firmness in texture to maintain their integrity and finished in a light soupy mix. No mushy or pasty beans for me. My wife prepares beans superbly—the greatest, though a son-in-law chef dishes up a scrumptious pot of beans too. I appreciate all dry bean varieties, especially when cooked and served with cornbread made with shortening and seasoning provided by cracklins, bacon or ham grease.

Many are the virtues of well-prepared beans—besides great nutrition and flavor they also can provide that extra boost to get over the hills. The most graphic description of beans is "musical fruit."

Bill Happel, an interesting bachelor who worked for Dad occasionally, wanted to have his noon meal with us as part of the labor agreement. My mother had whomped up a nice batch of cornbread, but when proffered to Bill he snorted and promptly stated, "My, can't stand cornbread, it scratches my throat", so Mom had to scurry around and warm up some biscuits, left over from breakfast, for Bill.

Mom made biscuits from scratch (other than using some rising dough always prepped on the back of the kitchen stove) every morning for breakfast. Bread was mostly biscuits or cornbread.

Lard, bacon or salt-jowl grease were conventional shortenings, and a lot of the lard consumed was rendered from the fats of the hogs we butchered.

The fats removed from intestines and other organs were converted to soap by saponification, using lye (potassium hydroxide) as the alkali agent. Some people produced crude lye by leaching the alkali from wood ashes. We used commercial lye. A large black iron kettle was used as the reaction vessel. Fat and water were placed in the kettle after a wood fire had been started under and around the kettle, which was mounted outdoors on foundation rocks. Then lye was added as the mixture became mostly fluid. Lye was proportioned to fat by estimation and experience and more might be added as the reaction proceeded. Frequent stirring and observation was required. When the operator deemed the reaction was complete, the fire would be quenched and the mixture allowed to cool and solidify. A kettle full of white soap was a satisfying sight. To insure full conversion of fat to soap some excess of lye was added with the result that a small amount of thick liquid would form at the bottom of the kettle. This fluid was alkaline with enough lye content to sting the skin. If not too strong it might be used to launder items heavily soiled by oils and greases but caution and judgment gained by experience had to be exercised to avoid skin burns or deterioration of fabrics.

After the soap was well solidified in the kettle it was cut into bars layer by layer until the bottom and jellied layer was reached, then removed to storage. This soap was used mostly for laundering heavily soiled garments such as overalls and outerwear and it performed marvelously.

A lot of garden ground was worked and planted in anticipation that yields could be reduced by dry weather and pestilences. Also, commercial fertilizers were not affordable and the amount of manure removed from the barn and henhouse was not adequate to satisfy the nutrient needs for high yields from all our gardens.

The story is told about Harry Truman using the term manure in one of his tirades against the Republican Party and a listener informed Bess Truman that he should refrain from such language. Bess replied, "Don't you dare mention it to him, I've just finally induced him to say manure".

Beans, corn, Irish and sweet potatoes, cabbage, tomatoes and onions were garden staples. Cucumbers were grown for both fresh salads and pickling. Sour, dill and sweet cucumber pickles were prepared. Dill and sweet pickles were canned in glass jars. Salt and sour pickles were preserved and stored in large stone type jars, covered but not sealed, and kept in the storm cellar located in the side of the hill below the house.

Lettuce and radishes were grown until early summer when the usually drier and hotter weather diminished response and yield. Cooked cabbage was often on the menu for a good part of the year because heads of cabbage would keep well into the winter when stored in our cellar. Some cabbage was processed into sauerkraut by salting and fermentation in large stone crockery jars in the cellar.

Dad always planted cantaloupe and watermelons that normally yielded well when rainfall was adequate and when fertilized well with manure. Annually, Mom insisted on raising citron melons for making tasty preserves and candies. The citrons were grown in our valley truck patch, and with malice aforethought, seeded in a small area conspicuously close to the county roadside. Nearly every year a passerby helped himself or herself to a citron thinking it was a watermelon. Some of the melon thieves would later sheepishly admit to the taking and how they were fooled. Citrons are bitter tasting and not edible fresh but they withstand dry weather much better than watermelons.

Gardens were planted as early as possible after the danger of frost was past in order to get maximum growth before dry hot weather set in. One year when the valley truck patch was in early and doing exceptionally well, the geese slipped through a hole in the fence, and by the time we noticed them they had eaten or pulled up most of the sweet corn shoots and other vegetables that had emerged. We replanted, but the delay resulted in a later maturing crop that got hit with a hot dry July and didn't do well at all. Of course, the fence was fixed, but Dad threatened the existence of the geese. However, Mom prevailed with a plea that more feathers were needed for bedding. I wonder if the "feather-bedding" term for goof-off employees originated from the softness and comfort of feather beds.

Oftentimes, when light meals or just a snack was planned cornbread crumbled in milk would be the main part of the menu. It is still a favorite of mine, though I often substitute salted soda crackers for cornbread.

Persimmon trees grew in many places on our farm. They bore fruit most years, though late spring frosts occasionally deny a crop. Fruit begins to ripen in the fall, and some people think the fruit isn't edible until after a hard frost, but that is not true in most cases. Marked differences in the size, quality and date of maturity are evident for a variety of species. The unripe fruit is very astringent to the palate and can put a pucker in the best of faces.

Persimmons grow best in open areas away from heavy forests. Both male and female genders thrive together and male trees are necessary for fertilization and fruiting of the female trees. Persimmons are used for pies or in other baking recipes, but we did not care that much for them and ate them only from the trees while on an outing in the fields or woods—not too bad when hunger needed quenching late at night on a coon hunt.

Pawpaw trees were found along the major-sized creeks, but often we forgot to go searching for the fruit at ripening time. The fruit didn't last long because birds and tree-climbing animals such as squirrels, raccoons and possums began eating the fruit as it ripened. Even the groundhog or woodchuck liked pawpaw fruit, and believe it or not, woodchucks do climb trees. I have knocked a couple out of the tops of large trees with a .22 rifle.

The flavor and consistency of the pawpaw is similar to the tropically growing papaya but not as large in size. Most people would say it has a flavor similar to the banana. It also reminds me of the avocado though the skin of the pawpaw is not as thick and the flesh is of softer character when ripe.

No mulberry trees grew on our farm but a neighbor had three large trees in their yard that bore white fruit. My older brother and I visited these folks and climbed the trees to eat the very sweet fruit. The summer I was going on nine I ate so many of the white mulberries that I became sick and foundered on them. To this day, I cannot bear the taste of the mulberry, white or red.

When Sunday company was expected most families if possible, chose to have fried chicken as the main course for dinner. They raised chickens both for frying and for laying flock replacements. We had a chicken house for laying and roosting, but the chickens were free to roam, so when we wanted fryers to eat we had to catch them. If enough help was available they might be shooed into a pen for easier snatching. Transpose our system of raising chickens to this day and we are in swing with the environmentalists advocating free ranging for the birds along with limited chemical supplements. They might be right about chickens but not their vaunted support of organic gardening.

Killing the chickens was usually accomplished by wringing necks or by chopping heads off with an ax or hatchet. I could not wring a chicken's neck successfully and usually resorted to the ax. Dad could take a chicken's head off every time with a quick wring and a snap. Sometimes I tried to shoot them in the head with a .22 rifle, but usually failed because of the difficulty of hitting a constantly bobbing head.

We always kept a flock of guineas that were as good or better eating than chicken when the young were fried. Also, the eggs were tasty. At night the guineas roosted in trees, normally not far from the house. They were great alarm birds—setting up a loud high-pitched racket of cackling and screeching when animals, birds of prey or human predators intruded on our property. Apparently endowed with the nature of the wild to some extent, they were very difficult to herd or catch. With patience and bait a long rod or stick with hook attached to one end was effective for snatching them by snaring a leg. Trapping was another means for catching them.

Small flocks of both white and bronze turkeys were raised and all marketed unless a wild turkey could not be bagged for Thanksgiving and Christmas dinners. Turkey polts are very susceptible to the ravages of disease and predators, especially during the first three weeks of life. This is also true to a large extent for the wild turkey broods, and I often wonder how the wild flocks proliferate as much as they do, particularly today when wildlife predators are more abundant because of less trapping and hunting for furbearers.

Our fare of wild game consisted mostly of rabbits and squirrels with a treat of quail now and then. Mom cooked up a possum once, and the consensus after sampling the rather dark, sinewy and gamy meat—once was once too much. During fall migrations of ducks some would settle in on our pond or neighboring ponds and creeks. Often we could sneak up on them and nail a few with the shotgun providing a welcome supplement to our diet. Teal migrated first but the significantly larger mallard that arrived later was the preferred species. The migrating wild geese didn't land on the small waters but would come down to a picked cornfield or a green patch of fall wheat. When Dad had time to lie in watch, he managed to knock off a goose now and then. As table fare they are inferior to turkey.

The very edible and easily identified morel mushrooms were eagerly sought in the spring. Dipped in an egg-cornmeal batter and fried, morels are a tasty complement to breakfast, lunch or dinner. We were not familiar enough with other mushroom species to choose the edible types. Most people were very cautious and feared that poisonous species would be mistaken for edible varieties. Years later, I learned from my wife's Uncle Alvin Benad how to select an edible species of the chanterelle family of mushrooms. I picked a passel of the orange late spring variety, took them over to my parents and suggested that Mom fry up a mess. She prepared them in a fashion similar to morels and all except Dad had a big feed—he wouldn't touch them. Puffball mushrooms are quite edible and easily identified. They pop out in meadows and open areas during spring and summer after rains, growing quickly into large white ball-like stools. The younger growth stools are more tender and less rubbery than the larger balls and only the white balls should be selected—when browning begins, the quality has deteriorated. I'm not fond of them because of mildness and lack of distinctive flavor, tasting mostly the batter used to fry them.

Jams, jellies and preserve sweets were supplemented with molasses. The timeworn expression, "please pass mo molasses", was often heard at our table. We purchased or bartered for molasses from local farmer-producers who grew the sorghum cane that supplied the sugar. After the cane was cut and stripped of leaves it was run through a rotary vertical press, which was driven by horse or mule, hitched to a long pole extending from the press. Usually, one of the producer's kids had the assignment of leading or riding the animal around and around to turn the press rotor. Cane juice was collected from the press, poured into a large pan and heated to drive off copious amounts of moisture, reducing the juice to the desired consistency. Pans were fired with wood placed around and underneath. The final viscosity of the product was a matter of choice by the producer. Some preferred thin molasses and others wanted thick molasses. The lower viscosity or thinner product required less firing and consequently, less production time and fuel consumption. Two different systems were used for evaporation. In one case, an open pan was used and the juice stirred frequently by hand paddles. The other system also employed a pan, but it was hooded with an exhaust stack and exhaust damper control. It was called an evaporator and purportedly produced better quality molasses due to total pan evaporation control with fewer hot spots that could cause over-heating and charring of sugar.

The merits of "pan" versus "evaporator" molasses were indeed a contentious issue. From a consumer's viewpoint, I couldn't discern much difference in quality if the compared units were operated properly. In my opinion, if the open pan was stirred frequently and well, and fired uniformly, its product was equal to that of the hooded pan. Moreover, the evaporation rate was higher from the open pan. Much depended on the skill and attention of the operators. Though indefinable, the quality of the cane undoubtedly affects the flavor and texture of the molasses. Soil fertility, plant varieties, weed control, rainfall and growing temperatures are determinants of cane quality just as they are for any crop.

5/   The Great Depression

Dad was a radio fan in the 1920s, beginning with use of crystal sets, and then graduating to the tube sets as they developed. He was in the vanguard for our community, and often neighbors came to our house in the evenings to listen to the Grand Old Opry, Amos and Andy and other programs. Sports fans visited during daytime to listen to broadcasts of the St. Louis Browns and Cardinals baseball games. No night games in those days. Today, few people know that St. Louis used to have two major league teams.

Anyway, we knew when the stock market crashed in 1929 by tuning in to news on the radio. Certainly we didn't own any stocks or bonds, so really hardly noticed the economic disaster until the effects of bank and business closures began to filter down to us.

Dad maintained a small bank account for store use and didn't lose much when the banks folded. He remembered very clearly though, the statement by the president of his bank, "Oh, this bank will never be closed." Two weeks later, the doors were shuttered. Subsequently, he wrote money orders to pay invoices for store merchandise. Besides, postal money orders were just as convenient since he was postmaster of the Seaton post office located in his store. Wages for postmasters of fourth-class offices were small but nonetheless, helped us very much to survive the depression.

At times we thought things might be better if the store was closed and Dad got a job with the WPA (Works Progress Administration—a federal government make work program) instituted by the Franklin D. Roosevelt administration during the depression.

Dad's store accounting system was simple—two sharp-pointed hooks mounted on the shelving behind the service counter. Accounts receivables from customers went on one hook while bills to pay hung on the other in order of receipt.

Daily receipts were tabulated at days end and entered in a ledger. Also, records of goods purchased were kept in a ledger. Operating cash was stashed in a drawer under the serving counter.

Income taxes were no problem whatsoever in those days. I doubt that anyone in our community knew what a tax form looked like.

As the depression deepened the receivables hook became more laden. When customers were allowed to run a charge account their tickets were pinned together on the hook. It was difficult to refuse credit to people truly in need and Dad empathized with the financial travails of his customers. Earnings from the store were meager but Dad had too much pride and concern for customers to close up shop and he hoped for better times.

Dad hustled to earn a penny any honest way possible. Produce such as chickens and eggs were purchased from customers and then sold to wholesale markets in St.James and Rolla. The produce was collected in crates and hauled in the back of the Model T to town. Egg crates were exchanged so empties could be hauled back to contain future purchases. We owned chicken coops and hung on to them for future hauls to town.

I always tried to go along on trips to town and often had to sit on the laps of adult passengers who begged a ride. A drugstore was located just across from the St.James produce market, and during the summertime trips Dad would give me a nickel to get an ice cream cone. Remembrances of how good the cream tasted still linger, especially the chocolate. I was on my best behavior before and during the trips in anticipation of the possibility of the treat.

Dad preferred to buy chickens, rather than fowl such as ducks, geese, guineas and turkeys because they were readily marketable, while the other were more seasonal or limited in demand by the consumers. All purchased fowl were stored in coops and housed in the warehouse most of the time before they were sold.

There were good people who became chicken thieves during the depression in order to put some food on the table—folks so proud they were more comfortable with stealing than asking for a handout. Most didn't eat the stolen chickens, but bartered or sold them to get the minimum of essential groceries such as flour, cornmeal, salt, sugar and lard. Dad empathized with their hardship—he never installed a really secure lock on the warehouse door. When he was awakened by noises that sounded like thievery in progress, he might fire his shotgun in the direction of the warehouse, but always aiming high. Some scattered shot pellets could be found embedded in the upper framing above the doors. The shooting induced a bit of deterrence for a while.

Dad had purchased two burlap bags of chickens—carried to the store by the seller. When he put them in coops he liked the looks of one of them, a perky, friendly little brown hen, so he turned her loose to the outdoors. The little hen hung around the store area and scavenged the grain spilled from handling bagged feeds in and out of the storeroom attached to the store. She began laying and selected the storeroom as her preferred place to nest. Thereafter, Dad left the storeroom door ajar so she could regularly deposit her eggs. One day the little brown hen turned up missing. She had roosted in the warehouse above the caged chickens to be marketed. About three or four days later Dad purchased a sack of hens. Chickens were bought by weight and the price per pound determined by type and age. While weighing and examining he thought one hen looked mighty familiar. He put the hens in a coop until the transaction was completed. After the customer who had sold him the hens was gone, he opened the door of the coop and released the familiar-looking hen which promptly made a beeline to the storehouse and laid an egg at her former nesting place. Indeed, he had ransomed his own little hen. The purveyor of illegal chickens eventually got work with the WPA and remained a good customer.

Dad was a buyer of furs and cottontail rabbits. If the rabbits had not been eviscerated cleanly or were not freshly killed they were unacceptable. Rabbits were purchased only in the winter when they would keep for a few days without spoiling. They were sold to the same wholesale market in St.James, which bought chickens, or sometimes buyers from St.Louis came to the store to purchase directly. Dad paid 5 to 15 cents per bunny, and they might be retailed in St.Louis for 25 to 50 cents, depending on the economic vicissitudes of the ongoing depression. The whole carcasses, unskinned but eviscerated, were packed in burlap bags for shipping.

Fur buying required considerable expertise to be profitable. The market was tenuous as it is yet today. However, PETA (People for the Ethical Treatment of Animals) was not around to harass the trappers, processing and marketing systems. Quality of raw furs is quite variable as it is taken from the animal, and also affected by handling procedures when skinning, cleaning and stretching to cure. Opossums led the list in quantity of pelts purchased, and valued the least. Skunks or polecats ranked next in numbers. Generally, skunks were graded by categories of appearance; white, broad stripe (much white), narrow stripe (white stripe down the back), short stripe (white on back of head and neck an part way down upper back) and black. Value increased in order with black being most valuable. A black would be valued at as much as three good possums and a white or broad stripe might be worth one good possum.

The supply of raccoons would be equal to or greater than the number of foxes (gray and red). Mostly, prime fox pelts were worth more than raccoons, but either was twice or more the value of the best skunk. Mink pelts were most valuable of all, and the supply was considerably less than that of raccoons and foxes. Once in a great while some hunter or trapper brought in a civet cat (much smaller than a skunk, but with a similar secretion of an unctuous substance with a strong musk odor). The civet was not prone to eject its secretions and may not have the ability to do so.

A sighting of coyotes was rare, and muskrats or beavers were not found in our vicinity. Now, coyotes are thriving while muskrats are active in many ponds and streams, and beavers are busy on most of the major flowing waterways.

Furs were priced within ranges in relation to size and quality. Fur quality was affected by animal habitat, weather, diet and handling by the hunter or trapper. The animals usually produced prime coats when the fall and winter weather was colder.

Dad sold his furs to St.Louis fur houses, and he liked to haggle with the buyers in person, but sometimes he had to ship them by rail or by one of the local truckers who hauled livestock and freight to and from St. Louis. The furs were packed in tow or gunny (burlap) sacks or other type bags for shipment. He was an astute buyer and made some money in the trade if the market didn't deteriorate unexpectedly. Actually, predictability of the market then was not as difficult as today. Though the depression economy caused instability, we didn't have the influence of animal rights organizations that today try to control or prohibit the consumption of furs in clothing and other articles.

Just about everyone living in the countryside hunted and trapped during the depression, and many survived through these activities. Consequently, the wildlife population was severely reduced during the worst years of the depression. Turkey flocks were decimated, and seeing a deer was a rare sighting, eliciting much attention and conversation within the community. The quail population was greater than now because the cost of ammunition was expensive in relation to the amount of meat that could be harvested with it. Also, quail habitat was plentiful and more hospitable because every Tom, Dick and Harry didn't have a herd of beef cattle overgrazing the landscape.

Literally thousands of acres of timberland, brush and weed-covered areas that I hunted on as a youth are now pasturelands by virtue of the bulldozers and herbicides.

We owned an old Stevens Crack Shot single shot .22 rifle that Dad had bought and used while he was growing up. The bore of the barrel became so worn that we couldn't hit the squirrels (now, I have other excuses). Eventually, enough money was scraped together to buy a new .22 single shot bolt-action rifle for my brother, Wib. His harvest of squirrels increased significantly, and I learned to shoot his rifle. At nine years of age, I was deemed proficient and safety oriented enough to qualify for my own .22 rifle, and again with saving and sacrifices I got a new Bearcat bolt-action single shot rifle. Dad ordered it from Shapleigh Hardware (wholesale merchandise house) in St.Louis and it cost $5.75, vintage 1932.

My first foray with new rifle, my brother and I were hunting rabbits along a small creek, looking in drifts and other places where they might be bedded. I located a rabbit close up and deep in the middle of a drift, and he just lay there watching me with big brown eyes. I couldn't stomach shooting the bunny smack in the face and backed off to the side, and shot through the debris. Of course, I missed, and as the creature leaped out and ran away, Wib shot at the leaping target with his .22 rifle. I yelled, "Why didn't you hit him"? Irately, he hollered back, "What's the matter with you, can't you even hit one sitting under your nose"? I didn't confess the true circumstances.

My Bearcat rifle was very accurate and remained in use until stolen when Dad's store was burglarized in 1986. He liked it and I left it with him to use.

Our Model T Ford gave up the ghost in late 1934, and we were without a motor vehicle for a year or so. Two brothers of Dad were in the trucking business, and they hauled merchandise for his store from St.Louis. Also, they transported the produce that Dad purchased to St. James, Rolla or St. Louis.

In addition to normal walking during hunting and working on the farm we walked a lot to visit neighbors while without a car. My brother and I rode our old horse, Baldy, to deliver groceries and other store merchandise to some customers. Others without horses, wagons and buggies, walked to the store for supplies. It was not uncommon to see them head home bearing a 25-pound sack of flour on a shoulder and a gunnysack of items in hand or on the other shoulder.

Most rural roads were just dirt-rock based and surfaced, seldom graded and surface drainage was poor. Many were just wagon trails through the woods and fields. Model T Fords maneuvered these primitive roads pretty well and the later Model A Fords did okay too. Roads to Salem, St.James and Rolla were graded to some degree to provide drainage and a bit of roadbed, but mainly dirt based with some gravel applied to the softer spots. Journeys to towns during rainy periods or spring thaws proceeded with trepidation, not knowing whether you might get mired down and require someone with a horse or mule team to pull you out of the muck and water.

Finances improved to the extent that Dad accumulated enough money to start browsing for a car. His trucker brothers located a 1928 Chevy in St. Louis, a four door that they thought was suitable, and at a negotiated price of $120. When they made their next haul to St. Louis, dad gave them the money to purchase and drive the car to us. Though the Chevy couldn't maneuver the cow path trails with the agility of the "T" it was luxurious in comparison, sporting a roof, glass roll-up-and-down windows and four working doors. It was equipped with mechanical band type brakes but only on the rear wheels. The brakes didn't last long and I began driving lessons at the ripe old age of eleven. I'm still learning but not without brakes.

One nice summer day Dad, Uncle Willie and I headed out for St. James. By this time the road to St James had been designated highway 68 by the Missouri Highway Department and improved by grading and graveling. Dad was putting the pedal to the metal on the '28 Chevy, hitting a speed of about 45 miles per hour when we came upon a herd of cattle around a bend in the road just before reaching Winkler. Without brakes, he down shifted through all gears, cut the ignition, and then at the last moment rammed the transmission into reverse. We stopped in the middle of the road just inches from the snouts of about ten cows. Luckily, the gearbox was not stripped and we eased through the cattle, continuing on our way. Ultimately, Dad got the brakes rebanded but those old mechanical brakes required a lot of foot pressure to be effective.

Death does not stop for a depression. With limited money and resources, people arranged for the transition from the living to the dead as best they could. It was common for a family of the deceased to prepare the body for burial and a coffin was either constructed from wood or perhaps hauled from town if money or credit was available. Very few could afford a vault. The body would lie in state at the home of the deceased while all-night wakes were observed. I attended more than one wake with one of my parents, usually falling asleep to spend the evening on a bed or on a pallet on the floor until Mom or Dad took us home.

It was standard practice for two or more adults to sit with the displayed dead at all times. Visitors spelled one another so they could take care of their chores. Dad liked to tell about a wake he attended where some young men discovered home made wine in the cellar of the expired and proceeded to whoop things up, creating a right spirited wake.

The do-it-yourself mortuary methods did not include embalming, so it was imperative to proceed with burial as soon as possible, particularly during the warmer seasons. One hot summer I remember over-hearing some women conversing at a funeral and commenting, "Did you see how she was swelled up, and they just barely got her in the ground in time."

Gaining promptness of burial was no easy task. Communications to some people came by foot or horseback and grave digging, which was done by hand, could be a problem. Soils in many Ozark cemeteries are rocky and tough to excavate by pick and shovel methods. Such locations often were selected because of low groundwater levels and access routes with more stable roadbeds. Sometimes it became necessary to use explosives to bust up the rocks enough so excavation could proceed to an adequate depth. Diggers with access to or experience in proper dynamite handling techniques were not always available. In one case when a neighbor was digging a grave and used dynamite, evidently he cut his fuse too short for one blast and couldn't scramble fast enough to put adequate distance between him and the blastoff to prevent severe bruises and lacerations from the flying debris. He was fortunate that he didn't lose an eye or more. His spectacles were broken.

The United States never really recovered from the depression until after World War II began, but along in 1937 conditions had improved enough that Dad decided he could supplement our income and improve the logistics of obtaining goods for the store by doing some trucking. So, he traded the '28 Chevy for a used 1935 Ford V-8 pickup. He built racks on the bed and began hauling livestock for himself and neighbors to St. Louis, along with cases of eggs mounted on a front shelf above the calves and hogs in the pickup bed. In St. Louis he purchased merchandise to haul back for his store and sometimes delivered items ordered by other stores.

I liked to drive the Ford pickup. It had a flathead V-8 engine with a rumbling, chortling running sound that was music to my ears. Dad was never enthusiastic about the Ford name because of his travails with the Model T. He even said bad things about Henry. So, when the V-8 engine threw a rod he traded the Ford for a new 1937 Chevy pickup. Hauling capacity of the new truck was increased by dropping the tailgate to bed level and then extending the racks to the end of the tailgate. Also, he installed overload springs and switched to heavy-duty tires and wheels after busting a standard ply tire and splitting a wheel while hauling extra heavy loads.

Dad decided we all needed more to do so he built another side room on the store and installed a dairy cream-testing laboratory for buying cream based on butterfat content. Then he expanded the size of the upper platform on the pickup so cans of cream could be hauled with cases of eggs as he trucked livestock to the St. Louis yards. If he couldn't make up a load of livestock when the cream needed to be sold then the cream was sold to dealers in St. James. We didn't have cooling facilities, and during warm weather the cream quality could deteriorate rapidly—more about this later.

The '37 Chevy pickup served nobly and well but its capacity was very limited, so in 1940 Dad took the plunge and traded for a new red one-and-half ton dual-wheeled driven Chevy truck. He teamed up with his brother, Raymond, and Tom Malone, who was a blacksmith and carpenter in our neighborhood, to build a rack on the new truck chassis.

They did a bang-up job with tongue-and-groove sidings, slatted fronts and back gates for flow-through ventilation when hauling livestock in warm weather. Thus, a tarpaulin was needed only on the front and top for rain or snow protection. They painted the sides and racks white and the rig looked snazzy.

Livestock was hauled either directly to Armour or Swift meat packing companies on the St. Louis, Missouri side of the Mississippi River, or across the Mississippi to the East St. Louis, Illinois stockyards. Prices paid for the livestock was the major determinant but the extra time and costs involved in going over to the East side were always considered. In hot weather, to avoid heat stressing of the stock, we often loaded the livestock in early evening and drove to St. Louis in the cooler evening air.

The stockyards maintained bunkhouses where cot type bunks could be rented for 50 cents a night. Dad and I slept there one night after unloading our cattle. The facility was furnished with a large common wash and restroom. Next morning, for the first time, I observed a woman come in and relieve herself in a men's room. She was a grubby looking character to say the least.

The stockyards provided pads where trucks could be washed down. Being proud of his white truck racks, Dad was careful to wash off all the manure and extraneous deposits. Moreover, a clean truck bed was desirable for hauling merchandise home.

Grandpa Malone and "Bapoo" Watkins liked to visit in town, and tried to estimate when Dad was going to St. James, then meet him at the county road to bum a ride. Both carried ubiquitous chews of tobacco in their mouths. Just a short while after Dad had launched his new truck rig, those two gregarious gentlemen waylaid him, and off to town they went, merrily expectorating out the open passenger side window. Dad loved them and would not complain to them about their tobacco chewing and spitting, but he was more than a little upset after the trip to town and back with them when he discovered all the brown streaked stains along the passenger side of the white rack.

Maintaining a bull for the breeding of small herds of cows is not economical, and during the throes of the depression neighbors shared bulls. Some inconvenience was involved since we had to get our cows to the bull. But no big problem, my brother and I were sturdy and capable enough to drive or lead our cows to the neighbors—taking the shortest and most accessible route, whether along the roads and trails or across fields and woods.

One of our older Jersey cows was having a problem becoming inseminated. We were getting tired of trekking around with her, and when she came into estrus the third time, we vowed that if she was breedable we intended to insure it was done. We kept the cow and bull together all morning until the bull had topped her twelve times. Some veterinarians might question those statistics, but they can "believe it or not." We would have tested them further but were hungry for lunch and knew that our parents were wondering what happened to us. Anyway, our goal was accomplished—old Jerry bore a nice big calf at the end of nine months of gestation.

Dad's Uncle Walter Malone offered one year to lend us a bull for a while if we came and got him. The usual matadors were appointed to bring the bull in. Wib and I rounded him up at Uncle Walter's farm about three miles from our place. Immediately suspicions arose as we noted a ring in his nose. But undaunted, we put a rope halter on him and headed toward home cross-country. Less than a quarter mile from the barn, herr bull stopped in the middle of the field and wouldn't budge and inch. A rope was engaged with the ring in his nose and we pulled on it till his nose bled, but no go, and to be more obstreperous, he lay down. Cajoling, punching, kicking and tail twisting were ineffectual. Desperately, Wib said, "I think I'll build a fire under him", and he did. Dry grass and debris were collected, shoved against the bull's side and fired. We stood there astounded as he calmly lay there as the fire burned his hair and scorched his hide. Since he wasn't our animal, we were afraid to let the fire burn further, so doused the fire and admitted defeat. Taking the halter off and the rope from his nose, we left him to do his own thing. Those who have expounded, "I'll build a fire under so-and-so if he doesn't get crackin'" must not have experienced the recalcitrance of a bull.

By 1940, construction of Fort Leonard Wood 35 miles west of Rolla was going full blast, military installations and war materials manufacturing facilities across the United States were going up full tilt and the depression era was history. Pearl Harbor was around the corner.

Many stories were spawned by the depression, and in the face of travail and suffering, the people in our community were able to spin humor into their yarns. Long after the depression, one of Uncle Robey's favorite stories was elicited when he could find an unwary Republican to listen. He would expound, "Them Hoover times wuz bad, most of us hungry', then one morning I broke my arm having breakfast." The agog Republican usually queried, "How in the world could you break an arm eating breakfast"? The dry and triumphal answer; "I fell out of the persimmon tree."

Sister Kathleen and Father with 1928 Chevy

6/   Droughts of 1934 & 1936

Rainfall in the spring of 1934 was below normal and practically nil during June and July. Rains came in late August. It was indeed a long dry spell. Temperatures in July didn't drop below 90 degrees Fahrenheit except at night, and it was common for temperatures to exceed 100 degrees during the days of July and August. Highs of 110 degrees were reached twice. The countryside was like an oven during the day. So hot in the house during evenings that it was difficult to sleep. We spread quilts or other padding on the ground in the yard, and tried to get some rest while battling the flies and insects. Later in the night with some drop in temperature we retreated to the house.

Most people couldn't endure the heat of the afternoons for any extended period, and chores and work were accomplished as early as possible in the morning. We lay or sat in the shade during the more sultry hours and worked on small tasks that didn't require much movement or exertion. Naps were taken to recover sleep lost during the hot buggy evenings. Our reading supplies were limited and we often read some of the more interesting material more than once.

One small pond supplied water for our livestock, and it went dry in July. Dad envisioned that he might be able to haul water to the stock and handle their needs. He loaded the Model T with barrels and cream cans and took off for Norman creek to fill them, and then he came back to a barn lot of cattle with their tongues hanging out. A couple of galvanized tubs were set on the ground and one filled with water from the cans. An old cow ran over and sucked the tub dry in no time flat. As we emptied the rest of the containers into the tubs, the water was consumed just as quickly, and the cattle stood around mooneyed, some bawling and some with tongues half way out of mouths. It was obvious we couldn't satisfy their thirsts in this fashion with the means at hand. A tank wagon with an engine-driven pump for filling and emptying would have been adequate to supply the demand, but no such rig was available in our community. We couldn't afford the services of a commercial hauler.

We began driving the cattle to Norman creek once each day. The distance was about a mile and a half, and we drove them over the county roads as early in the morning as possible. Though it was a small herd of ten, the driving task was of considerable magnitude. My older brother, Wilbert (Wib) and I were assigned this duty. At the creek we worked to hold them near the water without wandering, so they would tank up. By the time we got home we were bushed and the cattle acted like they hadn't had a drink. However, with repetition of the process the cattle became acclimated to the routine and learned to drink to the utmost during the single daily exposure, and they survived, though not without considerable loss of weight. Pastures had dried up and other rations were limited. Milk production decreased severely.

To reach the creek we drove the cattle on the Bell Lane road that crossed the creek. Marion Bell pastured cattle in fields bordering the lane, and extra shepherding was necessary when our cattle observed the Bell cattle across the fence, but breakouts were avoided. The cattle were driven every day until rains filled our pond in late August.

Most farmers had one pond only, two at the most. Ponds were small, and laboriously constructed, using a team of mules or horses pulling a scoop, manually controlled and dumped by a man walking behind with his hands on the scoop handles and the team control reins looped around his waist. The clay soils were not easily worked.

In later years as conservation and assistance programs of the Agricultural Stabilization and Conservation Services (ASCS) came into play, farmers began building large ponds under guidance and subsidization by the ASCS. Construction was done with bulldozers and to specifications of the ASCS.

The ASCS ponds had to be fenced to exclude livestock, and piped so water flowed by gravity to a watering tank

54

outside the fence. A float valve controlled water flow and level in the tank.

Today the landscape is dotted with ponds that provide for increased cattle herds and also fishing. The pond building program was and still is one worthy government effort that has been of enormous benefit, not only to farmers but also ecologically. I believe that evaporation from this multitude of man-made reservoirs has helped to reduce the severity of droughts since 1936 by increasing moisture and heat dispersion to the atmosphere, particularly in the Midwest and plains states.

As the drought wore on, not only was there a shortage of water but also pastures had dried up, and only the very early hay had made anything like a crop. The situation was becoming desperate for many farmers when the federal government initiated a program to subsidize the sale of cattle made surplus by pasture and feed shortages. Market prices were extremely low because of the surplus and light demand for beef products. The government established a fair pricing schedule for participants in the program and subsidized the difference between market prices and prices received by farmers. Part of the deal between the government and the packers included government purchases of canned beef produced from the program cattle. This beef was distributed by the government to those enrolled in the federal welfare program. The old, thin, lanky cows were designated canners—I suppose because a large portion were processed into the canned beef distributed by the government. This cattle classification persisted through later years.

Dad and Mom were too proud to apply for the federal emergency food assistance program, but some neighbors gave us some of the canned beef—said they had gotten tired of it! We thought the meat was great, lapping it up and wishing for more. It was a wonderful diversion from a late summer meat diet of pork jowl and boiled squirrels.

The spring and winter hatches of young squirrels were skimpy and we were shooting mostly old ones for meat. An old bachelor (batchelor in Ozark lingo) we knew who lived by himself and carried his cooking water from a distant spring, told us he had about given up on squirrels for sustenance—he was worn to a frazzle from carrying water to boil them long enough to make the gravy tender. No pressure cookers in those days.

About half of our cattle were sold under the government program. Mom insisted on keeping the best milkers and a couple of heifers for future milkers. Enough hay had been put up early to get the remainder of the herd through the following winter, along with supplementary turnips that we chopped up with corn cutting knives. After the August rains fell we planted a large patch of turnips, and they had ample time to produce a bumper crop. Also, we ate turnips, but they never sated my appetite and I have not been enthusiastic about turnip dishes since the depression.

We had been hauling water for sanitary use, washing clothes, and watering our various fowl flocks in order to conserve our cistern water for drinking and cooking, but the cistern went dry before the drought ended. Then we began hauling our potable water supply from a spring on Norman creek, which supplied the water where the cattle drank from the creek. With concern about contamination we switched to hauling water from a good spring farther upstream on Uncle Willie's farm, but it was not as readily accessible, and getting there and loading containers took more time for each haul. We had to hew and dig a trail in some places.

With all the other drought related problems, my mother fell and broke her left arm, which limited her ability to handle some tasks. One job was clothes washing and we kids took over. All laundry was done by hand, scrubbing on a board, rinsing and wringing. Water was precious, so the underwear, light and fast-colored clothes were washed first, then the same water was used to wash the more heavily soiled work clothes.

Later, a used Maytag washer with roll wringers was acquired. Its agitator and wringer were power driven by a one-lunger two-cycle gasoline engine. A foot-operated crank was pumped to start the engine, which was cantankerous about starting. Nevertheless, the rig proved to be a great advance from the corrugated scrubbing board and hand wringing. Today those old scrub boards are considered antiques and sell for a handsome price. Replicas in the smaller sizes are available in specialty and antique shops. Though small in stature, my wrists are strong, and developed, I think, as a result of wringing clothes and milking cows.

While the cistern was dry we cleaned it. The single pulley-rope arrangement used to haul buckets of water from the cistern was our means of access to the bottom of the reservoir. One end of the rope was anchored at ground level, and then Wib and I took turns climbing down into the cistern. One filled a bucket with cleanup material and the other hoisted the loaded bucket to the surface. Actually it was nice to stay down in the cistern for a while to cool off, but I needed help to hoist Wib up when he wanted out. A multi-force reduction pulley system was needed to lift each other, but such a unit would have been slow and tedious for hauling up smaller weights of cleanup material and water.

Our cistern was only about 15 feet deep, but quite large at the bottom, being about seven feet in diameter. The bottom and the sides half way up from the bottom were composed of a rocky strata interspersed with a sticky clay. I don't think it ever leaked a drop. The top half of the cistern was cased with large shaped stones, and the cutting, shaping and laying of the stones to form this cylindrical section was a masterful piece of masonry work. The craftsmanship of some of those early stonemasons was a joy to see.

Later, after removal of an old back porch (the one on which I hid in the box used for a dog house), the cistern was enclosed within a larger kitchen and dining area addition. A pitcher type pump was installed and boy, we were living it up—water in the house. Had to remember to keep enough water on hand to prime the pump. With ten feet of water depth this reservoir contained about 3,000 gallons.

My mother was not psychic but she was familiar with a lot of the old superstitions of the Ozark Plateau and hill country. Sometimes you might observe her throwing a pinch of salt over her shoulder when something went wrong in the kitchen. Anyway, in the spring of '34 she had a premonition that a drought was on the way and insisted that every plot of suitable ground be plowed and planted to vegetable crops.

We didn't have a team for farm work, and borrowed Grandpa Malone's mules, Beck and Kate to plow and harrow the gardens in preparation for planting. My brother and I went with Dad to get the mules, along with the buckboard wagon for hauling the walking moldboard plow and spiked-tooth harrow. The mules were hitched to the wagon, the tillage equipment loaded, and we headed out to the county road to home. Just after entering the main road, something spooked the mules or they just plain decided to act up—they took off like they were "hell bent for election". Now, Dad was an experienced teamster and had worked these mules before, but he couldn't slow them. He thought the mules would wreck the wagon and the tillage tools, and he hollered to Wib and me to jump out. Wib jumped, but I stayed in the wagon. Dad worked harder yet to control the mules, but if anything, they increased their speed, so he jumped out too. He thought I had evacuated but saw differently as the wagon, load and mules went whistling on down the road. He tore after the wagon yelling at me to get out, but couldn't catch up. Those booger mules ran another 50 yards, and then just stopped right in the middle of the road. Dad came to the wagon breathless and hung on the tailgate panting. Finally, he could speak and asked, "Why in the world didn't you jump?" and I replied, "I didn't want to." I feared outrage at that point, but apparently he was so relieved and thankful that no one was injured and the wagon was still in one piece, that he just shook his head and grumbled. The mules traveled the rest of the way to our place just as docilely as you please and like nothing had ever happened.

Patches of garden were planted where none had been established before, and the mules performed admirably while all the grounds were plowed and harrowed. Then everyone went to work, sowing and planting for the next several days. Most seed germinated and emerged. Subsequently, enough rain fell to generate good yields of the early crops such as lettuce, radishes, peas and onions, and the early varieties of cabbage plants developed nice heads. Not enough rain was received at the critical growth period to fully develop the potatoes, and our diggings garnered only little boogers, hardly big enough to make creamed potatoes and peas. Mom's foresight paid off because some of the virgin plots held moisture well and provided additional yields before the heat and lack of moisture decimated everything.

As crops became more drought stressed the insect infestations also increased. The only pesticides available then were arsenic of lead and Paris green, and because of cost were not used as often as needed. We eradicated potato bugs by hand—knocking them off the plants into a bucket, and then killing the pests by adding kerosene to the bucket. We tromped on the bugs that missed the bucket and fell on the ground. By mid-July most crops were done for. We picked some early blackberries of small size, and the plum trees yielded a modicum of fruit. Peaches were small, but we peeled them, and Mom canned them whole, seeds and all. Tasted mighty good come wintertime.

The drought of 1936 began later in the summer than '34 and extended into September. It was not as severe as '34, and we harvested more crops before the heat and dryness clobbered the late plantings. Hay crops were of better quality and sufficient to supply most of our winter cattle feed. We drove the cattle to water for a few days, and the cistern was dry for a short time.

During both droughts the fishing lakes and holes in Dry Fork and Norman creek went dry. As the water levels dropped the neighbors got together and seined the holes, harvesting the fish before the holes dried up. I joined the crew and noodled for fish hiding under rocks and deadfalls along the edges of the stream where the seine wasn't maneuverable. I grabbed a couple of nice catfish without getting spiked by their sharp horns. Luckily, no snakes were grabbed but we saw some moccasins. The fish were a welcome addition to our diet.

We survived the droughts and never went hungry though there were times when we might have eaten more if available. The hustle and ingenuity of our parents in the growing and preserving of foods pulled and pushed us through. And, we survived without government handouts.

Today we are not immune from droughts but the effects are not so severe because most farms and country homes have deep drilled wells with capacity to supply the needs of the household plus livestock. Large farms may have more than one well. Moreover, more and larger ponds and small lakes have been constructed since World War II. There is little irrigation in our Ozark region because there is little row cropping any more. Most open land is grassland and used for hay cropping and pasturing of beef cattle. Only one dairy operation remains in our Phelps County.

7/   Hallelujah Chorus

The Highland (a.k.a "Blackjack") schoolhouse was the central meetings place for the community, Sunday school, bible school, church and sundry other activities.

The late 1920's and the thirties represented an era when roving and itinerant preachers, troubadours, evangelists and promoters were ubiquitous to our rural area. Most were out trying to garner enough income to live on or to acquire a stake to move on toward better opportunities.

No sooner would one preacher move on than another arrived to promote some sort of evening preaching or revival services. Some asked to board with members of the community while others traveled to and from the evening meetings. The longevity of their activities depended on the reception by the community, and especially by the contents of the offering plate. Their personalities and performances were as varied as those attending the meetings. One guy I remember well arrived with quite an entourage of family and friends. He flailed the air and preached with an apparent grasp of the Gospel of Jesus Christ, but I don't think he could read. He had memorized key texts from listening to others reading to him, and therefore the reason for group support on the road. Though enthusiastic and sincere, his grammar was atrocious and not compatible with our local dialect. After a couple of nights, attendance dropped off and we never saw him again.

Many of the nightingale evangelists were not associated with established religious denominations and had little or no formal theological training. Some didn't know the meaning of the word seminary. Nonetheless, I believe that a number of them, with the grace of God, were successful in bringing understanding of the mercy and grace of God in his word, and salvation through our Lord and Savior, Jesus Christ.

Our community was protestant oriented, but not denominationally aligned, generally tolerant of variations in theological beliefs. Doctrinal standards of the Baptist denomination were most prevalent in acceptance.

Before my mother was married a purportedly ordained Baptist minister baptized her, but record keeping was not a forte of people in those days, and some ministers gradually gravitated to thinking they were certified ministers and practiced thusly. It was common to baptize by immersion in ponds or creeks. Church services and sometimes dinners would be held at the water's edge, followed by multiple baptisms.

A baptism with a large audience present was being conducted in a pool of upper Dry Fork creek. The administration of the sacrament to one of the participants was underway when a large snake began swimming in the direction of the preacher and baptismal group. An observer on the creek bank yelled, "Somebody kill that damn snake". Pandemonium reigned in the water for a while, with screeching, splashing ladies and a few distraught men. With all the commotion the snake disappeared, and the minister eventually got the melee under control and resumed the rudely interrupted ceremonies. The baptisms were completed without any reappearance of the reptile.

For a year or so, church services were conducted at Highland schoolhouse ("Blackjack") by a more or less perennial preacher who claimed to be a certified Baptist minister. He scheduled a Sunday evening service once each month when possible. Fire and brimstone was the order of the day or night, and favorite bible verses and texts were expounded repetitively with theatrical emphasis and fist poundings of the air and the lectern. In a short while, he began to wear thin, and I heard my Mom say, "I'm tired of hearing—a city set upon a hill cannot be hid".

When the "Holy Rollers" asked to conduct services at the schoolhouse there was little opposition. Attendance at their meetings was notable because many were interested in the highly emotional activities. This sect was likely similar to the Pentecostal denominations, but little doctrinal clarification was presented. Some of our area young men who liked to "cut up" and horse around, while keeping to the back of the room, might join in with the babblings (speaking in tongues) and physical motions of participants up front, mocking their worship. As a youngster, I slept through many church services, but rarely did I sleep during the "Holy Roller" sessions.

An elderly man in his early sixties named Alfred "Hout" Golden bought a farm near the schoolhouse in the early thirties and moved in to work on his house, preparing it for family occupancy. He was interested in church and organized a Sunday school. Thereafter, bible classes and Sunday school were scheduled on a regular basis, and sometimes church services followed depending on availability of a pastor or minister. Attendance was noteworthy and young men from distances as far away as five or six miles rode their horses to Sunday school and church, attracted to the many young ladies who showed up. Horses, buggies and wagons were more prevalent than motor vehicles in the churchyard. Trees were used as hitching racks for the horses. Many times I saw men and girlfriends leave after church riding double on a horse. Those living within a mile or so of the schoolhouse often walked, and in some cases their feet were the only means of transportation.

One Sunday my cousin Charles Malone with his family was visiting us and he and I decided to ride old "Baldy", our horse, to Sunday school. I was only seven and he was six. We didn't have a riding saddle, so he sat behind me and held on to me while I held the reins in one hand and grasped Baldy's mane in the other. After Sunday school we led old Baldy up beside a stump and crawled aboard. A group of older boys were watching us and some dogs were hanging around. Just as we turned on to the county road one of the boys said, "sic 'em", setting a big dog into gear who then ran barking at the horse's heels. Now, the boys were not really malicious and didn't intend any harm. Practically everyone knew our old horse, and she had never spooked or gotten excited about anything—in fact, we had to thump her frequently to keep her traveling at a modest gait. But the hubbub spiked her that day, and with fire in her heels she took off down the middle of the road as fast as she could run with us hanging on for dear life. We met a car and she didn't give an inch, staying slap dab in the middle of the road—the driver took his car to the ditch. We were doing o.k. until we reached the turnoff at the store. I had no control whatsoever, and as she turned at breakneck speed to head for the driveway to the barn, Charles and I couldn't withstand the centrifugal force, and we became airborne to sail on down the dry, hard and rocky dirt road.

John Ketchum was at the store waiting for Dad to come from Sunday school, and hearing the loud clatter of the hoof beats on the road, ran out to see what the commotion was about—just as "Baldy" made the turnoff. Charles' head met a rock in the road. John grabbed him up in his arms and carried him to the store porch. He was knocked out for about 20 minutes, but with the exception of a large knot and gouge on his head he wasn't seriously injured and recovered quickly from the trauma. Like a cat, I suppose, I must have landed on my feet without injury other than my pride. But I was wide-eyed scared. By the time Charles was regaining consciousness most of the Sunday school attendees had arrived at the store to see what happened.

It was fortuitous that we flew off the horse because she blasted all the way to the barn and into her stall. The entrance to the stall was through a low overhead doorway, and if we had hung on we would have been creamed by the door casing, and likely I would have been killed. Old Baldy never moved so fast again, though my brother did his best to race her after we acquired a riding saddle.

Sunday school meetings were closed with the Lord's Prayer and Mr. Golden was Sunday school leader for several years. The King James Bible translation was almost the universal source for scripture readings, but other bible translations began to appear, and Mr. Golden liked the translation of the Lord's prayer that read, "Forgive us our trespasses as we forgive those who trespass against us", better than the King James version which reads, "Forgive us our debts as we forgive our debtors" (Matthew, Chapter 6).

Mr. Golden was a kind, gentle and honest man who had a pipe in his mouth when he was awake except in church or Sunday school. He bought pipe tobacco from Dad in big RJR sacks (for some reason unknown to me, the RJR brand had locally been dubbed, "Run Johnny Run", though the insignia was registered by the R. J. Reynolds Tobacco Co.) and on credit. He bought sacks periodically for a year before paying the bill. He was just a slow payer, but facetiously, Dad rationalized that the reason Mr. Golden didn't like the King James Version was that it reminded him of his debts.

In the drought summer of 1934 a Presbyterian missionary minister from Cuba, Missouri found Seaton and began church services at the schoolhouse on a regular monthly basis. Small, short and stout with a big wide smile and hearty laugh, he knew all the hymns and led the singing loudly and with gusto. Everyone liked Ernest E. Boyd. He traveled out of his way just to stop and visit with Dad and customers at the store. He loved to hunt squirrels and fancied our best squirrel dog, Carlo. Brother Wib named the dog, but where he dug up the handle, I don't remember. Mr. Boyd ogled over Carlo so much that Dad let him take the dog and keep him during the summers. Wib and I were not exactly pleased with Dad's generosity, though our other squirrel dog was quite adequate. However, you can't beat a team that knows to tree with a dog barking on each side to keep the squirrels guessing as the hunter or hunters circle the tree.

Mr. Boyd brought Carlo home in the fall, and our prodigal canine would be fat and sassy from pampering and select grub, turning up his nose at our mundane feed offerings, and even ignore us at times. After about six weeks Carlo had lost most of his excess weight and returned to a more normal cur attitude and with more attention to our commands..

The young people of our community received Mr. Boyd's summer bible schools enthusiastically. One of his daughters played a portable organ which they managed to haul in the trunk of his 1935 V-8 Ford to the bible classes.

She was 21 when I was 13, and I developed a secret crush on her—I doubt she or anyone else ever suspected.

Actor's groups were organized one summer session to present plays based on incidents described in the Bible. After practicing and at the conclusion of the summer school, we put on a show for the community in conjunction with church services and a big Sunday picnic style dinner on the grounds. I played the part of the traveler who got beat up by the thieves in the Good Samaritan story. Clubs used by the thieves were made by stuffing long stockings tightly with cornhusks, then sewing up the ends. In reflection, those kids were not so playful--the actor-thieves pummeled me very enthusiastically and vigorously—retribution perceived, perhaps with no malice aforethought.

The following summer we attended a week of Bible studies with other youth from the regional area of Reverend Boyd's missionary ministry. Meetings were conducted at the Safe, Missouri fairgrounds facilities. The fairgrounds exhibition buildings were used as dormitories, and cots and beds were moved in for our stay. One large building was adapted for kitchen-dining facilities. Local resident ladies and mothers were recruited as cooks and chaperones. All attendees were asked to bring some food supplies to contribute to the pot. Besides the bible classes, we had a great time playing games and attending get-acquainted parties. We carried our water from a gorgeous artesian well located on the fairgrounds—laboring under the memory of water supply shortages and conservation; I was fascinated by the abundance of sparkling clear water flowing to the meadow.

I participated in the sacrament of Holy Communion, and I did not understand this Service. My major criticism of the meetings and studies was the lack of explanation and instruction for communion. Grape juice and bread wafers were consumed as symbols of the blood and body of our Lord Jesus Christ, and that is not in conformance with Christ's words spoken at the Last Supper (Matthew 26:26,27,28; 1 Corinthians 11: 24,25). Also, I took communion at a military chapel in England while serving in the U.S. Eighth Air Force and the chaplain did not explain the sacrament before communing the airmen.

After marriage to a girl who was raised as a member of the Lutheran Church, Missouri Synod, I was impressed with the biblically sound doctrines and liturgies of the LCMS. After attending adult confirmation classes I became a member of this church in 1950, and was baptized at the time of my adult confirmation. We drink wine just as Jesus commanded during his Last Supper with his disciples, and we believe the bread and wine are his body and blood just as he said. Moreover, we accept and adhere to the admonition and guidance of St.Paul as he writes in First Corinthians of the Bible, especially chapter 11, where he deals with participation in the sacrament of Holy Communion.

Historically minded old timers with a religious bent, like to talk about "Brush Arbor" revival meetings. As a youngster I attended a few of those affairs. Usually, pole framed structures with brush-covered roofs and an open front were prepared for the preaching entourage. Benches and other available types of chairs were collected for seating the audience in front of the open side of the Arbor. Kerosene fueled lanterns were hung on poles and trees for lighting.

No question, we the audience were out under God's canopy of stars and planets (no satellites then), but our feet were on terra firma and our bodies exposed to a local atmosphere invaded with buzzing gnats, mosquitoes and other flying and crawling insects attracted by the lights. To say the least, conditions were not conducive to absorption of the proffered evangelical messages, no matter the skill and elegance of the presenter. And if you didn't have the itch before attending the hoorah, the ubiquitous resident ticks and chiggers of the summer and fall in the Ozarks would take care of that.

Today, the Highland schoolhouse and property belongs to the existing community and is used as a meeting place for Sunday school and church. Grade school was terminated in the early fifties when the district was consolidated with the St. James school system.

We have fond memories of those rural Ozark church services and related community activities. Today we see many mega church congregations with thousands of members, multi-million dollar budgets and multiple preachers or leaders who may not be any more effective in reaching out to bring salvation to the lost through the Word of God. Our Lord Jesus Christ said, "I am the way, the truth and the life. No one comes to the Father except through Me." John 14:6 from NKJV. There are many in the hierarchies of various established churches who do not accept this word of God as divinely inspired and infallible. They are reticent to preach that we all are sinners and to call sin a sin. "For the wages of sin is death, but the gift of God is eternal life in Christ Jesus our Lord." Romans 6:23 NKJV.

"Scripture is a two edged sword and penetrates where human cleverness and skill falter and fail" (author unknown).

8/   Cracker Barrel Philosophers

A man named Chamberlain established the first store in the vicinity of Seaton, Missouri some years before the Civil War. A succession of owners included Farmers Union, W. N. Adams, Mr. Broyles and K. H. Spradling. At the time of Spradling's purchase the store was located on the county road and just across from Highland (Blackjack) schoolhouse. The Seaton post office was also located at Spradling's store. Later, Spradling moved both the store and post office one-quarter mile east to another location on the county road that is now State Route JJ.

A new store building, a warehouse and residence were constructed using native oak lumber for all framing, siding and floors. Sidings were battened and heavy building paper was the only insulation on the inner walls and ceiling. The store and warehouse were roofed with galvanized-corrugated sheet metal and the house was roofed with asphalted type roll material. The store was built on layered rock pillar-type foundations and elevated well off the ground at about three feet along the frontal section in order to level the structure on an undisturbed site. Possibly the builders were concerned about termite exposure and also wanted good ventilation to avoid dampness.

When the tornado of 1947 struck, several trees near the store were uprooted but the only damage to the building was the loss of a few sheets of roofing. Uncle Robey surmised that the tornado just passed underneath.

Mom and Dad purchased the store and home with 66 acres of land from Spradling in late 1922 and moved there with my two-year-old brother in 1923. As mentioned in chapter 1, I was born there on December 29, 1923.Upon taking title to the store and farm Dad was also sworn in as post master of the Seaton fourth-class post office, which was located in a framed off area in the northwest corner of the store.

The store was a focal point for the community. Not only did people come for groceries and mail but they gathered for gossip, story telling, friendly banter, checker playing bartering and business dealing, commiseration and politicking. It was a communications hub.

A community telephone system had been in operation at one time. It used the old battery-energized line and phones with all subscribers on the same line. Individual residences were contacted through a system of hand-cranked signal rings. For example, one long ring plus two short rings may have been a call for us. All phones on the line rang when a call was signaled. The many potential combinations of short and long rings could more than accommodate the subscribers to the system. The most obvious disadvantages of such a system was inability to get on the line because of garrulous persons who hogged the line, and lack of privacy due to unsolicited listeners called "rubber neckers". As the number of "neckers" increased, transmission deteriorated until no one could hear conversations. Transmission under best conditions was only fair and lightning was a safety problem. Members of the cooperative system were responsible for maintenance and repair. Unfortunately, during the depression the lines were allowed to deteriorate and there wasn't a working phone system again until after World War II.

Dad merchandized groceries and dry goods plus a smattering of hardware, farm and home supplies. It truly was a typical vintage country store, more or less.

Kerosene (coal oil) was a major commodity since everyone used it for lighting fuel. Customers' containers (usually one or two gallon steel units, bailed and closed with screwed cap, and a pouring spout) were filled from a spigot installed at the bottom of a 55-gallon steel drum. I was happy when the fuels delivery company brought a 200-gallon tank with a pump, so all we had to do to fill containers was hold them under a spout and hand-crank the desired amount.

Vinegar was dispensed from a 100-gallon, wood-staved barrel that came with a wooden spigot, which was driven into a hole drilled in one end of the barrel near the lip or perimeter. We mounted the barrel on blocks or platform so the vinegar could be drawn into the customer's container by gravity and liquid head. Occasionally a customer needed vinegar badly, but forgot to bring a container. Dad tried to accumulate a few containers for loaners, but if they were loaned out he would send one of us kids to the house to see if empty fruit jars or other suitable containers were available. Empty vinegar barrels were in great demand and spoken for well ahead of time. Some suppliers accepted returns of barrels for rebates or in exchange when another filled barrel was purchased. At this time all vinegar was derived from the acetous fermentation of apple cider.

My father's given name was Albert, but universally, he was called Bert. One memorable lady customer would state his name with a delightful ringing purr, and I recall her saying, "Bert-t-t-t-t, I need a gallon of vinigger". What a pleasant vernacular. She also always asked for pickle seed when wanting cucumber seed for planting.

During my early experience in Dad's store most grocery commodities were purchased in bulk quantities, with the exception of tinned canned goods and some sealed glass jars and bottled items. Sugar, salt, flour, cornmeal and beans came packaged in 100-pound cloth bags. Flour and cornmeal also were shipped in cloth bags containing 25 and 50 pounds. During the mid-depression era several suppliers vied with each other to determine who could sell the most flour by promoting fast-color cloth fabrics for the flour bags. Many attractive patterns were offered, and much bartering and trading was common among the women searching for desired patterns and quantities of cloth. One of the perennial comments expected from local wags—"Wouldn't that cloth make a pretty pair of drawers for so-and-so"?

Not every household was gifted with an accomplished seamstress or even a sewing machine. My mother was a very talented seamstress and fabricated many dresses, blouses,

71

skirts panties, bonnets, etc. for herself, my sister and others who bartered for her services, often trading fabrics and accessories for her work. She eschewed making men's shirts—I never got to wear a colorful flour-sack shirt. An old foot-treadle Singer machine was used for all her sewing.

When about eight years old I fussed, wheedled, cajoled and begged Mom until she made a cowboy vest and pair of chaps for me. Immediately after completion, I went out and ripped the chaps asunder trying to ride a calf.

The 100-pound bags of commodities were stored behind and under the long service counter that was positioned in front of the shelves of canned goods, tobaccos and miscellaneous items. Products were scooped out of the sacks into brown kraft paper bags and weighed to the amounts requested with small-package type scales mounted on the counter top. Then the bags were folded at the top and hand tied with cotton twine.

To satisfy a diversity of customer palates, dry whole beans were stocked in several varieties, usually navy, pinto, and Great Northern white. Whole roasted coffee beans were purchased in bags containing 100 pounds. The bags were huge and unwieldy for one person to handle due to low bulk density of the coffee. They were constructed with a liner of crinkly-like high-tension paper snuggled inside a tightly woven type of burlap with extra strength to provide protection from snagging, and spillage of a relatively expensive product. The liner was designed to preserve the quality of the beans, reducing migration of extraneous materials through the burlap, and reducing loss of flavor by transpiration.

A large hand cranked grinder was mounted on the counter for grinding coffee beans, if requested by the customer. Most customers preferred to buy whole beans and grind to suit their beverage preparation method, and grind in lesser quantities as used. A small hand-cranked kitchen grinder was almost a standard accessory in households. Usually two brands of beans, differently priced, were stocked in an effort to satisfy a range of customer tastes. It's doubtful that many persons, if put to a taste test, could discern any difference when both brands were brewed the same way.

I liked the smell of coffee beans, whole or ground, but we didn't drink coffee beverages. Dad said it wasn't good for us, and always pointed to a family that drank coffee, as fanatically and often as the British drank tea, saying, "Look how brown their complexion, that's what coffee will do to you". He may have been right then, but several years later, he became a coffee imbiber and never acquired even a tinge of brown. What coffee type and brand was best, how much grinding, how to make the beverage, etc. were subjects of enthusiastic debate by the customers.

Dried fruits such as raisins, prunes, peaches and apples were bought from wholesalers in boxes containing 30 pounds. The boxes were constructed of light gauge wood slatting and lined with waxed paper, and stored on a large shelf behind the counter within easy reach. Later, these fruits were shipped in boxes fabricated of heavy pressed paper fiberboard. The fruit pieces packed together rather tightly, and scooping was difficult, so often we just dug the fruit out by hand, dropping it into a paper poke for weighing and packaging. People were not so finicky then and besides, most of the dried fruits were cooked before consumption, though I didn't hesitate to take some in hand for a snack, without washing beforehand. Anyway, we didn't have a sink with tap water to run to. Raisins and prunes were stocked all year but dried apples and peaches were carried seasonally.

Soda crackers were purchased in large round ribbed light-gauge sheet metal cans with friction lids and 30 pounds of crackers capacity. Waxed paper lined the cans and separated the multi-layered sheets of crackers. The cracker sheets were impressed with a pattern so they could be broken into small square individual crackers. We broke the cracker sheets with ungloved hands to place them in paper pokes for weighing and packaging. Wonder if today's hygienists and state food inspectors would get apoplexy if they observed this or the aforementioned handling of dried fruits. Cracker inventory was kept as low as possible during the humid summer months because of moisture absorption with resultant softening. Though the friction type lid helped reduce the problem it had to be removed for access, and during the hot humid summer months, excess moisture would enter the crackers during extended storage.

Lard was purchased in tinned sheet metal cans with friction type lids. The cans held 45 to 50 pounds. Lard was ladled from the cans into the customer's container, quite often a half or one-gallon metal syrup bucket with friction lid. The large containers were called lard "stands", why I don't know. Dad sold the "stands" to an ever-present waiting list for the magnificent price of 15 to 20 cents during the depression era. Of course lard was selling at only about 5 cents per pound and dry beans going for a similar price. An equivalent "stand" can be bought today in variety and specialty stores, but at a much greater price. They are excellent storage for many things and my wife uses two or three in our house.

Dad's candy showcase was of nice size with glass top and sides. Sliding doors were positioned on the backside where only the proprietor could get at the candy from behind the counter. Three or four brands of candy bars and a similar number of loose candies were normally stocked and displayed in the case. During the Christmas season more varieties of loose candy and striped canes were offered. Loose candy was sold by the pound, but Dad was generous to the kids and might add extra to the poke without weighing. Hot summer weather caused chocolate type candies to deteriorate and the inventory was minimized at that time. Air-conditioning, as we know it today was just a dream then.

Cooler weather at Christmas enabled the stocking of some fruits, meats and cheeses that would spoil in warmer weather. Oranges, bananas, bologna, knockwurst wieners and a block of American cheese were often purchased for the winter holidays and seasons. Bananas were purchased on the stalk as grown and what an attractive sight then, but rarely seen now.

Electric power was not available in our region, so no refrigeration other than cooling by the use of ice, and that was a problem because ice had to be hauled from Rolla or an ice plant at Maramec Springs. During the worst of the depression era we just made do without ice, but later, Dad made trips to town often enough to keep ice in a soda pop cooler with room enough for both pop and some lunchmeat such as bologna or braunschweiger.

In the late thirties Dad bought a used Servel refrigerator that operated on kerosene energy, and installed it in the house. The Servel performed well but could be cantankerous if you didn't maintain the burner and trim the wick periodically. Later, liquefied petroleum gas (LPG) burning models were not as prone to burner problems and performed handsomely for many years--in some cases longer than the electric motor driven compressor-cycle refrigerator units. At the Missouri School of Mines (now UMR), in a class dealing with heat and energy cycles, our professor avoided discussing the energy transfer cycle of the old Servel type units. He said such systems were not of commercial interest anymore (1947) and our time could be better spent on other systems, but I had the feeling he didn't understand the cycle very well. Some Servel refrigerators are still in use today.

Tobacco was an important item in the stocks of a country store. Most males over eighteen smoked or chewed, and a few females clandestinely used the weed in one or more ways. Some men never smoked but were not seen without a chaw in their mouths. No one native to our area used real snuff, the finely powdered tobacco that literally was snuffed in the nose. However, an outlander moved in and asked Dad to get snuff for him, and he obliged, then the guy soon moved away and Dad was stuck with a stock that sat on the shelf untouched for years, except for my handling. I was fascinated with it, and the idea that anyone would put such material in their nose. The snuff was packaged in cute little round cans that I coveted—finally, I sneaked a can but never tried any in my nose.

The tobacco product that is stuffed between the lip and gums, and quite popular today, especially with the younger generations, was rarely used in our community. Sometimes, it was inappropriately referred to as snuff because it wasn't chewed. Unlike snuff, this tobacco is more coarsely ground and glycerin or emollients added to prepare a sort of sticky mix that will hold together in a wad. It was souped up with other additives to enhance the flavor and taste.

Plug or flat tobacco was the most popular chew, but twists also were in demand. Dad usually stocked at least three brands each of plug and twist. The plug tobacco came from the supplier as 9 x 12 inch flat pressed slabs of ¾ to one inch thickness, and pre-marked with indentations for measuring and cutting the slabs into 2 x 3 inch pieces. The tobacco companies supplied special cutters for this purpose. Years later, after pre-packaging of individual plugs had become the order-of-the-day, these cutters were sought after as relics and antiques. A cutter was one of the few items in the store that I wanted for a keepsake, but by the time I got around to asking Dad for one, the scavenging antique hounds had separated them from him.

The slabs of chaw tobacco were packaged in very nicely made wooden boxes with mitered joints and a tongue-and-grooved sliding lid. We kids had nibs on the boxes, but now and then, someone outside the family in special favor, and after entreaties, might be favored with a box.

One customer chewed Old Kentucky twist exclusively for as long as he lived (91), and he didn't die of cancer. This brand is sold today, and is as potent as ever. I couldn't chew it without getting dizzy and sick unless it was diluted with the much milder cut-type chews that entered the market while I was in my teens.

During the worst years of the depression most smokers rolled their own cigarettes, and Dad stocked tobaccos that were satisfactory for both cigarettes and pipes. Prince Albert, Velvet and Half and Half were dominant brands and packaged in small pocket tins—the empties are often displayed for sale in today's antique stores and flea markets.

My wife has a whole carton of fresh-as-new empty Prince Albert tins inherited from an uncle. Someone with deep pockets might go whole hog and buy a fancied-up large round tin of tobacco. Those containers also are peddled at many collectibles shops.

The most economical brands of pipe and cigarette tobacco were packaged in small cotton cloth bags along with a larger economy-sized bag. Both sizes were closed with pull-and-tie strings and sealed with a glued paper strip. RJR (R.J.Reynolds Tobacco Co.) was the dominant brand in bags. The renowned Bull Durham brand was not popular in our locality, and Dad did not always carry it. Free papers for roll-your-own cigarettes were furnished with many of the packages and most smokers were adept at this game.

It was common knowledge then; long before we had an intrusive Federal Health and Human Services Agency or a Surgeon General, that smoking could be harmful to your health. When a smoker lit up a cigarette it was not unusual to hear some wiseacre say, "Lighting up another coffin nail, eh?" The rejoinder might be, "Yeah, but I'll die happy". More people smoked pipes in those days and many inhaled as much as when smoking cigarettes. Two veteran, inhaling pipe smokers whom I remember, died at the ages of 70 and 79. I have no idea how much their lives may have been shortened by the smoking, but both inhaled and blew smoke like a coal-fired steam engine. They didn't die of lung cancer and there was no autopsies to tell what the lungs looked like inside. However, I would speculate that they were black.

A large glass showcase on legs and in line with a long counter was located in the store on the west side. Behind were shelves for storage and display of dry goods and sundry items. The showcase displayed items such as dress shirts, ties, hankies, pens and pencils, knives, small toys, trinkets and other merchandise. Chambray work shirts were shelved along with denim overalls and cotton khaki type summer trousers. Socks and hosiery were stored in boxes on the shelves. Bolts of cotton fabrics and muslin were shelved and the counter was used to lay out, measure, and cut off yardage—when the counter sitters would be shooed off. Two bolts of "oil cloth" with different patterns were offered and shelved with other cloth yardage. This cloth consisted of a cotton fabric made waterproof by being treated with oil and pigment, for use as tablecloths, shelf coverings and the like.

Similar but more durable and attractive cloth is made today by treating fabrics with polyvinyl type plastics. We use it on our kitchen table and I love it.

Items for what ails you were stored on shelves in a section contiguous with the groceries and canned goods. Liniment for cuts, bruises, aches and pains; mineral oil for lubricating the internals; salts (magnesium sulfate hydrates) for the constipated and soaking of limbs or swollen feet; turpentine disinfectant and healer; other laxatives; salves and ointments for soothing and healing; tonics and elixirs for the low spirited; cough syrups and drops or lozenges; castor oil for constipation and punishment; iodine and mercurochrome for disinfecting, poison ivy, rashes, ticks and chigger bites; Carter's Little Liver Pills and Carter's pills of different colors for many other ailments; and aspirin, the only analgesic. Vicks Vapo-Rub was used to treat head and chest colds and to thwart pneumonia. While confined to bed, Vicks-impregnated cloths were affixed to your chest, and if pneumonia didn't kill you, Vicks Vapo-Rub would make you wish it had. "Black Draught" was a bottled black liquid that was advertised as a stimulant and cure for a broad array of ailments. It was popular and no wonder, it contained a substantial concentration of alcohol as did many of the then so-called patent medicines.

Red and white corn syrups were staples and stocked in half gallon and one gallon tinned buckets with bails and friction lids. It was consumed with baked bread, biscuits, pancakes, cornbread and butter when available, and used as a sugar substitute. Much debate ensued among customers as to which color syrup was best. I preferred the red and it was priced 5 cents less per half gallon than the clear. From my evaluation, the clear (some people called it white) syrup was just red syrup refined by filtration and oxidation to remove color and some impurities. I figured the natural ingredients beyond the sugars content was the flavor enhancer in the red stuff, and perhaps provided a small amount of vitamins to boot. Empty syrup buckets were treasured and used as containers for many things—doggoned good berry pickin' buckets for one thing.

Besides ground peppers, spices for pickling were stocked. Spices were relatively expensive and not used then in cooking nearly as much as today. Cloves were added to canned peaches and nutmeg was used in applesauce and for baking. Dad carried the whole nutmeg nuts, which had to be grated to have freshly powdered nutmeg—loved the smell. Sage was stocked because many liked it as a flavoring for pork sausage—earlier I wrote about Mom's heavy hand with the sage—it takes just a delicate touch.

Standard wire-drawn steel nails in the range of penny sizing and wire fence staples were stocked. They were packed for shipping in small wooden staved kegs containing 100 pounds. My wife uses one of those kegs, all painted and decorated, for potato storage in our kitchen.

Dad ordered fencing wire only on demand by customers. Everyone made fence posts by splitting white oak or post oak logs, cut to length and sharpened on one end with an ax. Posts were driven into the ground with 12 to 16 pound steel mauls. Now, swing one of those all day and you'll know what physical labor means.

Timber and firewood were cut by hand using axes and crosscut saws, so Dad stocked some axes and replacement handles, plus files for sharpening axes and other cutting tools. The woodsmen of our area frequently debated the efficacy of the single bit ax in comparison to the double bit. A majority favored the double bit with a head weight of three to four pounds. Being of small stature I wielded the lighter three-pound head better. I'd say the chain saw is the most important advancement ever for the timber industry, and anyone who has had to rely on the ax or crosscut saw would surely agree. I handled an ax quite well but didn't like to saw. I always accused my brother of not pulling his share.

Floor platform weighing scales on wheels were used for weighing produce, feeds, etc. in the store. They were beamed readouts with add-on beam weights to provide a capacity to 300 pounds. Contests were held to see who could pull the most weight by sitting on the platform, holding bottom rails with a hand on each side, then pushing down with feet and body. Once, while exerting thusly, something popped in my head and I felt some dizziness, thereafter putting a damper on my inclination to strut my lifting prowess.

Rainy days, wet fields and woodlands or other inclement weather byproducts fostered the congregation of a potpourri of idlers at the store.

Politics frequently highlighted the conversations, but serious controversies didn't develop often because most residents supported the Democratic Party. They might occasionally harangue about an isolated republican or two who appeared to be weathering the depression better than they. Dad referred to some republicans as black-assed republicans, and I'm not sure just how derogatory that expression was meant to be because he didn't elaborate a lot. His grandfather fought on the rebel side during the Civil War and was wounded in the battle of Wilson Creek just south of Springfield, Missouri. Dad was influenced enough by his grandfather that he had little good to say about Abe Lincoln.

The store was graced with only two chairs; so nail kegs, bags of commodities, boxes and the counters were improvised seats. The chairs were often reserved for checker players. I learned to play checkers at an early age and imagined I was pretty good until my rooming house landlord, Ernie Stackhouse in Kansas City, Missouri, took me on, many years later, and severely deflated my ego. He not only beat me every game, but refused to teach me his expert moves.

Religion was a popular topic of our country philosophers. Members of a sect group known as the "Millennium Dawns" had been soliciting in the neighborhood, trying to peddle or exchange their literature for about anything that could be carried or hauled in their beat up vehicles. They had engaged in conversation with one of our neighbors and he was relating the encounter to a group at the store. Succinctly, he said that their beliefs centered on the doctrine that Jesus Christ would return to earth and reign for a thousand years or a millennium. A listener, Harvey, took a long drag on his pipe, blew a string of smoke rings, then slid from his perch on a counter and announced, "There ain't no one going to make me believe that it is going to rain for a thousand years". Mirth erupted from the other loafers while Harvey glowered, but nothing further was offered by anyone either in explanation, confirmation or denial.

During another rainy day session, Harvey was present when the chatter turned to the dietary benefits of fruits and vegetables. At one point, Harvey inhaled, blew a big smoke ring, and said, "I like all vegetables except cherries, and I can't stand them."

Hot weather was a trying time for the egg buyer. Women brought eggs to the store in baskets or buckets and indicated a certain number in the container. Dad handed them to me, directing that they be placed in an egg case. We were prepped to take our own count, check quality and candle any that looked doubtful. We examined the eggs as we put them in the 30 dozen case. Dirty or otherwise questionable specimens were set aside for cleaning or candling. It was not unusual to find eggs that had not been gathered soon enough, had been taken from an abandoned nest, or partially incubated. With experience, most egg faults can be detected by the naked eye, but if in doubt, we candled for confirmation.

Our candler was a closed black box with a dry cell battery operated light inside. One side of the box contained a door with a hole, slightly less in size than the diameter of a large egg. Flexible but sturdy black fabric hinged the door, so no light could be emitted when an egg was placed in the hole and pushed in to contact a switch to turn on the light for illumination of the egg. By revolving the egg in the hole, any dark spots or blood veins could be detected and the eggs rejected. Bad eggs were presented to the seller with an offer to demonstrate the candling process should they appear skeptical. If they had miscounted, we showed them the partitioned dividers in the egg case that made an accurate counting more feasible. Now and then a customer's count was understated. Courtesy and diplomacy was the name of the game, and the training was great for a young feller.

As written in chapter 5, Dad began buying dairy cream in 1937, and I was trained to test the cream for butterfat content, which established the basis for calculating the value. The old Babcock test was applied, whereby a weighed amount (50 grams as I recall, and my first exposure to metric weights) of cream was poured into a small glass flask with a long graduated neck, then sulfuric acid solution was added, the bottle shaken by hand, then allowed to sit until the acid-cream reaction was complete. The flask and contents were centrifuged in a hand-cranked unit until all the butterfat as oil had been released. More sulfuric acid solution was subsequently added to the flask until the butterfat had risen into the graduated neck of the flask. Measuring with calipers the butterfat content as a percentage based on the calibration shown on the neck completed the testing.

The testing room was located at the far end of a large storage room, and partitioned off with a screened entrance door and screened windows above the front workbench. Customers could observe operations through the windows. The remainder of the side room was used for storage of cream in special ten gallon steel cans and other bulk food commodities, cases of eggs and platform scales for weighing cream, cream containers and other items.

Patrons brought cream in small covered metal containers, mostly of two to five gallons capacity. Some might bring two small containers at the same time, and a few who milked larger herds used ten-gallon cans like those we kept for storage and transport.

We weighed the patron's container with cream, then thoroughly mixed it, and took a sample for testing. After testing was completed, results were given to the customer. If they were unhappy with the results, we offered to retest if they cared to wait their turn again. If everything was satisfactory, the customer's container would be emptied of cream into one of our storage cans and the empty weight of the container determined.

Among patrons, cream quality and butterfat content varied widely. Fat content ranged from 40 to 55 percent. I hated to handle the high concentration stuff because it was so thick it could hardly be stirred, especially at cooler temperatures. But some prideful women were determined to develop as high a testing cream as possible, and then boast about it. Some women monitored my activities throughout the process, from receiving to the completion of testing. They were not allowed in the testing room, but those beady eyes were on me, especially while I was measuring the fat concentration in the test bottle, so I held it up to them so they could see the measurement. Even so, if the figure didn't come up to expectations, I could see doubts in their expressions, and they might comment, "But this was just like my last batch", or "This was from the same cows as last time, and I didn't change the separator setting". I tried to assure them that the best of creams could vary in quality. Perturbed customers usually were offered a retest if our schedule was not full and they were willing to wait for the rerun.

Many small producers did not have mechanical cream separators, and collected their cream by skimming the risen cream, after the milk had sat overnight or longer in crocks and pans. Such cream contained more milk, and depending on the skill of the skimmer might drop as low as 40 percent butterfat test. Those producers recognized the problems, and usually accepted test results without equivocation.

Not only butterfat content varied widely, but also the amount of extraneous material ranged all over the map. Crud content could pretty well be estimated by eye, but by state law we were required to run sediment tests on each patron's products on a monthly basis, and grading charts were supplied by the state. This testing was a lot of work and we were lax about fulfilling the quotas. State inspectors might threaten with license suspension for lack of sediment testing, but they checked only about once per year, and we never lost our buying license. Sediment test results were posted until the producer saw the tests, and evidence of excessive dirt and sediment would induce some customers to improve sanitation handling procedures, especially when we notified them that because of state requirements we might have to reject their cream.

The cream buying business went into a decline during 1940 when a neighbor started a whole milk pick-up route with delivery to a processing plant in Salem, Missouri. After World War II, Dad stopped buying cream as milk production declined markedly, and delivery of packaged fresh milk and other dairy products became available by truck delivery to his store. By then, the REA had installed electrical service, so he had power to operate refrigeration equipment.

John Parry was a farmer and customer who lived about three miles from us by horseback routes. He owned a beautiful riding horse with a nice saddle and other equestrian gear. He loved to visit, and many times after making purchases in the store, he mounted his steed, then sat there and visited an hour or more with new arrivals at the store who were willing to talk. On one occasion, Dad and I were hauling livestock of John's to St. Louis and John went with us. Early in the morning, somewhere about half way to St. Louis on old Route 66 there was a lull in the traffic, and we didn't meet a vehicle for quite a while, then suddenly a car whipped around a curve ahead. As we passed, John turned to Dad and inquired, "Now, who do you suppose that was?"

Normally, snowfalls in our area were not heavy enough to accommodate a lot of sledding, but when the white stuff piled up enough for such outdoor sports, John drove to the store with wife Julia in a horse-drawn sleigh. A pretty, well maintained rig it was, built similar to a buggy but on runners instead of wheels. He never invited me for a ride in the sleigh and I sure wanted to try it..

Another philosopher who liked to tarry at the store would often walk to the store, arriving around four p.m., and then sometimes stay until dark visiting. He would make several starts for home, stopping at points between the store, porch, porch steps and the road to converse with us. He might interrupt the discourse to say, "I better go, the wife needs this kerosene to fuel the lamps", then renew his conversation. Maybe an hour later, he pauses to ejaculate, "Doggone, I got to go, I have to cut wood for the cook stove so the wife can make supper". Then he tarried until dusk was coming on, and finally, moved toward home, commenting as he left, "Well, I really do have to go, we won't have any lights until I get this coal oil home". He still had a mile and a half to walk. We liked to talk with him and contributed to his dilatory nature by suggesting new topics for dissertations.

A young man named Boone Moreland was one of the more interesting characters who traded at the store on rainy days. We never knew where he came from. He surreptitiously moved on to a small wooded patch and stayed for about two years, then suddenly, he was gone without any adieu. He didn't receive mail at the Seaton post office, but bummed rides to town to apparently transact business of some sort. A taciturn and laconic person, he appeared at the store one morning with a large hoot owl hanging to the barrel of his single barrel 12-gauge shotgun. One of its wings was broken and it didn't try to escape. He departed in the same manner and never apprised us of what happened to the owl. Visitors had been observed walking in to Boone's place after parking cars on the nearest roads, but they were unknown to our neighborhood. Boone, a skilled woodsman, apparently spent a lot of time hunting and scouting the area. Rumors abounded as to what he was up to. His cabin was near the abandoned Smith iron ore mine and some speculated that he was an agent for a minerals exploration company. Others thought he might be on the lam from the law or hiding out for some other reason. Anyway, he remained a mystery man to us and left us full of intrigue for several years..

After Valentines day there would usually be more than one gathering of loitering, gregarious prognosticators at the store to conjecture and equivocate about who sent nasty valentines to certain people. Rumors were rife. Great care was taken to camouflage and conceal the preparation and mailing of these missiles. Some were recycled year to year until practically worn out. Rarely did the recipients correctly identify the real culprits, but the banter and speculations were mostly well taken. Anyway, no lasting grudges developed.

No one in our neck of the woods was concerned about Sunday "blue laws". Dad did eschew business on Sunday and tried to take the day off for rest and recreation. Nevertheless, customers would ask him to open the store on Sunday and he seldom refused. When Sunday school or church was in session at the schoolhouse people frequently asked for something from the store, either before or after the services. To get a real retreat from the store, he simply took a trip away from the vicinity.

Young men from other communities who attended evening church at the schoolhouse often stopped at the store before services to buy a snack for supper. They usually dined on soda crackers with cheese; canned Vienna sausage or potted meats, eating the victuals with fingers or pocketknife after spreading the feast on wrapping paper placed on the store counter. I hung around with a hungry look, hoping that a benevolent diner would offer a Vienna sausage to me, a special treat from my viewpoint. Hollis Bingham was my favorite benefactor, a cheerful, loquacious young man from the Hobson community about five miles south.

After Dad installed facilities for gasoline, oil and tire servicing, Sunday shoppers became more prevalent. Often, we found customers waiting when we returned from a trip. Gasoline was dispensed from hand-operated equipment. Fuel was pumped into a 10-gallon reservoir constructed of transparent glass and mounted so it drained by gravity through hose and a hand-controlled nozzle into the customer's tank. A gallonage gauge was mounted on the side of the reservoir so the desired volume could be measured by eye.

Engine oils were drawn from 55-gallon steel drums (barrels) into glass quart containers with screwed spout attachments to facilitate transfer to the engines. Later, the oil supplier furnished a large drum with hand pump for filling the quart containers.

Tires were removed from wheels with hand tools and punctures patched with fibered adhesive rubber boots. All tires contained flexible rubber tubes. Tubeless tires would not become common until after World War II. Inner-tube punctures were sealed with adhesive backed rubber patches that might leak if not applied very assiduously, and quality-patching material paid off with less failures. Later, we purchased vulcanizing equipment and supplies that were more effective for patching tubes and tires. Electricity was not available to power motor driven compressors, so air was supplied to the tires by hand pumps. Gasoline engine driven compressors were just too expensive to contemplate in those times.

Dad was not only the resident merchant, postmaster, counselor and pharmacist of Seaton, he was the barber. He was selective, limiting his barbering services to certain people. Also, recipients of his shearings had to accommodate his schedule. Operating tools consisted of hand-actuated clippers and scissors with a barber styled comb. He cut my hair for many years, and some times when he was tired or in a hurry the clippers pulled and I complained. Depending on his mood, he either laughed or told me to hush. I didn't have an alternative, so I grimaced and bore it.

Probably the most poignant experience of Dad in the role of counselor and medical expert was his efforts to console and help a young woman who had walked two miles to his store carrying her baby that had fallen from a bed. The infant was dead on arrival.

Seaton store building (pre 1956)

STATE OF MISSOURI
DRIVER'S LICENSE R LICENSE NO.
839525

NAME _Albert Malone_
STREET AND NUMBER _Phelps_
COUNTY
CITY OR P.O. _Seaton_ , MISSOURI

IS HEREBY LICENSED TO OPERATE A MOTOR VEHICLE UPON THE PUBLIC HIGHWAYS OF THIS STATE. EXPIRES TWO YEARS FROM DATE.

AGE	RACE	SEX	WEIGHT	HEIGHT
16	W	M	125	5'7"

COLOR OF EYES	COLOR OF HAIR	DATE ISSUED
Blue	Blonde	BO MAR 25 1940

SIGNATURE OF LICENSEE _Albert Malone_

Author's first drivers license

Seaton store building (after 1956)

9/   Mail Call

I don't know the establishment date for the Seaton Post office, but my father was postmaster from 1923 to 1965 when the U.S. Postal Service closed the office. My mother served as associate postmaster and handled postal services when Dad was absent.

Seaton was classified as a fourth class post office, and anyone using a Seaton address picked up their mail at the post office location. All mail coming in to Seaton arrived via a rural star route that ran from Bangert, Missouri to Seaton over selected county and state roads. A post office and store were located at Bangert, which was situated on a branch of the St. Louis and San Francisco railroad that connected Salem and Cuba, Missouri. Bangert received both its mail and Seaton mail as it was routed through Salem, Cuba and Steelville. The star route carrier delivered the Seaton mail, plus mail to boxes of anyone on the route who used Star route Seaton or Bangert addresses. Though domiciled on the Star route, residents had the option of picking up their mail at the post offices, and some living away from the road made that choice. Outgoing mail from Seaton would, of course, be in the reverse flow.

Mail carriers for the star routes were selected by contract bidding. Anyone 21 years or older was eligible to file a bid for a three year contract with the U.S. Postal Service. Bidding forms and instructions were available at the post offices and it was a closed bidding process. Both Bangert and Seaton postmasters along with the successful bidder were notified when the Postal Service selected the carrier. The low bidder would be the winner unless the Postal service was apprised of some reason to consider rejection. To my knowledge, none of the lowest bids were ever rejected during the years Dad served as postmaster of Seaton. Apparently, the Postal Service didn't make much of a background investigation in view of the fact that one man who successfully bid the route on at least three different occasions could not read or write. He solved that limitation by taking a reader with him—usually one of his kids in the summer. However, not being literate was not a big handicap for him because the number of route boxes was only about 20, and after a while he became familiar with those names by the appearance of the writing, and he could detect the correct box if the addressor's writing wasn't too unusual. Occasionally, when no one traveled with him and he couldn't determine the right address, he brought that piece of mail to Seaton and said he had missed that item in his mailbag. So, this item went out on the return trip next day, and Dad told the carrier the identity of the addressee. Most people on the route were aware of his disability and met him at their box when expecting important mail or in some cases when they wanted to send mail.

Mail was carried on horseback or horse-drawn buggy on those days when the condition of the roads became difficult to traverse with a motor vehicle. This happened frequently during the spring thaws or when heavy snow fell. And sometimes a horse could cross Norman creek at flood stage when a car or truck could not. As the WPA (Works Progress Administration) got into gear during the early part of the depression this government make-work organization did a lot of work on county roads, and improved them to the extent that carrying the mail was not interrupted by bad road conditions. Of course, a rising creek remained a problem.

Shortly after World War II the county road department poured a concrete slab across the Norman creek bed at the old ford location, and crossings became smoother and less hazardous at low water flow. However, driftwood and other debris washed on to the slab and impeded travel until cleared away. And still the creek could not be forded safely at levels more than a few inches above the 18-inch slab.

In 1963 the Missouri State Highway Department constructed a bituminous paved road (JJ) from state highway 68 to Seaton, and installed a fine all weather access concrete bridge spanning Norman creek at the site of the old ford. And lo and behold, the Feds closed the Seaton post office, effective December 31, 1965. You can bet your bottom dollar that the state highway department was not apprised of the Fed's intentions or they would not have paved the road and it would have remained a county road. JJ is state maintained.

Today, The state of Missouri has little interest in improving rural roads, but loves to build freeways, bypasses and other grandiose projects more politically appealing. The counties are on their own. Thousands of miles of rural Missouri roads are poorly constructed with bad drainage and terrible roadbeds and surfaced with gravel or crushed stone. Better than the dirt roads of the depression era by a lot but the rural populace deserves equity in relation to state roads.

Throughout this book you will note references to electrical power and road improvements as the major forces enabling the renaissance of many rural areas of Missouri. The Rural Electric Associations (REA) are still in the vanguard as promoters and developers of a better rural economy and life. But the Missouri Department of Highways and Transportation has dropped the ball and at this writing shows no inclination to pick it up. Unfortunately, the county administrations (commissioners) are not inclined to organize politically so the necessary pressure can be brought to bear on legislators to provide equity in distribution of revenues for county roads.

Uncle Joe Burleson lived about two miles south of us on the old Burleson family farm where my mother was raised. He was a World War I veteran who had been exposed to poison gas in the European conflict, resulting in some damage to his eyes. He liked to read and his eyesight was adequate with large thick corrective lenses for reading. He received a small veteran's service-connected disability pension, and was financially able to subscribe to the Springfield, Missouri Daily News, even during the depression era.

Uncle Joe's daily paper was mailed to Seaton, and each day he walked the two miles to and from Seaton to get his paper and mail. He could have had his mail delivered on another route closer to home, but he liked to come to Seaton. He was interested in us and we all liked him. As a baseball fan he sometimes came to our house to hear radio broadcasts of the Brown's and Cardinal's games.

Uncle Joe often opened the paper at the store and let us read too. One day the paper headlined a big story about a young woman who had given birth to a girl out of wedlock, and had stowed the baby in a blackberry patch for a while. Accused of abandonment and in trouble with the authorities, someone in an official capacity had ruled that if a man would marry the woman and assume responsibility for the child, she would not be charged with a crime.

We noticed that Uncle Joe appeared to take more than a casual interest in the news story. We didn't realize how much until we heard he was home with a wife and baby. He had gone to Rolla, hired a man to drive him to Springfield where he married Rose and brought her and baby to his home. We took to his new family right away and chivaried them as soon as we could herald the message and get people together.

A short time later, Rose's parents and brothers came to visit. Then within a few months they decided they liked our part of Missouri and moved to our community. Everyone liked them and we were glad to have them as neighbors. The men were craftsmen and musicians—all played the violin (fiddles to us) and guitar well, also strummed the banjo. They began building violins and sold several. Their musical talent was in considerable demand to make music for parties and community meetings. Likely their repertoire was a mixture of what we call bluegrass today, and old folk songs.

Well, Uncle Joe got busy with other things, got a radio and dropped his paper subscription, so he didn't make as many trips to the post office. Later he bought a "Whippet", and said the car sure beat walking. He let me drive it once, and I was disappointed with its performance—it wouldn't pull the hat off your head. I much preferred our old '28 Chevy but didn't tell that to Uncle Joe.

The business of the Seaton post office included a lot of money order transactions. Dad filed the sales records and receipts in a large metal box, which he carried to the house for safekeeping each night. When all the family was away from the house, this box and contents was stored in a special hiding place. Neither the store nor post office was burglarized until about a year before Dad died (1987), and though the post office was not in operation then, he used the partitioned space as an office for bookkeeping and records storage. No money was stashed in this office but the burglars messed up everything looking for money and other valuables. The event was very stressful for Dad after 65 years without such problems, and I believe it hastened his departure. He customarily kept his old trusty double barrel 12-gauge shotgun at the house, but left it at the store the night of the burglary, along with my "Bearcat" .22 rifle. Of course, the guns vamoosed with the "ninjas". They didn't find a pistol and several silver dollars he had stashed away. Ironically, after his death, we looked high and low but never located the silver dollars. He must have selected another hiding place completely unknown to any of his family.

Few people had bank checking accounts in the depression era. When they had any money to make purchases and payments by mail, money orders were the legal tender. This mode of payment was beneficial to the fourth class postmaster who received a small flat salary, but also was paid a stipend for writing money orders, which increased proportionally to the number of orders written above an established minimum and for a specified time period.

While we were growing up, Dad wouldn't let us mess around in the post office, but let us watch at times as he opened the mailbags and sorted the mail into the various customer slots in the storage racks. Many times mail arrived with the proper Seaton address, but the intended personal or business recipient listed was not or never had been a Seaton resident. First class mail was returned to the sender, but junk mail and magazines could not be returned, and was to be discarded by postal regulations. Therefore, we kids watched for anything bound for the waste box that we might find interesting. We were always hungry for reading materials, and didn't subscribe to magazines other than the Missouri Ruralist, which our mother obtained by bartering an old hen to an itinerant salesman for a three-year subscription.

The former postmaster of Seaton, Curt Spradling, had left a leather civil war vintage pistol holster in the post office when he resigned the office. I coveted the holster and unrelentingly wheedled and begged Dad to give it to me. Ultimately, he succumbed to my persistence. As a kid in the cowboy infatuated stage, I cherished this artifact and carried toy pistols in the flapped case. What happened to the holster after I left home I don't know. Likely, without use and cleaning, mold accumulated followed by decomposition and destruction by mice, then to disposal by my mother. Today, in good condition, such holsters are eagerly sought after and command handsome prices.

I have a prized memento from the Seaton post office— the postal stamper used for canceling outgoing mail. It is still set up with the Seaton insignia and date of the last day of operation, December 30, 1965.

It was good to have been raised in the aura of a rural post office.

Postal stamper set with last cancellation date

Joe Burleson, mid twenty age, before World War I

Nora Malone
Author's Mother and Associate Postmaster of Seaton

10/   Roamin' in the Gloamin'

At the ages of twelve and nine, my older brother and I were roaming and hunting the countryside within a radius of three to four miles of our home. No one posted their land in those days, and most neighbors didn't consider us trespassers unless we discharged firearms close to residences, or didn't respect their livestock and other property.

In the summer and fall we hunted squirrels and used dogs for treeing. At times during the fall when the hickory nuts were maturing, we left the dogs at home and sneaked up to the known heavy-bearing trees, catching the rodents feeding on the nuts. It was not unusual to find several in the same tree. The large fox squirrels are not as wild as the smaller grays, and often we were able to shoot two or three in the same tree before the remainder fled. The grays are prone to scamper to their den trees or hide in the leafy tops of tall trees as soon as they see you, so stealth is essential for consistent success in putting meat on the table.

When the hickory tree mast was slim, we always hunted with dogs. Our best squirrel dogs were mixed breeds, dominated by feist bloodlines. We wrote about "Carlo" in chapter seven, one of our favorite squirrel dogs and of feist breeding. He was stubborn as a mule at times, refusing to put out, as he should. Overall, he hunted well for several years until the motor vehicle chasing fever got to him, and as a result, Dad accidentally ran over him with one of the dual wheels on the 1940 Chevy truck. His hip was fractured, and after that, Carlo limped and was lackadaisical about hunting, but he quit chasing vehicles. Laddie was not quite as good a hunter as Carlo, but he was steady and not as temperamental. Together, the two were unbeatable. When one treed a squirrel the other took up a barking position on the opposite side of the tree while my brother and I covered opposite sides of the tree at positions ninety degrees to the dog's stands, so the squirrels exposed themselves as they slipped around the tree trunk or large limbs in an effort to hide from us. We usually located them quickly unless they had gotten to a den tree and escaped into a hole in the tree.

We hunted squirrels mostly with .22 rifles and long rifle ammunition. We aimed to hit them in the head for a quick kill and less damage to meat. Headshots were difficult to make—we didn't have scopes and our open type iron sights were not conducive to such fine accuracy at treetop heights. When "still" hunting without dogs we fired .22 short ammunition that produced less discharge report, so not to disturb the squirrels as much. The squirrels became more alert and evasive as the hunting season progressed, so one of us carried our 12-gauge shotgun to shoot the rodents that wouldn't sit still long enough for us to get on target with the .22 rifle, or if we crippled one with the .22, we might get him with the scattergun as he scrambled to reach a denning hole. We loaded the shotgun with medium charges of number 4 or 6 lead shot. No. 5 shot is a good all-around loading for squirrels but cartridges containing that size shot were not available to us then, and still are not found in many stores except for the more heavily charged turkey loads. As a reloader, I now build whatever loads I like within the ballistics limitations of components.

Squirrels young enough for frying were most sought after, but it was not always easy to differentiate between young and old when they were sticking to a limb 100 feet up in a leafy treetop. When we needed meat and the squirrel crop was thinned out, we intentionally harvested some of the old bushy tails. The old boogers were more difficult to skin and so tough that boiling was required to tenderize the meat. A pressure cooker will do a much better job of cooking and tenderizing tough meat, but such was not available then.

One person can skin a young squirrel relatively easy, but skinning moves twice as fast when two persons work together. You can skin an old squirrel by yourself but it is a mighty tough peel, and two can do it easier and faster.

Once in a great while we rousted a flying squirrel. Smaller than a gray squirrel, they effortlessly sailed from tree-to-tree or to the ground. Furtive and elusive, they were rarely sighted and we didn't try to kill them. They are endowed with folds of skin connecting the fore and hind legs that enable them to take long gliding leaps.

During the winter we hunted at night for fur-bearing animals such as possums and raccoons. Our squirrel dogs were not good night hunters, and at times we hunted with folks who had hounds. As we got older we occasionally got together with neighbors of our age group to night hunt, and if the dogs were not hitting any trails we might build a fire, then sit around it telling tales and just yakking.

One hunting night we trekked near the Morrison Cemetery in Dent County. My brother Wilbert, Cecil (John) Bell, my cousin Charles Malone and I made up the contingent. We got to talking about cemeteries and spooky stories, and then arrived at a consensus that we would walk through the Morrison Cemetery. We had progressed to the middle of the cemetery, boldly talking loud and joking, and we were nearing some large evergreen trees in the center of the graveyard. Just as we walked under the largest and tallest tree, there was a tremendous roar as a huge flock of birds flew off their roosts—probably starlings. We bolted like stampeding cattle, running into one another and the tombstones. Almost breathless, we stopped, collected our wits and realized what had happened. Sheepishly, we regained our composure, moseyed out of the cemetery and headed homeward.

Superstitions about cemeteries were plentiful, especially what happens in them at night. A report had been making the rounds that a bright lighted unknown something was appearing in the Adams cemetery on nights when there was a full moon. Several witnesses had testified to a phenomenon, and some were fearful of traveling the road that passed by the cemetery. Dad was not superstitious and believed in getting the bare facts and letting the chips fall where they may. He was helping a younger brother, Clarence, haul a truckload of cattle in the early evening, and they would have to travel the road by the Adams cemetery. He decided he'd get to the bottom of the reported eerie mystery light. Approaching the cemetery from the south, you had to drive down a long hill, cross Norman creek, and then climb another hill as the road skirted the cemetery on its left. A full moon was out and well up in the night sky as they started down the south hill. Dad opened the passenger side door of the truck and stepped out on the running board, announcing to Clarence that he was going to see what this spook light was all about, and asked him to slow down. Clarence told Dad to get back inside, but Dad stayed put on the running board, and as he watched, he solved the mystery. The moon was shining on a small pond to the east of the cemetery, and at that particular time the moonlight reflected from the surface of the pond water at just the proper angle to strike a large polished granite tombstone with remarkable light reflective characteristics. It was indeed a striking sight worthy of being heralded as spooky. Clarence was driving and unable to observe as much as Dad, and his confidence was not buttressed enough by Dad's explanation for him to stop to confirm the diagnosis. Besides, Clarence said he had a load of cattle and wasn't about to stop on the rough hillside road and have to start up again. The word got around and the mysterious light became mostly history as the years rolled by.

Wib (Wilbert, my older brother) and I trapped during the winter months when the pelts of furbearers were in prime condition. We ran the trap lines daily and early in the mornings before school. We couldn't range out as far with our lines as when hunting because of doing chores and attending school. Mostly possums and skunks were caught because the night hunters got most of the raccoons. Minks were trapped mostly on the larger creeks and rarely encountered in our trapping area. We didn't get sprayed directly by the trapped skunks because they would expend most of their fetid repellent before we reached the trap, and we terminated the animals with a shot to the head from our .22 rifle before release. Even so, our clothes, hair and skin absorbed vapors from the oily liquid ejections of the skunk. Also, the processes of skinning, cleaning and stretching the pelts for curing left more of the fetid odor on our clothes and body. Skunk trappers were not always socially acceptable at home or in school.

Cousin Charles and I dug a skunk out of his den, and as we dug close to his lair—could feel him and retrieve hair on our punching stick. We let Charles's little dog go into the den. We had restrained the dog from entering the den as we dug and enlarged the hole in the hill.

At a certain point we released "Lucky" and he hit the lair like a cyclone with flailing claws and ripping teeth. In about one minute a tangled ball of dog and skunk shot out of the hole. Lucky took a full blast from the skunk as Charles and I scattered to avoid a direct hit. The animals rolled down the slope and Lucky tackled the skunk again while taking another dose of juice. Lucky then backed off and we shot the skunk. The dog rolled and rolled in the dirt and vegetation, and then got very sick and we thought for a while he might not make it. But after an hour Lucky gained enough stability to drag home with us, and suffered no serious aftereffects. If the Society for Cruelty to Animals or other animal rights groups of today were to get wind (pun intended) of such a caper as this we would be skewered and castigated in all the media and threatened with incarceration or worse.

We set leg-hold traps to catch fur-bearers and now and then a rabbit got caught in one of the sets. However, our strategy for trapping cottontails was based on box trap settings with bait attractants. We made the box traps from ¾ to 1-inch thick wood planks. The design was relatively simple; a front trapdoor attached to one end of a stick that rested on top of a forked or notched upright fastened to the topside of the box, and a notched trigger stick attached to the other end of the stick holding up the door. The trigger stick extended into the interior of the box through a hole near the closed end of the elongated box. The rigging for a set was adjusted so the door was up and open while the notch of the trigger stick engaged the edge of the hole. Heavy twine connected the trigger and door to the cross stick. When the rabbit entered the box and bumped the trigger notch off its setting the door dropped shut and we had him.

To remove the rabbit we jostled and shook the box (we called them rabbit "gums", but I don't know why) until the animal's rear was maneuvered toward the trap door, then we raised the door with one hand and grabbed his hind legs with the other. Pulled out, the bunny was terminated with a quick karate chop to the neck with the side of a hand. We usually sold the rabbits, but ate them if short of meat for the table. Rabbits are easily skinned and eviscerated. We ate the entire carcass except for the head and feet.

There were no fishing waters near our home. When enough spring rain fell to keep Norman creek running for a while, we could find some sunfish perch in the holes below the springs. But mostly we went fishing in upper Dry Fork creek in Dent County, which offered better opportunities, though its flow would cease in the dry summer months. One weekend Wib, Charles Malone and I trekked to a stretch of water on upper Dry Fork that we called a lake, and where a cave was located under a bluff above the water. We explored some in the front of the cave and caught perch from the lake. We didn't bring lunch or cooking utensils and becoming hungry, built a fire and tried to cook the fish on sticks above the fire. The cuisine was not attractive to me, but Wib and Charles ate most of the catch along with wild onions scrounged from the nearby fields. Thereafter, I planned to pack a more edible lunch to bring along on future sorties.

We hunted quail when the odds were in our favor; for example, when they were bunched in the weeds and grass or during a heavy snow that reduced their mobility. Measured by most criteria, we were unsportsmanlike, but today's critics who would judge us have not walked in our moccasins—they know not the trials of keeping food on the table under Spartan conditions—their resources not so limited that a single shot shell must produce more than one bird. Yet, we still managed a higher quail population than today.

As we grew into our teens and economic conditions improved we leaned toward quail hunting ethics more acceptable to today's neo sportsmen and conservationists. Dad acquired a double barrel 12-gauge shotgun; Wib started teaching school and earned enough extra money to buy a new Remington semi-auto 12-gauge ($35-$40 price tag in 1938). We took in a hand-me-down male pointer bird dog and were sort of prepared to find quail and take them from covey and single rises.

We went through several bird dogs, and had the most success with two Llewellyn setters obtained as pups from Dad's cousin, Hammy Malone. The smaller, little "Bonnie", was a natural and required little training to become a masterful performer in the fields. But Bonnie got sick and wasted away. The vet said he could do nothing and recommended putting her down. Dad didn't have the heart to do it, and Mom asked me to end her misery. It was one of the most distasteful and saddening assignments of my life.

I went barefoot during the summer until I was of high school age, enjoying the freedom from shoes in spite of painful stubbed toes and punctures from stobs, rusty nails and other miscellaneous hazardous objects. If my mother was aware that a nail or other sharp object had penetrated a foot, invariably our feet had to be washed in soapy water, then subjected to turpentine and other medicinal applications. Next, we had the option of wearing a bandage on the foot enclosed by an old sock, or wearing shoes until the wound didn't display any inflammation. An absolute was washing feet before bedtime, and certainly that was an appropriate action because we tramped barefooted on many things, known and unknown. Stepping on fresh chicken scat that squeezed between my toes constituted one of my most abhorrent missteps. I have disliked and eschewed live chickens ever since those encounters.

Copperhead snakes were a bit of a hazard for the unprotected footsies. One year they propagated prolifically around our house and yard. We killed six or seven—one found lying on the steps of the cellar under the house. During warm

106

weather milk and other perishable foods were stored in the cellar, and after killing the snake on the steps we thoroughly inspected the steps and cellar before entering. None of us were bitten, but a neighbor and Uncle Robey were bitten on the arm and leg respectively at their residences. The copperhead venom is not as potent as that of the rattlesnake. Nevertheless, the limbs of those victims of the copperhead bites were swollen almost beyond recognition, and the victims were nauseated, sick and weak for several days. They saw doctors, but several hours after being bitten. Antivenom injections were not provided and I don't remember if they were available and I don't remember what relief may have been provided. Possibly they arrived too late at the doctor's office for the antivenin to be effective even if available.

I was traipsing barefoot through a patch of woodlands one day looking for squirrels, and glancing up a lot into the trees as I walked, and then for some reason I quickly shifted my eyes to my feet. One foot was in the air poised over a four-foot copperhead. How one can spring so high so adroitly from one foot is difficult to imagine, but my raised foot didn't touch the ground until I was over and well beyond the snake.

I learned to swim in a pond on the old Cooper place, which was a part of Uncle Willie Malone's farm. The pond was larger and deeper than ours, and cattle did not access it much because of location in an isolated and poor grazing area. Also, we swam in the creeks, but the acceptable holes in Norman creek were small and swimming any significant distances was impossible. Nice lakes were available on upper Dry Fork, but a longer walk from home. Each swimming party of boys usually contained a "bank walker"—one who paraded naked back and forth on the creek bank, showing off his dangling attributes.

Bullfrogs were hunted in ponds, and our favorite pond was located at a woodland edge across a field south from our house and the county road. This pond belonged to Johnny Ketchum and he didn't mind our taking of the croakers. We shot them with .22 rifles, but also liked to slip into the water, submerge up to our chins, then gently ease behind the frogs that could be seen at the water's surface, and grab them by the long hind legs.

In my opinion, freshly caught frog legs when fried are fare to be acclaimed, and all in our family liked them. However, my mother was squeamish about the legs jumping around in the frying pan. Our catches were fresh out of the water, so maybe commercial frozen legs don't perform that way in the skillet. I have eaten legs prepared in restaurants but never observed the cooking operation. I don't recall frog legs being active in the frying pan when my wife cooked a package of frozen frog legs I purchased from the grocery store. However, she firmly articulated that she had fried more than her share of frog legs while growing up, and stipulated an end to my ambitions for home-fried frog legs. One thing I know, restaurant fare is not as tasty as the legs we garnered from our outdoor environment.

We worked at raising crows for pets. In the spring nests were located, and when the young birds had grown to the feathered stage, but not yet developed enough to fly, we took one or two to our house. We tried many diets, even digging worms and collecting insects for their substantial appetites, but they didn't survive to maturity. Likely, other factors such as environment and diseases contributed as much as diet to their demise.

Then one bright spring day I raided a nest in a tall black oak tree, bringing one small pin feathered crow down in my shirt front, and brought it home to a prepared nest of shredded paper in a cardboard box. I don't climb tall trees anymore, not for any reason. I don't think we handled this bird any differently than in previous attempts, but this fledgling survived to live long past maturity. Naturally, I dubbed this hearty survivor Jim, though we had no inkling as to gender.

Jim was with us for over two years and a delightful companion and object of our affections. His demise was caused by lead poisoning at the hands of "Redneck" Adams and his 12-gauge shotgun. Mr. Adams said he mistakenly took Jim to be a wild crow ready to scavenge his sweet corn. I had to believe him for he voluntarily admitted the deed, and we would not have known otherwise. He recognized Jim because of the ring we had fastened around his leg. Jim was about two miles from home when he met his waterloo—we knew he was ranging a bit too far, and should have brought him to earth for a while by clipping his wings.

It is very true that crows are attracted to bright and colorful items and snatch any they can carry to a hiding place. They visit the hiding places to pick up and play with or just admire their acquisitions. If we couldn't find a missing item, we discreetly observed Jim to trace him when he visited his caches. If he saw us watching, he wouldn't go near his loot. Items were recovered frequently, but we were cautious about leaving valuable things exposed to Jim's foraging.

Jim liked to perch on my shoulder and ride along, purring his raspy crow chatter and sometimes tweaking an ear. He somehow sensed to keep his distance when I was engaged in an activity that didn't need the intervention of a crow.

Jim stuck close by while I split seasoned wood boles into small sticks for cook-stove fuel, watching for grubs and insects to fall out of the cured wood. Once he got over anxious, sticking his bill in to grab an insect just as I brought a stick of wood down with the ax. As he staggered and flopped around, in anguish I thought he was done for, but the blow must have been a glancing one, for no blood was drawn and he recovered quickly. Jim was much more cautious during later scavenging.

We liked to play baseball and softball, and ready at the drop of a hat to get a ragtag group together to play a team in another community such as Hawkins Bank or Norman on a Sunday afternoon. Facilities were crude and cow pastures with minimum impediments served as playing fields. Each team brought their own bats, and each was obligated to supply at least one good ball for competition play, plus one for practice or emergencies. Turns were taken with the balls.

Not everyone had a fielder's glove, and softball was played without a catcher's mask, breastplate or shin guards. No one had spiked shoes, and played in everyday footwear or a few fortunate ones might have tennis shoes.

Representatives from both sides selected a friendly, tolerant soul, who was willing to withstand abuse and adjudicate disputations, as umpire. I could handle base and field positions, but too small in stature to be a heavy hitter. While at bat in one baseball game I tried to duck an inside fast pitch by pulling in my bat and stomach; but didn't tuck enough and the ball caught a finger on the bat. I still have vestiges of that maneuver showing on a fingertip.

Destruction of wasps and hornets nests was another sport in which we indulged, and it could be painful. These stinging insects build nests extensively in shrubbery and brush scattered in fields or in open wooded areas. Our game entailed the collection of handfuls of rocks, approaching the nests to throwing distance, then cut loose with a volley and run pell mell away from the nest. Some participants claimed that a wasp could follow the trajectory of a rock back to the source, and the best evasive strategy was to hit the ground, lie flat, and the aroused attackers would fly over you. I didn't buy the theory about lying down, but I learned they could find their target almost as quickly as lightning. After I raced about 50 feet from one bombarded nest, stopped and turned to look back, a big red wasp immediately spiked the middle of my forehead, causing a knot the size of a hen egg to develop, and it ached severely for and hour or more. Today, to take out nests around our buildings, I use insecticides packaged in pressurized containers with the capability of making heavy pinpoint applications to the nests.

In all our wanderings and escapades we were never seriously injured. Cuts, bruises, scratches, tick and chigger bites galore, mosquito bites, sunburns and bellyaches we got, but no major accidents or illnesses.

We informed our parents of planned destinations, but didn't reveal all our plans unless they became inquisitive. We had demonstrated that we were able to care for ourselves in the rural environment, and they did not get overly concerned when we didn't return home right on schedule. In comparison with today, no drug problems existed—tobacco, yes. Dad didn't smoke or chew tobacco, and he would have smoked our behinds if he caught us using tobacco in any fashion. Nevertheless, we managed to sneak some tobacco for an occasional and clandestine smoke or chew, but with considerable trepidation and worry for the future.

I did not take up smoking seriously until away from home, and never became a heavy smoker. Many years later I quit cigarettes, pipes and cigars in that order and over a period of about ten years. Chewing tobacco was something else. I enjoyed a chaw when outdoors working, playing, fishing or hunting. I used to leave a trail of amber through my hunting territories. Some outdoor writers declare that deer are repelled by the scent and will evacuate from the area. Well, I have killed a lot of deer while chewing every step of the way, and my success rate has not improved one whit since I quit chewing several years ago.

Assigned chores and school attendance occupied a lot of our time. We would have roamed the countryside more if not for such activities and special projects like brush cutting and getting up a supply of firewood.

Author's Father with harvest of ten squirrels
all from one hickory tree

11/ Café Society

There was no TV in the thirties. The first time I saw TV demonstrated was during World War II while in the Big Apple. As a part of a directed tour of Rockefeller Center I visited a studio equipped with a demonstration unit of the new concept. We were invited to stand before a camera and at the same time view ourselves on the CRT tube. It was an opportunity for the showoff and pseudo-actors to perform. It was interesting but I haven't been on TV since except for some isolated news bites and cam cording stuff. And the news interviews were not too charming since I was under the gun about environmental controls of emissions at some of our company operations.

Radio was our medium for keeping up with regional and national news. As written at the beginning of chapter five, radios were sparse in our community, and neighbors often visited on Saturday night to listen to the Grand Old Opry and other programs on the radio. Apples, when in season, and candy were passed around, and often, homespun tales competed with the offerings on the radio.

The community was well complemented with folks who played the guitar, violin and banjo. Uncle "Woody" (Woodrow Wilson) Burleson was accomplished with those instruments, plus being a virtuoso with the harmonica. He could render the best emulation of a railroad steam engine at full throttle that I have ever heard. Our local musicians congregated periodically at different neighborhood homes to make music and entertain visiting families and friends. Neighbors took turns hosting the music fests. Folk and gospel songs dominated, but fiddlin' tunes were popular too. One of Dad's favorites was the fiddler's "Leather Britches".

Uncle Woody joined the CCC (Civilian Conservation Corps) when it was organized at the beginning of the depression to create jobs for youth, and we lost his musical talents for a while. After settling in with his CCC job he came home on weekends when he could hitch a ride. He was assigned to Indian Trail National Forest near Salem, Missouri, so he was not far from home. He and Uncle Tom Burleson made their home together in the Watkins school district.

Marriages provided opportunities for the community to party a bit. A chivari would be arranged, supposedly without the newly wedded couple's knowledge, and on the selected date people began arriving early in the evening at the couple's abode for visiting and sometimes a music fest. About 10 p.m. most of the gang went outside and set up an uproar with a cacophony of noise, ringing cowbells, blowing horns, banging on pans and tubs and rattling anything else that could be conjured up by the imagination. Shotgun blasts were also discharged into the air.

At one celebration one old boy fired off his 12-gauge single barrel and half of the barrel ruptured. He wasn't injured and didn't know what caused the barrel to burst. He claimed the ammunition was factory loaded and the barrel was not Damascus steel. A consensus developed that a dirt dobber wasp had plastered a mud nest in the barrel, and he had not inspected the bore of the barrel when charging. He allowed as to how he would be more careful in the future.

After the ruckus, everyone came inside, and the groom was obligated to pass out cigars to the men, and the bride was supposed to have candy for the women and kids. If the men didn't receive cigars the groom might be taken to the pond for a dunking, but maybe receive leniency if he established that financially, he was embarrassed, and just not able to afford treats. And believe me, the old saying, "Got married on a shoe string" aptly applied in the 1930s.

At one point during the depression, when we were without a motor vehicle, we walked two miles and back to a chivari, and didn't think a lot about it, usually carrying a kerosene lantern to light up obstacles along the trails during the night. Though Dad didn't smoke but once in a blue moon, on this night he lit up one of the groom's gift stogies, and even let me try a puff, but I did not inhale (shades of 1992 election campaign days). Dad said not to get any big ideas from the experience.

Many rural schools would host a pie supper once each year. The event was justified as being part of the educational process; as the school children would acquire experience and training in speaking and expression through the performance of entertaining skits and plays. Also, local performers contributed accompanying music with special renditions offered by request. "Froggy Went a Courtin'" would likely be on the musician's agenda, and gospel songs such as "What Would You Give in Exchange for Your Soul", and "When the Roll is Called UP Yonder, I'll be There", were hammered out by the vocalists with the band.

The auction of pies began after school plays and music performances were concluded. All females were invited to bring a pie, or some might choose to bring a box of fruit and tidbits to eat. Young ladies considered to be in a matrimonial age range contributed most of the pies, and much effort was expended on decorations of the pie or box containers. A few matrons joined in, expecting their husbands to buy their pies—prompting some interesting bidding contests between husbands and guys who tried to stir up mischief for every-body's entertainment. Not every husband yielded to that form of usury, and some of the bidding gamblers paid dear prices for the pie they consumed.

It was incumbent on the buyer of the pie to eat it with the gal who brought the pie or box. Some louts gave the pie away after receiving the box and finding the owner's name, but most were real gentlemen, and it was not uncommon to see big young men eating with little nine or ten year olds—treating them like grown ladies.

The pies were brought in under cover to conceal the names of the owners, and stashed at the back of the stage behind the theatre curtains. A few young men would try to bribe the schoolboys, who had access to the storage area behind the curtains, to provide identifying characteristics of certain girl's pie boxes. Actually, ownership was often ascertainable from the progress of bidding and identification of the bidders. Some bidders were sly, and one night when the pie of Uncle Robey's girlfriend was on the block, he let another guy win the bid after he had run the price up exorbitantly. Always, a few free-lancer gals didn't tell any of the boys how to identify their pies. They added interest to the bidding game but their pies usually lost out on price.

Proceeds from the auction went to the school for special purchases or projects, so the auctioneers worked hard cajoling the audience to bid up. After the pies were sold, to create further interest and more revenue, contests were run to determine the best or worst of certain types of personalities. For example; nominations for the man with the dirtiest feet were solicited, and the winner was the person who received the most contributions of money. A bar of soap was awarded to the illustrious winner. The prettiest girl present was selected in similar manner, and presented with a more tasteful prize, a cake or other desirable item.

It was traditional that some character would assume the prerogative of starting the bidding on each pie with, "I bid one thin dime", and in isolated instances, that was it, resulting in some embarrassment to the pie owner, but fortunately, usually forgiven and forgotten in the ongoing hubbub. In the absence of a "thin dimer", and in better economic times, the bidding often opened with a ringing "two bits" (25 cents), and some sold for that solitary bid. Four bits and six bits were common calls as the bidding advanced.

Pie suppers were well attended, and drew people from surrounding communities and school districts. During my early years, I saw more riding horses and horse or mule drawn buggies and wagons tied to trees than parked motor vehicles in the yard. People looked forward to these events, and repercussions were possible if a teacher was reticent to organize, manage and direct such affairs.

An inveterate attendee at pie suppers, Bill Fiske, a bachelor and older man, had no transportation other than his legs, and if he couldn't hitch a ride, hiked as far as five miles to attend the suppers. He liked to dance a jig, and if not called upon to perform, both he and the audience were sorely disappointed.

I noted a recent announcement in the Rolla Daily News that an old-fashioned pie supper was scheduled at the Vichy, Missouri firehouse. Indulging in some nostalgia and reminiscing, I also wondered how old-fashioned it might be.

Ice cream socials provided another avenue for rural fraternization. Rural merchants usually sponsored these events, advertising, planning and managing the operation, with the objective of making some profit in addition to promoting good will and socializing within their trade areas.

Bottled soda pop was sold from ice-filled tubs and ice cream was available in either paper dishes or cones. Several pop flavors, still in existence today, strawberry, cream, grape, orange and lemon were offered. You could have any flavor of ice cream you wanted as long as it was vanilla. Chocolate cream didn't store as well as vanilla, softening more quickly, especially during the hot summer weather. However, if the proprietor expected a big turnout for his supper, he might bring in a smaller five-gallon can of chocolate to satisfy the tastes of the chocolate lovers.

Ice cream was obtained from the Rolla creamery in steel containers of five or ten-gallon capacities, and the price per gallon was less for the ten-gallon can. Cans were lined with a special paper that contained the frozen cream. The cans of cream were immersed in salted crushed ice, and all enclosed in a specially constructed heavy wooden stave type barrel. A heavy canvas cloth covered the top of the barrel. A substantial container deposit was required at the time of the cream purchase and was usually enough to inspire prompt return.

Usually, the socials were held in the evenings, beginning about seven p.m. and ended when appetites had been satiated, or when either the patron's money or the cream supply was exhausted. One of my fondest childhood memories is about getting up early in the morning and rushing down to the store to check the cream cans for any leftovers—and sticking my head inside cans to savor the wonderful smell. It seems that vanilla ice cream was better then and superior to products sold today.

In the mid thirties we acquired a hand-cranked freezer for making ice cream at home. That machine became the opening key to turn some summer evenings into localized parties—usually timed with the need to make a business trip to town when we could bring an extra block of ice home. Freezing capacity was only one gallon per batch, so the number of participants was controlled in order for everyone to get a crack at the first batch. Ice cream recipes were discussed and debated vigorously, with opinions and tastes as variable as the weather. Thousands of batches must have been prepared with our freezer—almost every family in the neighborhood borrowed it more than once. After ten years or more of use the last borrower returned it broken and it was not used again—it was done for. But by that time people had been wired for electricity and could store small packaged and commercially produced ice cream in freezers.

Graveyard workings were held annually at most rural cemeteries. The men were supposed to work on the cleanup and maintenance of their family burial plots, while the women and kids visited, and made preparations for a large picnic dinner. These gatherings were scheduled for the summer so the weather would likely be comfortable for outdoor work and visiting, barring a summer rainstorm. After World War II, attendance at these get-to-gathers declined and the large communal lunch-dinners were discontinued. People still came to visit old friends and maybe bring individual picnic lunches, but by then, most cemeteries had developed organizations for soliciting gifts and donations, so the cemeteries could be maintained better and on a regular basis by contractual agreements.

My parents and many other deceased relatives are buried at Morrison Cemetery in North Dent County, Missouri. It is now organized as a non-profit corporation with by-laws, members, a board of directors and officers, who are responsible for care and maintenance of the cemetery. The corporation's annual meeting convenes at the cemetery on the third

Saturday of August, and serves also as a time for visiting and renewing of friendships. When vacancies occur in the board of directors, it is the responsibility of the members to propose and elect replacement directors during the annual meeting. Operations and maintenance are funded by donations, memorials, bequeaths and income from reserve funds.

As we mourn the passing of friends and relatives, we also reminisce with some nostalgia the loss of the grand old dinners and all-day fellowship at the cemeteries.

To enlarge and expand our social spectrum, we began taking short motoring trips after Wib bought a used 1935 Chevy standard—he had been teaching school at a one-room rural institution, and was in the chips. Twice, we visited Forest Park Zoo in St. Louis, observing animals, birds, reptiles, snakes and other living things we had never seen except in pictures. We were enthralled with the chimpanzee shows.

My mother loved flowers and grew many species both in and out of the house. She wanted to see Shaw's Gardens in St. Louis, so we visited there twice in order to see all the displays. We drove to and from St. Louis in the same day—making a long day and tired feet as we tried to cover as much territory as possible in our allotted time. The trip took over three hours from our home in the '28 Chevy and traveling mostly on old route 66 but better time was possible with the '35 Chevy. Today you can do it in about half that time.

The year Dad traded for the new '37 Chevy pickup we took in the Missouri State Fair at Sedalia, and enjoyed it immensely, though we did the tour in one day, leaving early in the morning from home and returning late in the evening. That was a day when the cows didn't get an evening milking. Mom, Dad and sister Kathleen, rode in the cab of the truck, while Wib, Alfred (Bozo) Golden and I rode in the truck bed. The bed was enclosed with a high wood rack to contain cattle and other animals, so when we wanted to get a better view of the scenery we climbed the rack until our heads extended above the top.

Alfred was eight or nine years older than we boys, but he was full of stories and we liked to run around with him. Often he night hunted with us and was captain of our cow pasture baseball teams. Later Alfred married Verba Golden and they had two daughters. Verba was a daughter of Ed and Bessie Happel (see Chapter 1) and sister to Gladys who was older and reminded me more than once that when about 10 years old she stayed with us some and helped my mother take care of me while a baby. Gladys married Luther Adams, a young man who farmed about three miles from Seaton and Luther became one of Dad's best friends and customers.

The barker for a girlee show at the State Fair mesmerized Wib, who quoted the barker thusly, "Hey, hey, hey, watch these dollies shake that hay." I don't know how I missed that but he must have sneaked away from me.

Roller-skating had become a popular evening recreation for young folks during my mid teens. Frank Watkins, a guy in his mid twenties, then lived in our neighborhood and had a nice four-door '27 Chevy. He was friendly, courteous and interested in helping the kids, so he offered to take us to the St. James roller skating rink. My sister Kathleen, our cousins Irene and Charles Malone and I went skating with him, and had a grand time. After a couple of trips we were getting the hang of the sport, then Frank moved away, leaving us stranded for transportation. I have not tried any type of skating since.

No sartorial elites lived in the Seaton community. During our sashays to parties, church and other affairs we dressed as neatly and comely as circumstances allowed—but most of us owned only one good Sunday-go-to-meetin' outfit, and one pair of dress shoes that often served as school shoes too; certainly, a striking contrast to the clothes-horse attitudes of today, when many kids flaunt an excess of garments, yet not thankful enough for their bounty to present themselves attractively.

Holiday observances and celebrations were Spartan. New Year's eve parties were infrequent and few people journeyed to town to participate in activities. We might listen to radio broadcasts of big city party exuberance.

We didn't celebrate the birthdays of Presidents Washington and Lincoln, but duly noted their contributions on their respective days. Too bad it is not so today.

Valentine's day was mildly acknowledged with some tomfoolery as mentioned earlier in Chapter VIII, "Cracker Barrel Philosophers." Unrequited love was not a problem because few men had resources to present girlfriends and wives with purchased gifts. Schoolteachers usually allowed time for students to make valentines to present to each other during a party at the school, and the teacher might give some candy for a treat.

Memorial day was observed much as today, though we didn't get to watch parades and bands or hear all the memorial speeches and testimonials by military officers and politicians, unless we went to town. We visited country cemeteries and placed homegrown flowers for decorations and remembrances.

We were patriotic when July fourth rolled around, but did not own a flag to fly, and rarely had money for fireworks. Depending on the day of the week we might go visiting, fishing, get up a ball game or listen to the radio. Yankee Doodle Dandy we were not. We just might have to work in the hay or search for a stray cow.

Thanksgiving day was a time for family dinners and visits. My mother was a great cook, and more often than not, the hostess. Chicken and pork dishes or wild game provided meat and we grew large longneck squash (better than pumpkin, easier to raise and best storage characteristics) for pies. Though we raised some domestic turkeys, they were for market only, so no dining on turkey unless Dad got lucky and nailed a wild bird around Thanksgiving time. Cranberries were a luxury—we made do very well with preserves and jellies made from wild berries and domestic fruits.

As a "youngun" I never believed in Santa Claus and, "there ain't no Santa Claus" is a fitting epithet for me today in more ways than one. The stark reality of our "hard scrabble" existence was a sufficient deterrent to belief in myths and shibboleths of an ephemeral and benevolent white-bearded man in red delivering gifts in abundance to all good children. There was no fireplace in our house, and the imagination of even a three or four-year-old child was not adequate to perceive a man entering our house through a six inch stove pipe exhaust.

In a nutshell, we celebrated Christmas as the birthday of our Lord and Savior, Jesus Christ. We believed the biblical description of this event and the giving of gifts to be observed as a part of this story of God's infinite love for us.

The range and character of Christmas gifts was narrow and functional. During early childhood, we kids were pleased if we received one single toy. Generally, we got gifts that were attainable at little or low cost—oranges, bananas, apples and nuts in our stockings hanging on the wall near the stove (yes, that part of the Santa Claus myth was an accept-able fun thing) or a needed item of clothing. How excited we were one Christmas to find a small wire-wheeled hauling wagon under the Christmas tree. I saw one like it recently at an antique shop sporting a price tag about 100 times the cost of our wagon. I was always pleased to get a new pocketknife, even though it might not be made with solid metal bolsters. Kathleen was thrilled to get most any kind of doll.

Today, my wife and I often admire and remark about so many well-designed containers of various foods and other commodities that are discarded and destroyed. We examine the bottles and boxes and say, "Wouldn't I have loved to had these to play with when I was a kid, and some would have served as great gifts for us." Even now I can hardly part with some of the small boxes that contained primers for reloading of ammunition cartridges...but I can't figure any other earthly use for them.

Christmas trees were cut from a large selection of red cedars growing unattended in a field on the old Cooper place about a half-mile from home. My brother and I carried them home. Tree trimmings consisted of a few purchased baubles, preserved from year-to-year, and handmade decorations including popcorn strings.

Our one-room country schoolteachers usually developed a Christmas program including presentations by students about the biblical Christmas story. Mothers of the students and preschool children were invited to the parties, which were scheduled for Friday or the next to the last day before Christmas day. A Christmas tree was installed and decorated a few days before the programs by teacher and students. The teachers provided a small gift along with some candy and an orange (usually, funded out of their own pocket) for each student and visiting child. Students were allowed to place gifts under the tree for the teacher.

Mercy, can you imagine anything like the foregoing activity taking place today? If today a public school teacher even hinted about sponsoring an occasion to celebrate and present the history of Christ's birthday the administrative bureaucrats would hemorrhage and likely mess their britches in fear of the atheists, Americans United for the Separation of Church and State, the American Civil Liberties Union and other organizations.

Our United States Constitution says nothing about separation of church and state. It does state that the State shall not abridge or interfere with the rights and freedoms of citizens to practice and follow their religious beliefs and education. Woe unto the people if they don't do more to stand up for the Bill of Rights and the rest of the Constitution.

Our State and Federal Courts are increasingly prone to make law rather than interpret the law and these incursions must be challenged and defeated if we are to remain the republic the majority desires.

Bits and Pieces

…A Special Friend…

During the early part of the depression era, through an advertisement in the Missouri Ruralist, my brother, Wib became a pen pal with a man named Logan Finley. Logan was a bachelor, in his mid thirties and living on a small farm near New Bloomfield, Missouri. He had aspired to be a doctor of medicine and for a while had attended the Kirksville College of Osteopathy, but with the onset of the depression did not have enough assets to continue his education.

Logan hitchhiked down to visit us and we enjoyed having him very much—a great storyteller, and he pitched in to help everyone with chores and major tasks. He stayed about a week, then went home to check on things at his farm, and arrange for a nephew to keep tab on his place while he was gone. Shortly, he arrived again to stay a month while we were getting in a winter supply of wood for fuel, which was a major job in those days when the ax and crosscut saw were the principal instruments for timbering. He was handy with these tools, and encouraged Wib and me with his energy and enthusiasm.

We cut poles of wood, and then hauled them to the house using Grandpa Malone's team of mules and buckboard wagon. After accumulating the required amount of poles for a season of heating, a neighbor was engaged to bring his powered saw rig to cut the poles into stove size pieces. The rig was sort of like a large bench saw, but powered from a jacked-up rear wheel on a Model T Ford. A flat surfaced pulley was installed on a hub bolted to the wheel of the "T" and power transferred from the hub through a wide flat belt to a flat-faced pulley installed on a shaft that drove the circular saw blade. It sure beat hand sawing or chopping, many times over. Some boles sawed from the larger poles had to be split to a size suitable for charging our stoves. So, we still had plenty of work to do with axes, mauls and splitting wedges.

We augmented our pole wood supply with wood derived from larger trees unsuitable for lumber or deadfalls created by aging or windstorms. Here we had to trim branches with the ax and cut the trunks into boles with the crosscut saw. Splitting of boles and chopping of limbs was done on site and the wood then hauled by buckboard to the stockpile at the house. Later after Dad acquired a pickup truck, we hauled wood with it, but had to be more selective of cutting sites to allow access without getting bogged down or busting a tire. We would have been ecstatic with a chain saw and a hydraulic splitter. Today, we have a wood burning stove for supplemental heat in our house, and I do my wood splitting with a Monster Maul and sometimes wedges and an eight pound driving maul. Great exercise!

We cut and sawed our wood supply during the winter, so it cured or seasoned for six months or more before use in the following winter. Considerable moisture is lost during curing, resulting in a wood of higher heating value, and promoting higher stack gas temperatures, which help to reduce deposition of tars and resins on the inner surfaces of stove exhaust ducts and chimney. Excessive deposits can ignite, creating heat and temperatures so excessive that adjoining structures may catch fire if not designed properly. We checked our pipes and chimney periodically during the heating season, and cleaned them if buildup appeared excessive.

Logan hunted with us, helped skin and prepare animals and birds for the pot, and for curing and sale of the fur-bearer's pelts. He joined in community activities and parties. All the neighbors liked him. He visited us periodically over a period of three years, then he met a woman about his age who lived eight miles from us in the Norman area, and after several months of courtship they married and lived at his place in New Bloomfield.

We drove up to visit them, and dined on squab for the first time. Logan had gotten into the business of raising pigeon squabs for meat. I had never before or since seen so many pigeons in one place. He was moderately successful with marketing in the regional area and in the larger cities. After a few years, he tired of the pigeons and sales promotion, and obtained a factory job in Jefferson City. Though acceptable, squab is not one of my meat choices. However, in some circles, it is highly acclaimed.

The last time I saw the Finleys, I had been released from the Army Air Forces, and drove to New Bloomfield to see them. He gave me a tour of the defense plant in Jefferson City, where he worked in the production of military apparel. They were in good health and he continued to house some pigeons in his barn but not as a commercial venture. The Finley's remained friends with my parents as long as they lived.

...Making Hay While the Sun Shines...

Our small cattle herd was mainly for milking, and we put up hay to provide forage for them during the winter. Enough farm acres were reserved for growing the required amount of hay, while remaining acres, excluding woodlots, provided pasture for grazing.

We didn't own haying equipment and relied on neighbors to do the cutting, raking and hauling. If Grandpa Malone's team and wagon were available, we borrowed them for the hauling. All equipment was horse or mule powered—no tractors, haybines or tedders, and few balers. When convenient and agreeable, work in haying or other farm activities was exchanged for the neighbor's services.

Our barn was small with a correspondingly small hay-loft, and without the capacity to hold all the needed hay for winter-feeding. The remaining hay requirements were stored in stacks at field locations, where they could be fenced and positioned for convenient feeding. Hay was cut with a horse

126

drawn sickle-bar mower that utilized a geared ground wheel to drive the reciprocating sickle through a pittman arm and head. The sickle was similar to those used today, but present machines, like my New Holland balanced head sickle bar drive, takes power from the tractor power take-off shaft and is a significant improvement. Today, haybines are used to combine the functions of sickle bar cutting and roll press-crimp conditioning for quicker drying.

Either of two methods were used to transport hay to the stacking areas; wagons were hand loaded, using pitchforks to toss hay from the windrows to the wagon, hauled to the stacking area, then unloaded by pitchfork to the stackers; if wagons were not available, but plenty of help at hand, shocks were made from the windrows, then after settling, dragged to the stacking areas. The shocks were encircled near the base with a drag chain arrangement attached to the traces of a harnessed horse, and someone rode the horse pulling the shocks to the stacks.

It takes more than one stack and lots of sweat to learn the art of stacking hay. A successful equation includes the ability to gauge the quality and amount of hay involved plus estimating dimensions needed to build a stable stack. Some people covered stacks with tied-down tarpaulins, but functional covers added significant costs, and a properly shaped stack will shed water well, minimizing hay spoilage.

Loads of hay hauled to the barn were unloaded with pitchforks to an overhead door in the loft. One or more workers in the loft distributed the hay over the storage area and tramped the hay to compact more into the space. It was hot and dusty work to say the least.

We built extra sturdy barbed wire fences around the haystacks and spaced them far enough from the stack perimeters to discourage reaching in by strong long necked cattle. But there are rogues who will not be deterred by five or six strand wire fencing on strong oak posts spaced at five-foot intervals. In spite of the barbs, they will push, shove and twist with head and neck until they loosen the fencing enough to establish access. We had one cow that could loosen any barbed wire fence ever built—and finally sold because we couldn't keep her out of the haystacks.

...Fire on the Ridge...

Throughout much of the Ozark plateau, in the spring it was traditional to burn the woods and some fields. If firing was done regularly on an annual basis, damage to timber stock would be light, and some undesirable underbrush was controlled. Much of the tick and chigger population would be destroyed. In the fields, native grasses were invigorated, and some undesirable weed seeds were rendered inert.

Controlled burning is the key to success. If years of leaf fall and other accumulations of deciduous tree discards and deadfalls are allowed to build up in the understory, then a firing will cause immense damage to both new and old growth forests because of the intense heat generated by so much fuel on the ground.

Some say that Easter was the time chosen by the old-timers to begin their burns, but this was not an association with us. Dad burned when weather conditions were conducive to controlling the burn, and before possible damage to new growth of desired species.

Today, if you burn without sanction and supervision of the National Forestry Service, or the State Departments of Conservation, you can be in trouble. It is well that they have brought this management method under control, but now the woods and fields are so populated with ticks that they will literally eat you alive if you stray from a cleared and beaten trail, or have not bathed in repellents such as the old reliable "Deet", introduced first to many G.I.s during World War II, and now available in aerosols of many brands and concentrations. I have brushed a sleeve against a bush, and watch it come away covered with seed ticks—looking like it had been sprayed with gray pepper. The seed tick's venom seems as potent as an adult tick—in fact, their bites on me cause itching for ten days or more.

Lyme disease was unknown in the era when the forests were burned annually. Now, this potentially debilitating affliction is prevalent in several northeastern states, and found in southeastern and some midwestern states. For a while, the medical community and biologists of Missouri were not sure as to the presence and distribution of the disease, but now documented cases have been reported, mostly in the southern half of the state. There is consensus that ticks acquire the disease from deer, which have been infected by a specific type of flea that is the true carrier. The tick species believed to be the dominant host has been designated the generic "deer tick" and is comparatively of small size, slightly larger than seed ticks referred to earlier. With an abundant deer population to host the disease carrier, coupled with horrendous annual crops of ticks, Lyme disease is expected to spread to more states.

Rocky Mountain Spotted Tick Fever was identified in Missouri before I was born, but has become more prevalent since burning of forests has been restricted.

The wisdom and experience of the settlers, and the Indians before them, was great. They were much aware of the benefits to the ecosystem effected by burning, and they did not burn indiscriminately.

... Don't Cry Over Spilt Milk...

Near the age of six, I learned to milk cows. Soon after becoming proficient in this activity, assisting with the milking of our herd became a part of my chores. This task was assigned to Wib and me, and peace and harmony between us was not always the order of the day. Each cow displayed an individual personality (bovineality?) and bickering between siblings could be engendered by decisions as to who milked whom. Some cows were prone to kicking, or planting a foot in the milk bucket just as it was about full. Skill and extra effort was required, plus foreknowledge of the proper technique for discouraging kicking by burrowing your head into her side, just so. Our stall capacity was limited, so some cows were milked outside the barn. Outsiders were fed protein supplements in a pan or trough to hold them more or less stationary, but if milking was not completed before the supplement was consumed, the cow's attention would divert in the direction of another cow's feed trough, whether empty or not, and you had to remain alert to the potential instability of your milking position. No one relished tackling the udder of the cow with a stub tail— having lost the longhaired end to entanglement in a barbed wire fence or other hair snatcher. That stub was a veritable club, swished in fly time or not, and woe unto the milker who neglected to duck his or her head. I was smaller and able to duck more easily, and so the family remonstrated with me to do my duty.

One morning the ground was covered with glare ice, and a cow is not any more stable than "a hog on ice". Our big, old gentle Jersey cow's feet flew from under her and she landed flat out, and then just stretched out as if dead. I was so concerned that I lifted her head up; and before you could say squat I was flat on my back, as she with great strength had flipped her head and me to the ground, knocking the wind out of me. I thought I had had it, but after a short while, with slipping and scrambling, both managed to get on our feet—she just had the wind knocked out of her without any damage whatsoever.

Often our cats came to the barn for a treat at milking time. When milking outside we squirted milk directly from a teat at them. They quickly learned to sit up and become adept at catching the stream of milk in their mouths, but could swallow only a small portion of the output. They would back off, and then return sporadically until they were satisfied.

Then there were milk fights between siblings, which were denounced by our mother because milk was being wasted, and too much milk on clothing promoted premature laundering.

We boys thought Dad was partial to our sister, Kathleen, because she never learned to milk. She became wise enough to eschew the milking scene since she had been subjected to streams of milk sent flying from cow's teats in her direction. Cows are prone at times to be obstreperous and roguish. I was trying to herd a non-cooperative bovine through a gate, and in response to her defiance, threw a piece of weathered board at her. The board bounced off her rump and smacked Wib in the head, knocking him sort of silly for a while. He staggered about while I was aghast and frightened. Shortly, he recovered, and with enough vigor to give me a blast of vituperation. He proved to be a sturdy survivor with only a hen egg sized knot on his head as a souvenir. Another time Wib was not helping me with the herding, and in frustration, I threw a frozen water-laden corncob at him. The cob was off-target, colliding with his head instead of his rump. Again I was scared that he may have been injured seriously, but he was okay. and I was surprised that he didn't take retribution.

Milking as a labor intensive activity has changed dramatically. Today, herds numbering in thousands of animals are milked rapidly and systematically by sophisticated systems operated by persons limited in number to the time required to place suction cups on the cow's teats while milking each cow twice daily. Few people even know how to hand milk a cow today. Many have little conception of the derivation of the packaged milk in grocery stores.

The modern dairy industry is a model of efficiency, and technology continues to bring improvements to operations and record keeping. Not many would want to revert to the days without pasteurization, homogenization and convenience of advanced packaging and storage. Consumers are blessed with abundant supplies of one of the most nutritious and sanitarily protected products, milk.

Have I ever cried over spilt milk? Yes, indeed, because every gallon lost reduced the small stipend I received from my mother as a portion of the money received from the sale of cream produced from the milk—especially during high school when I did the milking before breakfast and then walked three miles to catch the bus to St. James.

... Survival of the Fittest...

Health care during the thirties was rather primitive in comparison with today, especially in rural areas. Sulfanilamides and antibiotics had not been developed. Vaccines were scarce. Other than smallpox, I was not vaccinated for anything until I entered the Army Air Forces on active duty in February 1943.

Pulmonary pneumonia was one of the scourges of both old and young. Other than bed rest and comforting care, there wasn't any effective treatment, and you either made it through or you didn't, depending on your constitution and God's will.

Jim Hatcher and four sons lived for a while on the old Clayton place, about a mile northwest from us. Delmar, the youngest son, at age 13 was a large healthy boy, strong and tough, who would walk barefoot to the store in cold weather. One day in the winter he walked to the store in a chilly rain and without a raincoat. In a couple of days he came down sick with what the family thought was a bad cold, and the usual home remedies were applied, plus cough drops obtained from Dad's store. As a high fever developed, pneumonia was suspected and doctors were summoned, who could not or would not come from town. It is likely they were deterred by the poor accessibility to the Clayton place in winter weather, and might have had to walk or ride a horse in from the schoolhouse. Delmar was in no condition to travel, and succumbed to pneumonia. It was a sad time for family and schoolmates.

A Malone cousin, also named Delmar, who lived in the Clinton Bank area, at age 12, came down with nausea and pain in his lower intestinal region. A doctor came to his house, and since a fever had developed, diagnosed his ailments as intestinal disorder with possible pneumonia complications. I don't remember the recommended treatment, but Delmar's condition worsened, and a different doctor was summoned. It was reported that almost as soon as this doctor entered the sickroom, he exploded with an oath that it was a case of a ruptured appendix, and too late to operate—by as much as two days. The doctor departed angrily, still cursing, and Delmar expired within a few hours after the doctor's examination and diagnosis.

At the age of nine, cousin Charles Malone came down with pneumonia. At the beginning of his illness, the family suspected pneumonia, and called Doc Dillon who came from Salem as quickly as possible. To reiterate, there was no clear-cut effective treatment, but the doctors could check vital signs for regression or progression and give comfort to the family. I remember Charles' mother and my mother placing warm cloths, laced with Vicks-Vapo-Rub, on his chest periodically. The efficacy of such treatments might be questioned, but he was a survivor.

People were fearful of getting lockjaw (tetanus) from infections of cuts and punctures. No one in our community was stricken with lockjaw, and though anti-tetanus shots may have been available, I never heard of anyone getting an injection until vaccination programs for school children were introduced in the late thirties. Most families were very conscientious about open injuries, and treated them with antiseptics, then ointments and home made sterilized dressings.

Rabies was of concern to most people, and a dog or other animals acting strangely set off an alarm, introducing apprehension about approaching and handling the animal, especially if it was frothing at the mouth. Our commonly used term for rabies was "hydrophobia." Here again, I never heard of anyone in our area getting rabies, but the series of anti-rabies shots were available then.

A dog appearing to be rabid ran under the porch of Bill Happel's house, and he shot it with his .22 rifle through a crack between boards on the porch. When talking about the incident, he made the mistake of telling his nephews that he thought something might have struck his face when he shot, but no blood appeared. Perhaps a speck of wood or dirt from the porch may have touched his face. By intimating that saliva or other fluids from the dog might have gotten on Bill's face, the mischievous boys agitated and worried Bill so much that he went to Salem and took the series of seven anti-rabies shots daily for seven days. Bill was prone to worry, and most likely, his imagination had gotten entirely out-of-hand. We skinned fur-bearing animals, eviscerated and butchered wild game without wearing gloves, and rarely were concerned about rabies unless an animal did not appear healthy. If cuts or abrasions were present on our hands, we were more cautious about contact with blood and bodily fluids as we processed the animals.

Diseases of the heart and cancer are ranked today as the number one and two killers respectively. They were prevalent also in the era of the thirties but their effect on mortality may not have been the same as now. The available diagnostic and medical treatment capabilities would likely be considered primitive in comparison with today.

Many people were resigned to living with these diseases and let them inexorably take their toll. They lacked the resources and means to avail themselves of some of the more advanced therapies that might be available in the larger cities and medical centers, and even then radiation treatments and chemotherapy were relatively ineffective. Hepatitis (sometimes called "yellow jaundice") and diabetes also were often fatal when they could have been controlled with today's medical capabilities.

...Dental Dents...

Several teeth in Dad's mouth were gold capped before I was born. I used to sit on his lap when I was very young and ask him to show them to me. In middle age many of his teeth were failing and he had to resort to dentures. Periodically, as we were growing up he reminded us to always take good care of our teeth, and not neglect to visit the dentist regularly. I have appreciated that advice many times over. He steadfastly averred that Doc Ousley in St. James was the best dentist in the country, but my mother said Ousley was too rough, and went to Doc Towell in St. James. I respected Dad's opinion of Ousley's competence several years later when I was a senior at the Missouri School of Mines and Metallurgy.

We were preparing to go on our senior trip to visit industries in the St. Louis area, and I got a horrendous toothache. I went to a Rolla dentist whose name escapes me now, and he told me the tooth was abscessed, and likely would have to be pulled, but he would not extract it until the pain and swelling subsided. I informed Doc Conrad, chairman of the MSM Chemical Engineering Department about the tooth, and let him know that I still planned to go on the trip, though the pain was excruciating at times. He said I had gone to the most expensive dentist in Rolla and advised me to select another dentist. I might add that today, all dentists in Rolla are expensive, and they hang together on their pricing schedules. While living in or near much larger cities years later, I found just as competent dentists with significantly lower prices (inflation adjusted for comparison)—nothing like competition to level the playing field.

I drove my car on the trip taking three classmates with me. I got some relief from the toothache by taking aspirin every three or four hours. Gradually the pain diminished and then the area of the tooth began to get sore. It became so sore after the ache was gone that I could hardly breathe on the tooth without flinching. We managed the trip o.k. and after returning to Rolla, the soreness receded and I had no problems with using the tooth. Nevertheless, I decided to go see Doc Ousley.

I drove to St. James without an appointment with Ousley, and luckily, didn't have to wait. He questioned me about my problems, sat me in his dental chair, took a quick look, and then ejaculated, "It has to come out!" Without reservation, I said okay, because I had experienced a similar problem while stationed in England with the Eighth Air force, and had to have an abscessed tooth removed. Ousley fiddled around a bit with something on his instrument plate, then turned and said, "Open your mouth wide." I complied, he reached in and bingo, out came the tooth. I didn't know it was out till he triumphantly displayed it to me—no anesthetic. From previous experience I knew that anesthetics were not to be used on abscessed teeth, anyway not Novocaine and probably not later developed anesthetics either.

Ousley asked what I wanted to do about the empty space created by the extraction plus the space remaining after the extraction in England, when both teeth had been crooked and squeezed together. He said he could bridge the gap, but the cost would be rather much—he could make a butterfly plate for $20 that would perform very well. I elected for the plate, which he fabricated from plastic and had ready for fitting in a couple of days. The plate fit so well I hardly knew I was wearing it. The plate served beautifully for eight years until I lost it inadvertantly.

We were living in Des Moines, Iowa, when our son was born in 1956. After a couple of weeks, he became very demanding about feeding. Every four hours, like clockwork, he opened his mouth and with eyes closed began squawking incessantly until a bottle was stuck in his mouth— reminiscent of a nestling jaybird anticipating a feeding. When he was six weeks old my wife and I both came down with intestinal flu and we took turns feeding Todd, still on his four-hour schedule. My wife got so sick she couldn't get out of bed to take her turn one evening. I was wobbly too, but managed to stop his yowling with a bottle for a while, then I got so sick I had to vomit. I crawled to the bathroom stool, hung my head over and let go—that's when my tooth vanished, down the drain with the flush. I didn't know I had lost the tooth until I had begun to recover from the flu next morning.

I went to a Des Moines dentist to get a replacement butterfly that I wear today—cost had escalated to $35. Though its fitting has been tolerable, comfort in use is far from equal to that of Ousley's production. Later, while living in Illinois, I engaged a dentist in downtown Chicago for some dental work, and he volunteered that the craftsmanship of my butterfly plate was exceptionally good. I responded, "Thank you, but you should have seen the one made by Doc Ousley of St. James, Missouri."

My teeth were subjected to a lot of filling type work while I was in military service, and after separation from active duty, I had to have most of the Army dentist's sloppy performance corrected. A lot of Army dentists did their internships on a captive clientele.

...Bringing in the Sheaves...

Oats and wheat crops were grown on many farms in our area, but acreages were generally small—normally just enough was raised for feeding horses, flocks of chicken or other fowl. Some wheat was sold for milling into flour or mixed feeds. Oats and wheat were cut and bundled by a horse drawn machine called a binder. Bound bundles of grain heads and stalks dropped from the binder to the ground to be picked up and shaped into shocks by hand labor. Farmers shared the use of a binder or contracted with a binder owner to cut their grain.

Most of the bundled grain was processed through a threshing machine that was owned by a custom operator who went from farm to farm. Individual farmers were responsible for organizing a threshing crew and providing the necessary wagons and equipment for hauling bundles to the threshing machine and taking the grain to storage. The grain was caught and collected in gunny (burlap) sacks as it discharged from a spout on the threshing machine. Straw and chaff were blown from the machine to a stacking area, where a couple of men with pitchforks worked steadily to shape the straw into a stack—a hard, hot and dirty job in a highly dusty atmosphere more intensive than when handling hay.

During the late twenties and early thirties, Levi McWhorter handled the contract threshing in our neighborhood. His threshing machine was pulled and powered by a steam engine until around 1929. It was exciting to see the steam engine coming down the road and I'd run out to greet them. Levi would blow the steam whistle but charily; it took fuel to produce steam, however little might be used for the whistle.

Then Levi acquired a gasoline engine powered tractor with large wide lugged steel rear wheels to pull and power the thresher. It was a Case tractor. Some one asked Levi if his tractor was a Case, and he replied, "By juxner, it is indeed a case"—it had been having some operational problems. The roads were surfaced with dirt and gravel, so the lugged steel wheels did not cause deterioration.

While working on his stalled truck on what is now State Highway 68 and at a location about one mile south of St. James, a passing car struck and killed Levi. His wife, whom everyone called Aunt Jane, continued to live on their farm about two miles northwest of Seaton, along with four grandsons whom they had raised from an early age. She traveled by horse and buggy to the store with one of the boys to pick up mail and supplies. She lived on the farm into her nineties and until all the boys had left home. I wonder what her reaction would have been to traveling in a jumbo jet instead of her beloved horse and buggy.

...Blind Luck?...

Elijah Register and wife, Fannie, lived about three miles west of Seaton and were good customers of Dad's store. He was in his eighties and known as Lige. I first remember seeing him when I was age five. I liked to go with Dad to deliver supplies to the Registers. Lige and Fannie had a blind daughter, Ida, who lived with them, and she ordered items exclusive of Lige's order and paid for them herself. She received a small pension for the blind from the State of

Missouri. I was fascinated by her ability to differentiate between the various denominations of U.S. currency. She took bills from a box with lid, and while swishing back and forth in her rocking chair, carefully and meticulously ran the bills through her fingers. She never made a mistake as she selected the proper amount of money to pay for her goods.

We never knew exactly how Ida identified the different bills, but we speculated that she somehow marked the bills and placed them in a designed order in her box at the time Dad cashed her check. At her insistence, Dad counted out her money by individual bills and coins for the value of her check. Then, she put away the receipts from her check into several pockets on her apron and paid for her delivered goods with money from the box. Her memory must have been very keen and exceptional. We couldn't get a good look inside that mysterious box.

...Canary Blues...

I will always marvel at the initiative, ingenuity, patience, persistence and energy of my mother as we were growing up. From daylight to dark and beyond she was busy, though she liked to read, and would interrupt her activities at times to rest and read. She loved birds, animals and other critters, and at one time or another engaged in the breeding and raising of most domesticated species, plus a few wild creatures that we adopted and adapted to our environment.

One of Mom's enterprises for a period of six or seven years was the raising of roller canaries. Annually, she sold some of the males (the singers) to pay expenses and earn a few dollars for some special product or project in planning. Dad located a couple of markets for her birds in St. Louis and transported the birds to market in a covered cage in his truck cab on his way to deliver livestock to the stockyards in St. Louis. A well-marked singer sold for six to eight dollars and that was a good return on investment in those days. Occasionally, she sold females to reduce her breeding flock, and their value was much less at two or three dollars each. When she tired of the business two pairs were retained for her own pleasure.

A male, Billy, was Mom's favorite, and he sang frequently and eloquently. Inadvertently, she left the house door ajar one day. One of her many cats slipped in, managed to climb to the cage on its stand and knocked Billie's abode to the floor. As the cage crashed against the uncarpeted floor, the force of the impact released the door latch. The cat reached through the opened door, caught and consumed Billy without any compunction.

When Mom came upon the scene, a yellow feather was still sticking out of the cat's mouth. Aghast and shocked, she immediately took revenge on one cat. I had never seen her harm a cat or abuse any other animal before, but she picked up that feline, ran outside, grabbed it by the tail and began whirling it and herself in circles until the cat was flat out in the effects of centrifugal force, then whammo, she moved to bring the cat's head in solid contact with the trunk of an oak tree in the yard. That cat had not nine lives. It barely quivered after she tossed it with smashed head over the nearby yard fence.

...Stuffed to the Gills...

Mom ventured into taxidermy at one point. From an ad in Capper's Weekly magazine she obtained a self-study course in taxidermy, and after some study, she challenged her boys to bring in specimens for practice; with admonishments to minimize damage to the furs, feathers, etc. An opossum was selected for her first shot at applying her skills of the trade, and it turned out quite well. A wild duck, an owl and a fox were mounted, and then she decided that becoming a professional taxidermist was not her crock of cream, and not of enough interest to pursue as a hobby. Moreover, it was a problem to find time to work—and space to store materials and display the finished products.

I didn't develop a yen to try taxidermy. After skinning, cleaning and dressing birds and animals that we hunted and trapped, I was not enchanted with the idea of further handling or manipulation.

We were proud of Mom's accomplishments and encouraged her to continue but she had closed the door. I don't remember what happened to her mounted works.

...A Stitch in Time...

Many beautiful products of my mother's embroidery and quilting skills reside in the homes of her children and grandchildren. A few years before she died, she gave one of her best quilts to each, and after Dad died we siblings drew lots for all remaining quilts and handiwork. My prized possession is a quilt put together with 48 blocks, each representing one of the United States with embroidered name, state bird and flower (pre Alaska and Hawaii). We have not used it—likely it will be handed down the genealogical chain. I put in my bid for this particular quilt as a kid, and she did not forget.

Mom did most of her quilting and embroidery work in the winter, during periods of inclement weather and in the evenings by kerosene fueled lamps.

At the age of nine I was smote with inspiration to piece a quilt top. Mom lined me out with materials and directions for sewing seventeen piece blocks of the churn dasher pattern—relatively uncomplicated to cut and sew, but offering the potential for using materials scraps in a kaleidoscope of designs and colors. The pieces were sewn together by hand stitching, and I managed to complete all the required blocks over the many nights of one winter. Then my mother sewed the blocks together to make a quilt top.

That sewing session sated forever any desires of mine to sew, and I have not sewn since, with the exception of a few patches while in the armed services and emergency repairs while out on the range. Later my quilt top was put through the quilting process wherein backing fabric plus padding was hand stitched to the top. My fabulous quilt has been moved from state to state, but we have used it only a few times.

Mom quilted mostly during the winter. She used hand hewn and drilled wood frames to stretch the quilt top with backing and inner padding in preparation for hand stitching of those layers together. The frames were adjustable in both directions in the horizontal plane so quilters could work from two sides, and as quilting progressed, the quilted portion was rolled on to the working cross frame to allow working access to the remaining area. With each move the remaining unquilted area was retensioned and aligned to provide a stable stitching surface.

Dimensions of quilts varied widely being sized generally to match the anticipated use. An 86-inch by 76-inch quilt would provide an average fitting for a standard double bed, but people's tastes vary in regard to how far the bedspread hangs down toward the floor. My wife may kill me for saying this but, "In our house, the spreads hang almost to the floor so all the stuff stored underneath the bed will not be exposed to view."

Mom's living room was the only space with enough room to hang the frames and allow quilters access to do the stitching. The radio was in that room and when several people wanted to listen, the frames were raised up near the ceiling by rolling up the light cables used to suspend the frames and quilt from the ceiling.

…Wising Up…

I didn't view a movie until the age of seven, and it was a silent western. Aunt Mary Malone married Fred Castleman, and they lived on a farm just east of Springhill School not far from where Fred was raised in the Elk Prairie neighborhood. Mary and Fred were visiting us in Seaton on a Friday, and they invited Wib and me to go home with them for the night, then they took us to Rolla for the Saturday afternoon matinee movie. We stayed with them Saturday night too, and on Sunday, Mom and Dad came to take us home.

While playing on the Castleman porch I found a small rubber item that just fit over my index finger, but it was not familiar to me. It appeared to me that the item had been discarded or abandoned, and I stuck it in a pocket for future contemplation. Next week, Aunt Mary and Uncle Fred were again visiting in Seaton, and I overheard Aunt Mary say that a nipple used to bottle feed a waif lamb from their flock had turned up missing, and then I realized what I had taken. I was mortified and chagrined—they had made a special trip to Rolla to buy another nipple. I confessed my sin and was forgiven—we had never bottle fed any of our animals, and all the mothers I had known nursed their babies. I was just ignorant of the process and equipment used for synthetic imbibing.

We enjoyed our visit with the Castlemans and liked the movie. I did not view another movie until of high school age. I have never grieved or felt deprived about that loss of exposure.

...Turpentine Twist...

There is an old story about the farmer with a stubborn mule, which quit on him at an inappropriate time. The farmer tried everything he could think of, from cajoling to ranting and beating, but to no avail, the mule wasn't about to budge, so dejectedly he sat down on the side of the road by the obstinate beast.

Along comes a loquacious traveling salesman, who stopped and inquired of the dispirited farmer as to his troubles. The farmer wailed a lament about the cantankerous beast. The confident drummer ejaculated, "No problem pilgrim, just let me handle it." He went to his motor vehicle, came back with a brown pint bottle, lifted the tail of old obstreperous and poured a liberal portion of liquid from the bottle into the mule's anus. The mule catapulted into the air and hit the ground with all pistons churning at maximum r.p.m. and manifold pressure. As the mule faded into the distance, the farmer turned to the drummer and inquired, "What in the world was in that bottle?" "Turpentine," came the response. "Well now," snapped the farmer, "pour some of that stuff in my butt so I can catch him."

Wib and I had heard about the stimulating characteristics of turpentine and were anxious to experiment. The summer day turned lazy, hot and humid, and our two sleeping squirrel dogs looked like they could use some stimulation. We administered turpentine in accordance with procedures as defined by the balky mule tale, and then stepped back to watch. The dogs blasted off for a short distance, and then proceeded to sit down and scoot back and forth on their rear ends. They alternated between pacing back and forth, and rubbing their rears on the ground, but ultimately, took off in high gear to the pond and immersed themselves until their posteriors cooled off. Not a yelp or howl was emitted during the entire ordeal. I suppose there was no energy to expend on talk with fire in the hole.

The Humane Society and PETA (People for the Ethical Treatment of Animals) and no one knows how many other organizations of today would have conniptions if they knew about a turpentining shenanigan like we engineered. Such perpetrators would be branded as cruel louts, inhumane boors, vilified, ostracized in the press and probably threatened with extinction, or at the minimum, incarcerated and excommunicated from the human race. So much for that, and a plague on them too. After all, those dogs could have been infected with worms and needed treatment. It may have been coincidental, but those dogs were better squirrel hunters after our experimentation—and they didn't sleep as much, at least not around us.

...Bending to the Plow...

After old "Baldy" died we were without a horse to ride or for pulling a garden cultivator. Dad bought one of those hand-pushed cultivators, and after manhandling it for a while, he got the bright idea that a pull-push arrangement would be more effective—and much less exertion than a mere push operation—forthwith, I was harnessed to the plow. We cultivated a lot, but I reached the age of cautious impertinence, and acquired temerity enough to decry the role of beast of burden.

Finally, Dad bought another horse. It was a young horse of Percheron stock with little training, a gelding, gentle but clumsy as an ox. Dad hitched him to the one-horse plow and cultivator, and quickly learned the horse's wandering feet were crunching half of the crops in the rows he was trying to cultivate. So, I was enlisted to be the monitor and tender of "Smoky", leading him to keep the horse and plow on the straight and narrow.

"Smoky" was an abominable horse for riding. His gait, whether walking, trotting or galloping was consistently jolting and bone jarring—one need not worry about going to sleep and falling off. After I was away from home most of the time, Dad sold "Smoky" and bought a gasoline engine powered rotary tiller—didn't take long for him to see the light after my absence.

...Bushwhacked...

A lovely little valley with adjoining woods was located on the Garrison place about a quarter mile from our house. My brother and our cousins liked to hunt across it, and it was a prime spot for finding the weed we called "life-everlasting". After fall frosts, the leaves on the main stalk of this weed dried to a crispiness that conditioned them for crumbling into a consistency similar to pipe and roll-your-own cigarette tobacco. After crunching, and then rolled into a cigarette, the weed leaves burned at a rate and with smoke generation similar to tobacco. The taste and flavor when smoked was more biting than and not like tobacco, but not disagreeable at all. Smoking this weed did not induce any hallucinating effects, nor did it appear to have any addictive characteristics, though we did not imbibe to any significant degree. And we did not inhale (there we go again).

The valley was part of a trail used by travelers during and after the Civil War, and our parents claimed that a horseman was waylaid and killed in the valley by bush-whackers during the lawless era after the war ended. We did not have historical documentation of this story, but the possibilities were enough to shift our imaginations into high gear as we tarried in and traveled through the valley.

...Dark Moonshine...

Uncles Robey and Clarence Malone operated a general trucking business in the late twenties and early thirties. In 1934, Robey opened a feed and farm supplies store in St. James, Missouri. About the same time, Clarence reopened the Clinton Bank store for a few months, and then returned to trucking on his own.

Clarence was not a jovial type, but did sally forth with a modicum of dry wit, along with snappy and tart rejoinders. In the era of street traffic cops in St. Louis, Clarence was driving his cattle laden truck on a downtown street and motioning for a left turn. In the middle of the intersection, and with both arms and mouth in motion, the cop thrust his arm out and bellowed, "You can't make a left turn here," and Clarence shot back, "I believe I can, if you'll get your arm out of the way."

On another occasion, while backed up to a dock, taking on goods from a wholesale grocer in St. Louis, a loquacious idler in the area was quizzing Clarence about this and that, and noticing the Seaton, Missouri address painted on the truck's doors, asked Clarence how big and what kind of place might Seaton be. Without missing a beat in his loading of boxes and cartons, Clarence responded, "Why, it's quite a city, we got bicycles and everything." In reality, there wasn't a bicycle in Seaton until 1945, when Dad bought one for my younger brother, Gilbert.

Dad recounted the time during prohibition when Clarence and he were in Rolla in the afternoon and headed down Pine street to a restaurant—a man stepped out of an alley and in a low voice said, "Psst, you wanna buy some good white lightin'?" Clarence, without breaking pace, yelled back loudly, "Hell no, I ain't got rid of mine yet!"

In 1937 Clarence and Robey opened a feed and produce store in Rolla with Clarence as manager while Robey continued to manage the St. James store. After a few months the Rolla store was in the black and sales were increasing steadily. Then one evening Clarence became very ill and had serious vision problems. He was rushed to Barnes Hospital in St. Louis where he died within a few hours at the age of 26. Attendees in the ambulance on the trip remarked that Clarence was suffering nausea, headache and internal pain and could not see, yet he could relate where they were on old route 66 most of the time—his years of trucking this route had imbued his senses with extraordinary sensitivity.

I was almost 14, and old enough to put two and two together and more, as my parents and Dad's siblings talked about the death of Clarence and surrounding events, all in hushed, subdued and furtive voices. I surmised that Clarence had imbibed some badly distilled or contaminated "white lightning", "white mule" or "moonshine" whiskey. They were concerned about what people would think and say. I couldn't see why the situation should be considered disgraceful since it was common knowledge that Clarence liked a snort of whiskey now and then, as did a lot of other people during prohibition. It was just tragic that some drinkers were not wary enough about the supplies of contraband juice.

The symptoms and rapid progression of Clarence's illness to death pointed strongly to considerable methyl alcohol contamination of his whiskey. Methyl alcohol is a killer when consumed in moderate quantities. Unscrupulous and sadistic purveyors of illegal alcoholic beverages had been known to "cut" potable moonshine with the lower cost methyl (wood) alcohol that was readily available since at that time it was used as antifreeze in the radiators of many vehicles—before the commercialization of ethylene glycol as an antifreeze.

...Jim Crow...

Crows were not protected birds when I was growing up, and we hunted them quite a lot because they were predators of quail and other bird's nests, and they pulled up young seedlings in our garden. A large flock could decimate an emerging patch of sweet corn, and they seemed to do it as much for amusement and aggravation as for the amount of corn they garnered from the sprouting seeds.

The crows propagated prolifically and at times congregated in flocks of one hundred or more. We located their choice daytime roosting sites that often also served as night roosts. Then we concealed ourselves in blinds made from woods brush and foliage near the roost tree until a large number settled in the tree. Then we targeted more than one with one single shotgun blast. Another tactic involved the use of relatively inexpensive .22 rifle ammunition and try to pick off more than one before the flock flushed. .22 short cartridges were used because the discharge report was less noisy—with all the cackling and calling of a large flock we might get off three or four shots before they wised up.

Crows are very wary birds and usually can't be successfully hunted at one roost more frequently than once a week.

We mimicked the crow's calls with our voices to attract them to our location. This worked for a while until the more mature birds began to recognize our calls to be bogus. The trouble call was effective until again, they became familiar with our style.

Finding a crow's nest provides good shooting opportunities because they are very protective of the young until they have been flying for a month or more. Sometimes when fledglings are still in the nest old birds will barrel right in to the nesting location even when shots have been fired.

I don't see large flocks of crows in the Seaton or Elk Prairie areas of Missouri anymore. They are now protected though an extended hunting season is allowed. I believe that the rarity of large flocks is due to more hunting, along with more effective long-range accurate varmint type hunting rifles carrying high magnification scopes. Crows are wily birds and not an easy prey. As mentioned earlier, they are persistent predators and with amazingly keen eyesight can spot mice, bird's nests and other prey from remarkable distances.

This past summer a friend was cutting hay and mowed over a turkey's nest. The setting hen flew before the mower reached the nest. He hoped the hen might return to the nest so he pulled away 200 yards or so to see what might happen. As he watched, a crow swooped down and snatched an egg from the nest. He had not noticed any crows beforehand in the area.

In the summer and fall crows sneak into my small orchard and pull off more fruit than they eat—just naturally mischievous. A watch crow is always on the ground, and rarely can I approach closer to them than 60 yards. They know the range of shotguns.

Have I ever eaten crow, literally? No, and I'm not about to start, unless a depression should arrive that is worse than that of the thirties of the Twentieth Century.

...Fire Away...

Many shooting matches were held at Dad's store. Some were impromptu affairs as a result of challenges brought on by bragging, bantering or wagering fever, but most were planned, and often run at night using lanterns and car lights to illuminate the target and shooting area--when a car with reliable illumination was available.

Night action was possible with minimum illumination because most of these matches were shotgun shoots where target clarity was not too critical. No one in our community owned any match quality rifles—money was not available for such. A few owned old .44-40 and .45-70 cartridge rifles, but most folks owned nothing more than run-of-the-mill .22 rifles, which were adequate for hunting because no big game habited the region anyway. Granddad Malone possessed two small-bore muzzleloaders, but he had quit firing them after the .22 rifle became more available and economical.

Pieces of cardboard with a large X in the center of each served as targets. The shooter who placed a shot pellet nearest to the center of the X on his target was declared the winner by the appointed scorekeeper. With this method of scoring, your chances of winning were at least better than playing a slot machine or punchboard. With all the variables involved I think it would require the services of an exceptional mathematician to compute the odds. I have seen shooters using an open bore scattergun win over shooters firing tightly choked guns that produced much tighter patterns. However, most theoreticians would agree that the more tightly choked guns had an advantage provided the shooter had patterned his tube and was a good marksman.

Targets were placed at 30 to 40 yards, and usually hung on a nail in a tree. A large hickory tree stood about 60 yards east of the store, and with a lot of use as a target holder it absorbed so much shot it eventually died.

Normally, any shotgun of 12-gauge or smaller gauge was allowed, and the individual contestant could choose his shot size and powder loading. Obviously, more pellets could be fired at the target by the larger gauges, and a greater number of pellets were ejected per ounce of the smaller sized shot. In some matches all participants had to fire the same gun and identical cartridges. Most contestants preferred to shoot a gun with a full choked barrel and high-based loads containing the maximum weights of small shot (such as no.

8) and powder. However, most shotguns have individual characteristics relative to ammunition and will favor a certain loading for best accuracy and patterning. Consequently, the shooters who knew their guns well might fire lighter loads that patterned better in their gun. Also, number 6 shot might pattern better than number 8 in a gun though the pellet count for an ounce of number 6 lead shot is only 225 as compared to 410 for number 8. Each contestant paid for his ammo whether it was his selection or a stipulated loading by the promoter of the match. Dad usually carried a good selection of ammo in his store.

Each contestant put a fixed amount of money into the kitty when he received his target card, and wrote his name on the card. The organizer and promoter of the contest required the shooters to select a committee composed of two or three shooters or observers to hang and take down targets, measure the fired targets and call the shooters to the firing line, so most possibilities of hanky-panky were eliminated.

Prizes varied over a wide gamut depending on what the promoter had to sell that attracted a lot of shooters. It could be anything from a banty rooster, extra good fox or mink pelt to a hat or gun. Sometimes they just competed for the pot.

The first match that I was allowed to shoot, I won a big Plymouth Rock hen. The entrance fee was 25 cents, and I shot Dad's single barrel, full-choked 12 gauge, using a high base load of number six shot. Recoil was pretty much, especially for a nine year old.

Usually you are not aware of recoil to any great degree when you fire a shotgun at game, but lay a 12 gauge loaded with maximum charges across a rest to shoot a target, and you jolly well will remember the hammer and shove as it is touched off. The experience hangs on your conscience and whelps that old nemesis of the gunner, the trigger flinch.

In those days no one had earmuffs for noise reduction during shooting, though now and then, some used homemade earplugs made of cloth wadding. Today, I don't target shoot without muffs, even when firing the .22 caliber firearms. Not only are they beneficial for hearing protection, but also they reduce the potential for flinching and trigger jerking. Recently, after checking my target I forgot to reinstall my muffs to fire the next round from my compensated (ported barrel to reduce recoil) .44 magnum revolver. After touch off my ear with already deteriorated hearing capacity rang and hurt for five minutes. The compensated design significantly reduces recoil but at the same time markedly increases the noise blast.

Many old timers swear by the theory that the longer the barrel of a shotgun, the harder and farther it will shoot. A 36 inch barreled "Long Tom" was a prized possession for conquests in the shooting matches, but I noticed that the odds did not necessarily favor this firearm. Lloyd Happel wrote to the Winchester Arms Company and inquired, "How much farther will a 36 inch barreled shotgun shoot than a 30 inch barreled gun?" He received this succinct reply, "six inches." Nevertheless, the long barreled advantage concept persists in some quarters.

I possess my Dad's 36 inch barreled Winchester and have killed four gobblers with it. However, after patterning it, I found it to be considerably off point of aim when using the original beaded sight, so I installed new sights to improve accuracy. It still does not perform to my satisfaction, so I reverted to using my old semi-auto 12-gauge that handles only two and three quarter inch cased ammo. But I reload cases with 1 ½ to 1 5/8 ounces of no. 5 antimony-lead shot to yield velocities of 1100 to 1200 feet per second. These loads pattern better at full choke then the three-inch cased loads fired from the single barreled Winchester, and kick a lot less. The recoil from the three inch cased loads is so heavy that I installed a resilient pad on the stock butt. Of course, my recoil-operated semi-auto does not kick as much because of recoil absorption by the ejection and cartridge feeding operations.

Dad had missed some turkeys with the "Long Tom" in his later years, most likely because of its inaccuracy rather than defective eyesight or faulty aim. Imagination and emotion played the major role in his actions during the episode I'll describe later.

Reams of writing discuss the effects of barrel length on shotgun performance, and I've read at least two reports describing results of shooting tests that involved progressive reductions in barrel length of a single barrel. A nutshell conclusion could be drawn from those tests, that in relation to velocity there was no significant increase above 30 inches, but drop-off occurred as length was reduced below 28 inches. Many variables influence performance, and a choke-controlled length reduction study would most likely show notable differences.

...Talking Turkey...

Dad was an inveterate and avid turkey hunter who quested for this alert and wily bird until his death in 1987 at the age of 87. He hunted during the Missouri spring season just two weeks before he died.

Dad preferred the spring season when gobbling, romantically inclined male birds may or may not come to man made imitations of seductive hen calls. For many years he used wing bones from previously killed birds to make his calls. Our oldest daughter, Terry, gave him a box call for a Christmas gift and thereafter, the box became his primary calling instrument. Dad went after turkeys using any tactics that could put one on his shoulder.

Until the early thirties a thirty-day spring hunting season for turkeys was in effect in Missouri, and hunters set up camps in some locations. By the mid thirties the turkey population was just about decimated, and seasons were closed until populations could be reestablished by a non-political and more effective Missouri Department of Conservation. Today, Missouri has the largest population of turkeys in any of the other states.

I cherish a story about one of Dad's most embarrassing hunting escapades. He was hunting with Uncle Robey and they had agreed to set up at specific points known to each, and try to entice a turkey they had heard gobbling in the vicinity. Both made calls, and Dad was adamant that he saw a gobbler come in, and he cut down on him with his 12 gauge Long Tom loaded with a three-inch cartridge containing 1 7/8 ounces of no. 4 shot.

It was the first turkey that he had shot at that immediately let loose with man-sounding yelps. Robey would later comment while recounting the incident to me, "Yeah, he shot an old turkey, alright."

The morning was chilly and luckily, Robey was wearing a canvas type brush coat over another jacket—it likely saved him from more serious injuries. As it happened, a few pellets penetrated to his rump and drew some blood. My brother Wib was in another location and heard the commotion. He arrived soon to check Robey's condition, and noted that when Robey removed his outer coat, no. 4 shot pellets rattled all over the dry leaves on the ground as he shook the coat.

Dad was eighty at the time. After that Wib sort of took charge of the planning for Dad's turkey hunting and made sure Dad was in a spot well known to anyone who would be in the vicinity. He had to be on his toes and conduct some surveillance, though, because Dad might move without informing anyone. Roby admitted after being shot that he had moved from the place where he had told Dad he would stay. He said he had gotten up from his ground seat and started to move to another location when the blast nailed him, and his left hand without a glove was swinging free, probably similar to the bobbing red head and neck of an old gobbler.

Dad has been long gone but I think about him today as I am at about his age when he busted Robey and I take a second or third look at strange appearing objects that might resemble a turkey when I'm hunting.

...What's in a Name...

The true origin of the Seaton name for the post office and Dad's store is not known. Dad thought the location may have been named for Sam Seaton, father of Alf Seaton, who lived 2.5 miles west of Seaton on the county road that runs between Seaton and Elk Prairie.

Alf and wife lived in a one-room log cabin on a small farm of forty acres. After their deaths, the cabin stood until two years ago, and was used as a hunting cabin by the owners. Since, a new owner has let this potential candidate for preservation as a national historical site decay and deteriorate, and enclosed the land with a 12-foot high steel mesh fence that also encompasses several hundred more contiguous acres. Purportedly, the fenced acreage will be a sanctuary for elk.

Alf was near eighty when I was five and visited them with Dad as he delivered groceries to the Seatons. Alf hauled drinking and wash water in wooden barrels with his horse drawn wagon from the Bell pond, which was located about a quarter mile away in the middle of a large tract of forest. No one knew for sure how this large pond developed, but most thought it formed after a spring opened up. There was no runoff except after substantial rains. Anyway, the Seatons thrived on the pond water, and no livestock pastured in its vicinity. We hunted squirrels around it and watched for ducks on it during the migration seasons. Later, the Missouri Conservation Department stocked the pond with fish that propagated and grew well until one severe winter the pond became heavily iced, and without anyone to break the ice, the fish died.

During this era the ownership of the pond property was questionable, and most people in our community used it like free territory. Here too, the origin of the pond's name is moot. We knew that it was not named after the Bells of our Seaton neighborhood. After 1948 I did not see Bell pond again. Dad told me that it just gradually dried up and disappeared--some time in the sixties, he thought. Its recession would seem to confirm previous speculation that the pond had been fed by a spring at the center of the lake, and perhaps a shifting of underground strata had closed the spring just as it had caused the spring to open. Another possibility is that the water table may have dropped and the pressure on the aquifer supplying the spring was relieved.

John Seaton, who married Ellie Adams and lived on a farm about equidistant from Clinton Bank, Winkler and Norman, was a nephew of Alf Seaton. They had a son, Virgil, and daughters Addie, Beatrice, Gladys and Deloris. Addie married Brewer Bottorf, and they had a daughter who I courted for a while.

I have searched the 1995 edition of the Rand McNally Atlas and found locations identified as Seaton in the states of Arkansas, Illinois and Texas.

With the demise of the Seaton, Missouri post office in 1965, Seaton has no longer been listed on official Missouri highway maps. However, it is listed on maps of several web sites that utilize satellite mapping data and United States Geological Survey topographical mappings. Using the latter sources I found another Seaton in Tennessee.

There is a Seaton cemetery located in the Doolittle, Missouri area just a few miles west of Rolla. I have not yet visited this site and have not tried to determine its history. I do know that the cemetery is still used for interments because of announcements in the local media.

...Home on the Range...

In our community most farmers had perimeter fencing during the decade of the thirties, albeit that some was of minimal quality, and a lot of split rail fencing was still in place. Those old rail fences provided great quail habitat, and were reasonably effective for constraining livestock such as cattle and sheep, but hogs rooted under and out—lots of power in a hog's snout.

Most posts for wire fencing were made by splitting white oak and post oak logs, and then sharpened with an ax so they could be driven into the ground with a 12 to 16 pound maul.

Some farmers did not fence their woodlands, and allowed some open ranging of livestock. Others with woven wire fencing of woodlots let hogs into them when the acorn mast was ample.

The passing of the open range era came about with improvement of roads and increasing traffic. Legislators were forced to take action from a safety standpoint, and rustling had become more prevalent with better vehicular access. So, open ranges in our vicinity were legislated away and appropriately so.

...Doctors Anonymous...

Veterinarians were scarce as hen's teeth in our neighborhood during the thirties, but even if there had been a surfeit in that profession, we couldn't have paid for their services. We were much on our own.

Cattle breeding improvement efforts were minimal and most of our bovines grew horns. Most farmers dehorned cattle as calves, just after the horns had emerged enough to clip them off with large hand clippers similar to bolt cutters. Cattle with mature horns were roped and tied so the horns could be sawed off. Blood flow from severance was stemmed with mixtures of antiseptics and alum, or some used cauterization. Dehorning was scheduled for execution before or after the heavy fly infestation periods to minimize irritations and infections but the wounds normally healed without complications or further treatment.

Castrations of calves was accomplished as soon after birth as possible while it was easy to clip the scrotum and cut out the testicles, and when the wounds healed quickly. Now and then, and aggressive cow made it difficult to get at the calf early and the calf developed to young bull status. Then, the "cutting" became a real chore, entailing roping and tie down of the animal. Healing and infection was also more of a problem. In some cases the larger males were just marketed as bulls.

We rarely used the word, castrate. You might hear, "we better get that calf cut before it gets any bigger, or it's time we got them pigs cut." A clasp type pocketknife was the universal instrument for emasculation.

I didn't know any name for castration other than "cutting" until Dad sent me to a neighbor to borrow an emasculator. We owned a young horse that was to be turned into a "gelding", and the emasculator tool was designed to crush the testicle cords, so the testicles could be tied off to control blood loss during severance.

Brother Wib and I usually castrated our pigs. We simply cut vertical slashes on each side of the scrotum long enough to pull out the testicles and cut the cords for removal. Hog's scrotums or "cods" don't hang down in a bag like cattle, horses and men, but are attached around the perimeter of the scrotum to the hog's rear end. After cutting the testicles loose we slapped some lard or other grease with antiseptic in the wounds and let the pig loose.

I had heard people joke about eating "rocky mountain oysters", and decided I'd like to try some. We had procrastinated and let a litter of pigs grow larger than normal for cutting, so they had nice-sized oysters. I told Wib that we would save their testicles for an epicurean delight and we did. We trimmed them, and then sliced the oysters lengthwise, as you might a hotdog or sausage, and Mom fried them. Dad and my sister declined the delicacy, but Mom and I really lit into the batch—very good. Wib, who usually devoured most fare, ate some but was not enthusiastic about this new dietary selection for our table.

One summer our cattle became infested with screwworms, and that was really something. Some worms got as big as the end of your pinky fingers, and caused ugly wounds and scars after removal.

We dug them out and filled the holes with a special ointment (I don't remember the ingredients), and the wounds usually healed but sometimes got bacterially infected. The worms even infested udders and teats (tits if you wish). The screwworm fly laid eggs in cuts, punctures and abrasions of the skin and in tender moist areas such as the nose, and then the larvae developed. Very repulsive boogers to me, and I shirked the treatment job if I could.

During calving time we had to remain alert to the possibility that a cow could have difficulties with birthing, and first-calf heifers were particularly susceptible to problems if they had been bred early. They often needed help or both the calf and cow could be lost. Also, it was not uncommon to experience breech deliveries that are very troublesome.

Dad was away from home when I found a cow trying to make a breech birth. I was not strong enough at age 12 to pull the calf, so I enlisted the aid of a neighbor, Ernie Watkins, and after much exertion we got the calf out. However, the calf was dead. It was a large calf, but might have survived if we had found the cow sooner. We used rope with slipknots. Today, special tailored rigs can be purchased for calf pulling, but skill with the hands is still required, especially if the calf has to be turned.

One of the pigs in a nice litter became ruptured a few days after birth. We let the pig grow for some time, but at about 30 pounds weight the rupture deteriorated. At first we thought about butchering it. Then, Wib says, "I believe I'll sew it up." I held the pig while he worked on it with a large-sized sewing machine needle and heavy cotton sewing thread. He did a neat job, especially without either experience or medical suturing equipment. Alas, after a couple of days the surgical operation had failed to contain the rupture. The split was long and the suture thread had pulled through the edges of the slit, but the thread itself had not failed.

Pigs are rambunctious critters, and it's likely nothing would have stopped his rupture from busting out, with the exception of a strait jacket, and we thought about improvising something on that order, but we relinquished our surgical and veterinarian role, and reverted to our original plan to have nice fresh tender pork for the table.

We tried setting and splinting broken legs of various species of fowl, but couldn't prevent them from destroying our handiwork. There is probably a way to succeed, but no "eureka" for us.

...Goaticides...

Before herbicides there were goats. A good goat can eat a sight of herbaceous materials. I never butchered one to see how its stomach was constructed, but it must be made of Teflon, Carpenter 20 grade stainless steel and Hastalloy C combined. Not only will they consume about anything that grows, but also will dispense with many items of metallic and synthetic compositions.

Grandpa Malone had a pet billy goat that not only displayed a broad appetite, but he was a terror to us children. Uncle Clarence was changing the fan belt on his car, and after removing the worn belt he reached for his new belt and found only half a belt. The other half was in Billie's belly. Billie died from something other than old age, and we suspected a powerful chemical poison—nothing else fazed him. We conjectured about the possibility that a nephew of Grandpa's, whose convertible's top was ripped badly when Billie jumped on top and rammed his hoofs through, may have done Billie in. Anyway, several oldsters and we youngsters gave thanks for Billie's demise.

You can cut the brush of most deciduous tree species for as long as you live, and sprouts will keep coming back from their stumps and roots for the next guy, but put an adequate fence around the brush, add goats and in time they will kill all brushy growth. A good heavy woven wire fence of three feet height with two strands of barbed wire on top is adequate for containing goats, and the height of the top wire does not need to be much more than that required for range cattle. A goat doesn't jump like a deer, but boy, can they climb. So, you don't use any slanted corner post bracings.

Dad converted about 100 acres of timberland into pastureland in about 12 years. Loggers removed the lumber quality trees, and then woodcutters removed the remaining timber and large brush, selling it for use as mining props, charcoal kiln feed and firewood. After fencing properly, he selectively grazed patches of the acreage with a herd of 25 to 40 goats. The goats were fed during the winter. Goats are very hardy, but they do much better with shelter from rain and snow. Dad built a small totally enclosed house with two egress and exit doors for his herd—no insulation, but the walls were battened.

Goating is an effective and economical way to clear brushy land for pasture—for those who are patient. The bulldozer and herbicides have mostly replaced the goat, largely because of less management requirements and time constraints. Ecologically, the goat remains the performer of choice.

Author with quilt that he sewed at age of nine

1980 photo of Bert Malone
author's father and proprietor of Seaton store

Alf Seaton's log cabin—circa 1970

Author feeding goats on father's farm in 1940

13/   Begats and B'Gosh

C. W. Payne married Cleo Lush and they had a daughter named Lilly. Lilly married John Welsh Burleson and from this union several boys and three girls were born. A son, Thomas, was one of my favorite relatives. He was a half brother to my mother, and considerably older. Uncle Tom's siblings included our Uncles Lee, John, William, Joe, Nate and Aunts Becky, Mattie and Mary.

Mary (Molly) Burleson was my grandmother and her maiden name was Norvel. She was born June 10, 1872 and died April 17, 1927, and the cause of death was believed to be diabetes with heart complications. Her parents were Vesta and Elias J. Norvel. Elias was born March 6, 1850 and died December 6, 1910. Wife Vesta was born February 10, 1857 and died August 4, 1899. They, along with patriarch John W. Burleson are buried at Morrison Cemetery in Dent County, Missouri. John, my grandfather, was born May 7, 1852 and died when I was about seven years old.

My mother was the second oldest child of John W. Burleson's union with his second wife, Mary A. (Molly) and was born on February 28, 1901. She died on March 2, 1969. My mother's siblings were; an older brother Dewey, then in order of declining age, Viola (we called her Aunt Oley), Sam, Clyde, Norma and Woodrow Wilson. Clyde, at age 18, was struck and killed by a train in St.Louis. Norma died at an early age of three years and nine months. In addition to Grandmother Molly, Clyde, Sam, Lee, Tom, Nate, Joe and Mary (Burleson) Denoon are buried along with father John in the Morrison Cemetery.

C.W. Payne and wife Cleo, and Lilly Burleson, are buried at the Coppedge cemetery located about two miles north of the old Hobson, Missouri community and store in Dent County. The store was closed many years ago. Hobson is accessed by state route FF and is just a mile or so east off of state highway 72.

The cemetery is accessed from Hobson via county road 305 and a tributary road that ends on private property through which one must travel the last quarter mile. One seeking the cemetery should check with local residents who are familiar with the location of the cemetery.

Dewey is buried in the Hartford, Illinois area. Rebecca (Becky) and husband Claude Hobson are buried in the Wood River, Illinois area. My mother, Nora Virginia, and her sister Viola, are in adjacent plots with husbands Bert and Raymond at the Morrison Cemetery.

Uncle Tom Burleson was a handyman and Dad occasionally hired him to handle projects for us. He was a craftsman in the art of splitting oak shingles and clapboards. He always selected the trees and helped with the sawing of the boles to be split. One year, he split all the shingles and helped with the roofing of our barn and crib. He lived about three miles south of us, and boarded with us while working on a job at our place. There was never a more gentle or kind man, and he had immense toleration for the shenanigans of us kids. We liked to hear him talk, and prompted him to speak about church because his pronouncement was "chutch". Uncle Tom never married, and died at age 57 when I was about thirteen.

Several of my mother's siblings from both family groups of her father, John Burleson, lived in our community and adjoining areas. Uncle Dewey married Gertrude Brewer from the Watkins school district community and then lived in Hartford, Illinois. They had one girl, Geneva, who married Kelley Saragusa. Geneva is near my age, and after Kelley's death continues to reside in the Wood River, Illinois area.

Aunt Becky married Claude Hobson and they had one child, a daughter Naomi, whose age was a few more years than my brother Wilbert (Wib). They lived in Wood River, Illinois, and Claude worked for the Standard Oil Company Wood River petroleum refinery. Naomi married Floyd Milford and is buried, along with Becky and Claude in

Bethalto, Illinois. Her husband Floyd, two sons and a daughter-in-law survive.

Uncle Sam lived in Wood River and worked at the International Shoe Company tannery in Hartford, Illinois. All these foregoing Illinois resident relatives would visit us in Missouri for a day or two each year. Uncle Sam might come more often because without a family to support he could afford a new car, and he liked to drive.

Uncle Sam was a quiet, slow-speaking individual who never became angry. He had a nice grin, but I think it would have taken a fire under him to shake his timbers. One evening we were sitting around visiting (after I was married) at my mother's house, and Sam was there. A large black bug ran under Sam's chair. Mom was preparing a nearby couch for sleeping, and yelled, "Sam, a big bug ran under your chair", and stood expectantly, wanting him to catch the bug. Sam didn't see the bug, and sat complacently without flexing a muscle, then laconically drawled, "What color was it?"

Lee Burleson married Lillie Pidcock and lived on a farm a few miles northeast of Salem. They had one child, a daughter Flossie who married Cecil (Cal) Wood, a cattleman in the Salem vicinity. After Cal died she continued to run cattle on their farm until about a year before she died on October 13, 1999. She and Cal are buried in the Salem cemetery.

Mary Burleson married Bill DeNoon and they had three sons, Hugh the eldest, Lee and Ira. Lee and Ira were a few years older than Wib and I, but they were congenial and loquacious and we liked to visit with them.

Uncles Nate and Joe were twins, but with little resemblance. Nate was very short and stocky, while Joe was a foot taller and more angular in stature. Facial features and personalities were strikingly dissimilar. We wrote about Uncle Joe in "Mail Call", chapter 9. Joe and Rose had three daughters; Charlene (Burleson) Pierce, Nancy and Juanita (Burleson) Thomas.

Nate married Kate Happel, a sister to John, Ed and Bill Happel. They had two daughters, Viney and Ester and two sons, Roy and Ken. Ken was two years older then my brother, Wib, and Roy was two years older than Ken. Both saw overseas military service in World War II, and Roy was killed in action in the South Pacific Theater of operations.

Uncle Nate owned a sprightly pair of mules (Dick and Bob) that he used for farming and pulling his wagons and buggy. His buggy was large and well equipped with a top and other accessories. It was used for trips when Kate rode along, and when he didn't have big loads to haul. Uncle Nate was an inveterate tobacco chewer, and prone to talk in your face. He took a shine to me and liked to regale me with stories till the waves of tobacco vapors sent me reeling. I learned to develop a list of ephemeral errands to do when Uncle Nate corralled me for more than a few moments. "Here comes Nate and Kate", we sang when they appeared with mules and buggy.

Viney and Ester did not marry. Viney is deceased and Ester now resides in Arizona. Her telephone number can be found by accessing an Internet search station.

John Burleson had one daughter, Elsie (Burleson) Brister whose address I do not have.

William Burleson had two daughters; Evelyn (Burleson) Wilson, now deceased and the status or existence of her descendants is unknown, and Velma Burleson whose last known (1979) residence was in Kansas City, Missouri.

Mattie Burleson married a Patterson and had three sons, Hubert, Kenneth and Gene (deceased), and a daughter Ruby (deceased). Gene had a daughter, Sharon (Patterson) Ptuut.

I have never met any of the families of John, William and Mattie Burleson. It is possible that cousin Geneva (Burleson) Saragusa knows the addresses of some of the descendants.

Thomas Malone of Kentucky married Elizabeth Best, and their children were; McCager, John Wesley, Thomas Jr., Samuel, William, and probably some daughters.

McCager served in the Confederate Army during the Civil War and fought in the battle of Wilson Creek near Springfield, Missouri. After the war he settled in Missouri, and married Elizabeth (Shoemate) Jones, widow of a Civil War Union Army soldier. Their children were: Willie (W.T.), who married Jennie Kitchens; Marion Francis, who married Amanda Ketchum; Walter, who married Clemme Lamb; Charley; Tode, a daughter; Eva, who married John Happel; Minnie, who married Wesley Roberts; Hattie, who married Marion Bell; and Mary Jones who married Caleb O. Parry Sr.

Dad was a son of Marion Francis (M.F.) and Amanda (Ketchum) Malone, and was named Albert McCager. Though he signed some official documents as Albert M., everyone called him Bert. His middle name was derived from his grandfather's given name, McCager, who was known as "Cage". Great Grandfather "Cage" died about a year after I was born. Dad's siblings were, in order of decreasing age; Bessie, Elmer, Raymond, Elizabeth (Lizzie), Erma who died at age three, Mary, Clarence, Robey and Earl. Dad was between Bessie and Elmer in age and born on January 25, 1900. Dad died on May 16, 1987.

Elmer married Mary Wills and their children were in order of decreasing age Kenneth, Dorothy, Herman, Delmar, Harold and Katherine. Harold and Katherine survive today. Dorothy was about the age of my brother Wilbert.

Raymond married my mother's sister, Viola, and consequently, my siblings and I are double cousins of their children, Irene, Charles, Francis, Lee and Eddie.

Dad and Raymond were always close, even though according to Dad, Raymond was a perennial prankster, and the brunt of many of his jokes fell on Dad. Dad related a story about returning home one night on his riding horse and in his Sunday-go-to-meetin' clothes. After removing saddle and blanket, he was proceeding to put his horse in the stable. As he grasped the latch to open the door to the stable, he found the latch thoroughly swabbed with fresh cow manure— Raymond was the only other person out that night.

Irene is about my age and Charles age is near that of my sister, Kathleen. We were always close while growing up, and our families visited together more frequently than with other relatives.

At a spot on the small creek that flowed through our farm, wild grapes grew in such profusion that the vines blanketed the tops of a series of trees along a stream bank during the summer. We cousins climbed to the tops of those vines and had a great time rolling and jumping on the mats of vines and leaf cover. Our parents were not aware of those escapades.

While farming on what was called the Jack Hale place on Norman creek, Uncle Raymond bought a used 1927 Chevy coupe with a rumble seat. In the flivver, they whistled up to see us, and everyone wanted to go for a ride on Sunday afternoon. Irene, Charles, Kathleen and I were allowed to ride in the rumble seat, while our parents rode inside— managing to fit on the one seat by having one lap sitter. We traveled on old U.S. Route 66 to Sullivan, Missouri (about 50 miles) before turning back for home. Only six and seven years old, we kids were sorely disappointed that we couldn't go farther.

In later years Raymond and Viola purchased the Henry Utter farm located about two miles south of us (see Chapter 2, Everything I Needed to Know) and we were able to visit more often.

Too many cats had accumulated, and Charles was assigned the task of dispatching a bunch of them. He calculated their demise could be effected by the frugal use of only one 12-gauge shotgun cartridge. He put a half dozen in a gunnysack, and then tied the sack of cats to a low hanging tree limb. Stepping back about 50 feet, he cut loose at the bag with the gun. With the ensuing boom the bottom of the sack opened up, and the cats fell out and ran off. At that range a full choke shot pattern doesn't open up much, and apparently his aim was such that the edge of the small concentrated pattern just caught the bottom of the sack, but not enough to incapacitate any felines. All cats beat him back to the house and barn.

Uncle Raymond had a good pair of mules, Jack and Kate, and Charles handled them well at the age of twelve. After moving to the Utter place they broke and prepared ground for our gardens in the spring, and helped us put up hay.

Uncle Earl Malone was the youngest of his family and only about five years older than I. He liked to visit us and often stayed overnight. He was a likeable person and Wib and I were glad to have him around. He hunted with us and helped with chores, and we were especially enamored with his tall tales and jokes. Usually he showed up with some new stories that had been garnered from his older brothers, Clarence and Robey who still lived with their parents while operating a trucking business. Sadly, in later years alcohol got the best of Earl and he lost much of his charm and humor. It is believed that he is buried somewhere in Oklahoma, possibly in the Vinita area.

Aunt Lizzie Malone married Robert Rigsbey, and they had a son, Bobby, and a daughter, Evelyn. Bobby was three years younger than I. He loved to come out to Seaton from their home in Illinois. After reaching his teens he stayed with us during the summer school vacation time as long as his parents allowed, or until we hinted that he ought to head home. He was usually a willing worker, but complained when I pushed him too hard on a job. My tutoring was not always beneficial, I'm afraid, and learning how to make smokes from the life-ever-lasting weed was certainly not and exemplary piece of teaching. He didn't like to milk the cows, and was not good at it, but his lack of skill was probably due to distaste for trying to develop proper technique.

Aunt Mary Malone married Fred Castleman, and I wrote about my visit with them while they farmed in the Elk Prairie area (Chapter 10, "Wising Up"). Later, they operated a store at Clinton Bank, and while there a son was born who died at 18-month age from pneumonia. Then, a daughter, Mary Lou, was born who is close to the age of my younger brother, Gilbert. After their store burned, they moved to Rolla, and Fred worked for his brother Herman Castleman, who owned the Superior Chevrolet agency. I boarded with Mary and Fred during my first year at the Missouri School of Mines and Metallurgy.

Husband Fred preceded Mary in death. She was born January 11, 1907 and died November18, 1987.

Aunt Bessie Elsie Malone was the oldest child of Marion and Amanda Malone, and married Warner Happel. They had the following children: Ervin, "Buck", "Teet", Herbert ("Hub"), Ruth and Rubie Lee. Today, I don't remember the given names of "Buck" and "Teet". We called them by their nicknames from the time of recognizance, and I don't recall the origin of their monikers.

The Happels lived in the Bangert area. We visited them occasionally and they visited us at Seaton. "Hub" and Ruth were in my age range, and we got along well. Their farm was located well off the beaten path, and contained a pretty valley with a spring-fed tributary to the headwaters of the Meramec River. They carried and hauled water from a lovely spring, and we wished we had one like it.

Husband Warner preceded Bessie in death. She was born May 11,1896, and died August 18, 1987. Hub, Ruth and Rubie Lee survive and they are faithful supporters and attendees at our Morrison Cemetery meetings.

Uncle Robey married Dorothy Condray who was my schoolteacher for a while as discussed in Chapter three. They had one child, a son Nolan who died at an early age of 33. His mother preceded him in death by several years. Both succumbed to a rare heart affliction. After Dorothy's death, Robey married Opal Licklider who passed away within a few years.

Robey operated a feed and farm supplies store in St.James for 40 years until retirement to the farm where he was raised. He was born September 29, 1912, and was the last surviving member of the clan until death on November 1, 1994. Prostate cancer with metastasis was the cause of death.

Willie Malone, son of McCager Malone, and wife Jennie had the following children: Bertha, who married Curt

Spradling who sold his store and farm to my Dad; Pearl, who married Charles Bynum and lived in St. Louis; Cage married Clara Ellis; Hammie married Bessie Plank and Ira, who married Thelma Plank.

Walter Malone, son of McCager, and wife Clemme, had the following children: Grace, who married Clarence J. Sisco; Ernest (EJ) who married Dorothy Dillworth and Claria, who married Albert Hale.

Eva Malone, daughter of McCager, married John Happel and they had the following children: Lloyd (unmarried); Lawrence (unmarried); Carl, who married Hazel Bowen; John, who married Bonny Will, and Marvin, who married Mary Crain. I attended Highland grade school with all these Happel boys who lived on a farm about 1.5 miles west of us.. Carl died August 19, 2003, Lawrence died March 31, 2006 and Lloyd died in August of 2006. All of the deceased family is buried at Asher Cemetery just north of Winkler on Missouri Highway 68.

Hattie Malone, daughter of McCager, married Marion Bell and had the following children: Opal, who married Cecil Plank, then Steve Huskey; Austin, who married Blanche Fink; Ostis, who married Marie Grey; Ora who married Ernie Watkins; Tim, who married Myrna Arthur; Dovie, who married Clyde Frey; Add, who married Marie Coppedge; Lovie (unmarried), and Roxie (unmarried). Austin and family lived in the Seaton community on a farm adjoining his father's farm on the north. Austin and Blanche had several children and I attended school with John (Cecil), Paul and Don. Don and sisters are the only survivors of these families.

Sam Malone, son of Thomas and Elizabeth (nee Best) Malone, married Lila Shoemate and their children were: John, Thomas, James, Emory, Henry, Lawrence, Martha and Bessie.

Thomas (Tom) married Artie Plank and Oliver, Maggie, Frank, Opal, Gladys, Agnes and Doreen were born of that union. After the death of Artie, Tom married Estella Ketchum and their children were: James (Jim), Maxine and

174

Eugene. Tom's families grew up in the Seaton area and Jim was my age. Maxine is the only survivor of these families.

Tom was a farmer, blacksmith and part-time carpenter. In Chapter five Tom helped build the rack on my Dad's new 1940 Chevy truck. He also helped to build the larger kitchen addition to our house. We took our horses to Tom to be shod, and brought other things that required smithing to him for repair and rebuilding. A nectarine tree grew on his farm, and Maxine gave some to me to eat. It was the first time I had tasted nectarines and I found them more desirable than peaches—peach fuzz caused me to shiver, and still affects me in the same manner.

Most of Tom's children grew up and moved to Illinois, but Agnes, who married Titus White, lived in the Seaton area for many years and was one of my mother's best friends.

Jim, Maxine and Gene attended grade school with me at Highland.

After Tom died, Gladys, who married Clyde Spann of Hartford, Illinois, bought the old home place and they used it as a vacation retreat.

James (Jim), son of Sam Malone and Lila (nee Shoemate) Malone, married Rurie Luster, and their children were: Opal, Virginia, Rebel, Dorothy, Nellie and Mary. They lived in the Seaton community for many years and I attended grade school with Opal, Virginia, Rebel and Dorothy. Rebul was my age and my favorite. She married Kenneth Morrison and lives in the St.James, Missouri area today. Ken died January 3, 2003.

Jim was a handyman and worked for farmers and in the timber industries of the area. Jim and family also lived in the Elk Prairie community near Dry Fork creek for a while and while living there Jim killed the first rattlesnake that I had seen in Missouri.

Emory Malone married Alice Broyles and they had ten children: Emmet, Roba, Wayne Alma, Edgar, Elsie, Ernie, Dortha, Norma, Warnie and Orville. They lived in the Salem area, and I was not well acquainted with them. Most of the deceased are buried at the Morrison (Dent County) cemetery.

Ernie and Wayne have been faithful attendees at the cemetery's annual meeting and both are now deceased.

Henry Malone married Mary Broyles and they had two children: Lonie and Lora. I was not acquainted with their family.

Lawrence Malone married Myrtle Sneed and they had three sons: Wilbert, Willis and Chester. They lived in the Seaton area for a while before I was born and I never knew them. Dad told me that Lawrence was found dead with a bullet hole in his head and a pistol beside him, along the Seaton-to-Clinton Bank road. Who pulled the trigger was not known but some people believed it was a homicide. I believe the boys grew up and lived mostly in the Rolla area, but I am not familiar with their current status.

Martha, daughter of Sam Malone and Elizabeth (nee Best) Malone, married George Plank and had three children: George (Pete), Bertha and Lloyd. I was acquainted with Lloyd only.

Bessie Malone, daughter of Sam and Elizabeth Malone married Dan Webster and had two children: Arch and Meredith. I was not acquainted with this family.

John Malone was a brother to "Cage" Malone and married Margaret Childress. Their children were: James Pat Malone who married Bessie Clayton; Sarah Malone who married James Grayson; Jerry Malone and Francis Malone. I am not acquainted with the lineage of these families, but I believe Pat Malone's family lived in the Steelville area of Crawford County, Missouri, and bounded on the west by Phelps County.

William "Bill" Malone, brother to "Cage", and son of Thomas Malone of Kentucky, married Cressa Adams and their children were: Artie, who married Lem Pidcock; Dora who married Fred Lamb; Jettie who married Arthur Adams; Charley who married a Bailey; and Lillie who married Tom Shoemate, son of Stanford Shoemate. My parents knew these families. Pidcock was the engineer of the Winkler Branch train engines.

At this point I have been unable to locate the genealogy of Thomas Malone Jr., son of Thomas Malone of Kentucky.

Marion Malone, son of "Cage", his wife Amanda, and sons Elmer, Clarence and Robey are buried in Asher cemetery, located on Missouri highway 68 about one mile north of Winkler.

To return briefly to the Burleson genealogy. Tommy and Jennie Adams lived about 1.5 miles north of us, and had two sons, Earl and Jonah. Jennie was a daughter of Andrew Burleson who was a brother of John W. Burleson, my mother's father. Earl and Jonah (Jonie) were respectively, ten and eight years older than I. But they often visited us when they came to the store, and occasionally we visited at their house. They were hunting one night and shot my big gray tomcat, mistaking it for a coon in the feeble light of their kerosene lantern. It was a long time before I forgave them for that miscue. Both Earl and Joney are deceased.

This writing is not based in any way on an in-depth re-search and study of the lineage and genealogy of the Burleson and Malone names. Rather, it is a brief presentation of four generations of genealogy, so my family and friends will have a working knowledge of their ancestry, and sufficient information to pursue a broader genealogical effort, if desired. I have recently received additional information relative to the Malone family that precedes that of Thomas of Kentucky but have not yet analyzed or verified the specifics of this later genealogy.

It should be noted that I have referenced "Our Ozark Mountain Neighbours" by J. Gilbert Lay in the development of some of the foregoing genealogy. I have found some errors in Lay's genealogy of the later generations. However, his work has been very helpful, particularly with the earlier generations, though I cannot vouch for the authenticity and accuracy of all data.

John W. Burleson Families of 1912: Identification by rows:

top back, L to R: Tom Burleson, Joe Burleson, Agnes (Hobson) Inman, Flossie (Hawkins) Moore, Beatrice (Hobson) Howard, Ves Shedd and Josie Carty; 2nd row down, L to R: DeweyBurleson, Clyde Burleson, Lily (Pidcock) Burleson, Flossie Burleson, Lee Burleson, Alf Patterson, Mattie (Burleson) Patterson, Claude Hobson, Nora Burleson, Rebecca (Burleson) Hobson; 3rd row, seated, L to R: Reverend Brown, Mary (Burleson) DeNoon, Bill DeNoon, baby Hugh DeNoon, Mary, a.k.a. Molly (Norvel) Burleson, baby Norma Burleson, John W. Burleson and Mrs. Mary Pidcock, 4th row, L to R: Viola Burleson, Sam Burleson and Lee DeNoon

Grandparents
Amanda (Ketchum) and Marion F. Malone

Bert and Nora Malone (left)
And Raymond and Viola Malone (right)
Circa 1920

14/   Patter and Pits
Euphemisms and Hyperbole

The etymology of Ozark dialects and stories about Ozark folklore has been presented in the writings of several authors. "Down in the Holler" and "Ozark Magic and Folklore" by Vance Randolph, are excellent reference books for those who would like to study the language and history of the Ozarks. However, these references are out of print.

My intent is to present some of the words, expressions and associated stories that were native to our Seaton and adjoining communities. Some of this information may be generic to much of the Ozark regions.

Many of our expressions and words will be found in Randolph's writings, and he relates conversations with people in the Rolla area. Randolph writes about a hyperbole that I heard from my Dad when I was just a little shaver. Dad would say to me, when I had done something I should not have done, or when I hadn't done something I should have done, "I'll kick you so high the bluebirds will build in your butt before you hit the ground." As MC for a dinner meeting of Pennsylvania, New York, New England and Delmarva plant managers, division and corporate staff of about 100 in attendance, I used the foregoing expression, and they almost rolled in the aisles with laughter. Outside of Missouri I have never heard anyone other than myself use that saying. Incidentally, I don't recall anyone using "little shaver" where I have lived and traveled, and I have been in all of the United States except Alaska.

Speaking euphemistically was a way of life in our territory, particularly in the use of scatological words. In certain company, the use of Anglo-Saxon four-letter words was eschewed, for example; defecation would be described as, "Have to go shake a bush," "Need to see a man about a dog," and flatulence would be, "passing gas," or "breaking wind." "Hockey" was used interchangeably for the act of defecation, or for excrement. Wonder what players and fans of the contemporary hockey leagues would think about that?

When animals were in estrus it was common to hear: "She is in heat," or in case of a cow, it might be "She's a bullin'," and for a sow hog, it could be "She's a boarin'." We didn't have any deer around then, and had not heard about the "rut". When it got down to the homo sapiens, the pseudo-sophisticates might take the high road with "the birds and the bees litany," but more likely the Billies would say, "Time to tell them the facts of life," or "about time they knowed where babies come from."

In the days when buffalo nickels were minted for legal tender, a penurious or stingy person might be described as "So tight, he squeezes a nickel 'til the buffalo defecates." Or the expression could be "Tighter than a bull's butt in fly time." Of course, less genteel and more scatological words were used in uninhibited conversations.

When a heavy deluge of rain poured down, some might say, "It poured down like an old cow pissin' on a flat rock." Now, some may say I have after all resorted to scatology, and I do use it with some reserve, nevertheless I am in good company with the old King James version of the bible wherein that word is written more than once. Moreover, if you have ever witnessed a cow committing such an act, you'll understand it is a marvelously appropriate analogy. I hope that those who don't know where to find the above word in the KJV and want to check my veracity, will let this be an opportunity to study all chapters of the Holy Word of God, inerrant and infallible.

Normally, bastard was considered as an angry, deprecating and denigrating swear word. If uttered in a literal sense and meaning, it likely was expressed in a confidential or advisory-like manner. Often the euphemism "woods colt" was substituted as a more intriguing synonym.

Death is an inevitable consequence of life and sin, and often a topic of conversation to be dealt with under many circumstances in our communities. Probably, no other word has sponsored as many euphemisms as neighbors, friends, family, notables and politicians make special efforts to express condolences and respect for one who has died. Even our contemporary Rolla radio station KTTR announces the reading of their list of obituaries as the "Regional Record." The final act of dying has been chronicled as; "He or she departed," "passed away," "gone to their rest," "deceased," "expired," and in a more jocular tone, "bit the dust," "kicked the bucket," "cashed in," "bought the farm," or one the English taught me, "He's 'ad it," and there are many more. No doubt the Holy Bible inspired some of these euphemisms for we read in the eloquence of the original King James version; Psalms 104:29, "Thou dost take away their spirit, they expire, and return to the dust;" and in Psalms 146:4, "His spirit departs, he returns to the earth."

I was always amazed by the fine eulogies offered by preachers at funerals, considering what they might have to work with, but I dared not say to my parents, "But you said, old so-and-so." Folks who had disliked, denigrated, maligned and castigated the deceased while living suddenly entered metamorphosis and couldn't say enough good things about the departed.

A drunken person was never inebriated. They were; "three sheets in the wind," "on a toot," "hittin' the bottle," "in his cups," or "on a binge." And others might say, "He's drunker than a hoot owl." Where the latter originated I don't know, and I wonder why the hoot owl got picked on.

Another expression involving the owl was: "slicker than, or as slippery as owl excrement." I never investigated the veracity of that one, and here again, the scat word was something different from excrement.

Dad disdained the imbibing of alcoholic beverages, and was inclined to cast a jaundiced eye at those who did, and especially two of his brothers, who when they got on a toot, often made a special effort to include Dad in their celebration tour. As they would chuckle, "It will get his dander up."

One of those brothers in company with a cousin got "tanked up" in St. James, and then headed out at night on old highway 68 for home in a Model A Ford. This happened in the early 30s, and the steel bridge that spanned Dry Fork creek a few miles south of St. James had been constructed earlier when traffic flow was less, and economics were more paramount. The shortest possible length of span had been selected, resulting in the south end of the bridge abutting against a bluff. Driving off the bridge on that end, you had to immediately make a ninety-degree turn to the left. A large glass reflecting eye about five inches in diameter was sealed into the rock of the bluff at about eye level, and directly ahead as you approached across the bridge.

As the two "sots" approached the bluff, the passenger said to the driver, "There's the light," and the driver responded, "I see it," then promptly drove smack into the bluff. One got a broken nose while the other had some cuts and bruises. They survived to "toot" again.

A similar incident is purported to have occurred in the Elk Prairie neighborhood. In that case, the feller on a "toot" was driving a new car, and not too familiar with all its controls. He was approaching a new gate when a passenger yelled, "Do you see the new gate?" The driver replied, "I see it," and then proceeded to plow right through the new gate.

Stirl Adams and family lived about three miles west of Seaton, and not far from Lige Register's farm. Stirl married Viola Ketchum and they had five children: Juanita (Wanny), Estena who was about my age, Norma, Elsworth and Wilma. They attended school at Highland. Stirl knew a lot of country lore, and one of his favorite expressions was, "Show me a politician that don't lie, and I'll show you a tree that the wind ain't blowed on." Many subjects other than politicians were substituted into the phrase, along with unsavory characteristics. Another novel expression of Stirl's was, "If you fry him for a fool you'll sure lose your grease." And I wish I could recall more of his wide repertoire.

Estena was in my classes at grade school along with Verba Happel. We were giving recitation in a history class, and the teacher asked me to read from the text about some ancient foods and cooking that utilized a brazier. I pronounced brazier as brassiere, promulgating an immediate series of titters and giggles from Estena and Verba, which continued after they had returned to their desks, and for days thereafter. I recognized my error immediately, which served only to exacerbate my discomfiture.

Nicknames were unceremoniously slapped on many persons in our communities. The origin of such monikers was not always discernible or traceable, but the genesis of some was a storied thing. When Ed Watkins' first grandson began talking, he said "Bapoo" for Grandpa, and thereafter, Ed became "Bapoo" to friends and acquaintances. Ed was a kindly gentleman and never appeared to be offended. He played the dulcimer and occasionally could be cajoled into performing for parties.

My family nickname "Ab" was attached to me at an early age. My wife and some relatives still address me thusly, though my wife spits out a sharp Albert when she wants to get my immediate attention, or is not happy with my performance. "Ab" may have been a condensation, because we called my older brother Wilbert, "Wib" and my younger brother Gilbert, "Gib." However, after retiring, and returning to Missouri, I found that some people of Ozark stock would pronounce Albert as "Abbert", so perhaps "Ab" is just a shortened version of "Abbert". I don't remember calling Wilbert "Wib" until after I became Ab.

The male name Marion was often pronounced "Mern". Both my grandfather Malone and his brother-in-law, Marion Bell, were addressed in that manner. In contrast, Marion Lenox, who lived west of Seaton about five miles on the Seaton-to-Elk Prairie road, was always addressed as Marion, but to complex the matter—his son named Marion, became known as "Mernie."

The memorable nicknames of "Slats" and "Highpockets" assigned to two young women in our neighborhood, originated with their suitors. It's not known what prompted the "Highpockets" handle, but the one dubbed "Slats" was definitely on the skinny side.

Raymond Shoemate, a farmer and part-time carpenter who lived two miles northeast of Seaton on Norman creek was often called "Moody", but I don't know the derivation.

After knocking around the northeast and other parts of the United States for thirty-five years, a lot of my Ozark dialect and colloquialisms had been lost. Under duress or in animated conversations, I often resorted to some congenital words and phrases, sometimes provoking quizzical glances from the easterners. However, I usually felt at ease, conversationally, with natives of the hill country and farming areas of Pennsylvania where dialects are often similar to Ozark speech and linguistics.

It was good to get back to Missouri on a permanent basis, and to hear some of the native-oriented patter. There are those residents who will say Missourah, and politicians are prone to take that route in areas of Missouri other than the Ozarks. When growing up, we considered such people "stuck up", with aspirations to be something socially that they were not cut out to be. Those Missourians wouldn't think about calling themselves Missourahans, now would they? Then again, maybe they would.

What a pleasant sound to hear "cher" spoken again— much better than chair-r-r, particularly if the latter is emitted with a nasal twang. In the Seaton area, some Ozarkians would say "cheer", but my family always stuck with "cher".

He was so scared he "shuck" all over, illustrated an Ozarkian use of "shuck" as a verb, rather than using shaking as an adjective. We would say, "Did you shake the tree?" but the answer would likely be, "Yeah, I shuck the tree, and if I hadn't, the wind might have blowed the apples off." "Blowed" was commonly used instead of blown.

The story is told of the Missouri farmer, who was having coffee at the snack bar in the train station, when a lady came in, sat down beside him and ordered coffee. Just as the coffee was delivered to her, the train whistle blew, and she said, "That's my train and this coffee is too hot to drink."

Immediately, the farmer spoke up, "Here, take mine, it's done saucered and blowed."

After riding several miles on one of our buckboard wagons without a spring seat, just about any of us would have declared, "After riding on this thang, I'm about done fur." In other words, that thing had about worn us out. And "done fur" could be used in an apocryphal sense. We'll be "done fur" fur shore iffen it don't rain. Some folks might say "shur" for sure and "shore" was a common synonym.

The era of the Model T and Model A Fords ushered in a lot of do-it-yourself education in the maintenance and repair of rubber tires and tubes. Many a soul in our community expressed his frustration with the quality of tires with a plaintive "I'm tard of fixin' tars." Easily I slip into that vernacular today, and though there have been remarkable improvements in "tars", tires ain't been made indestructible yet.

St.Louis was our destination when transporting produce and livestock to market and purchasing merchandise for the store. It was a rare occasion when anyone made a trip to Springfield, Missouri, but if they did, they would tell you they had been to "Sprangfield."

Both kids and adults relished ice cream cones when available at ice cream socials, or when purchased as treats on a trip to Rolla, St. James or Salem. It was common to hear a customer request a "comb". My wife, LauraBelle, still likes ice cream cones, and calls them "combs" with delight. However, she lacks the temerity to ask for a "comb" at McDonalds or other quick serve ice cream merchants. The derivation of this terminology was not of interest to me when growing up, but now I would speculate that some child, who thought the edible cup looked like honeycomb was the incipient trigger. Then again, someone may just have gotten their tongue twisted and launched the word "comb"—to become ensconced in the vernacular by teasers.

When living in the rural Groton-Lansing area of Upstate New York, our driveway exited to a main state highway. At the juncture of the road and driveway the culvert was deteriorated, and the highway department had contacted my wife one day to tell her they would replace the culvert, but we had to purchase and arrange for delivery of the corrugated pipe. She called a local supplier, and with Ozark elocution, asked if they had "culberts." She said a momentary silence ensued at the other end of the line, and then a burst of guffaws followed. Chagrined and nonplused at the merriment, she crossly said, "What's the matter, don't you have any?" Still chuckling, a man replied, "Oh, you mean culvert." I wonder what the merchant's reaction would have been if she had asked for a "tin horn", which now appears to be our local Phelps County Highway department's definition for a corrugated pipe culvert. Anyway, she got us a new "culbert", and she still maintains that "culbert" sounds much better than plain old culvert, and avows it is a corruption and miscue by the developers of the English language as in many other cases.

While living in Iowa, I worked for a guy who told me he didn't know how to pronounce chimney until he went down to Missouri, where they are called "chimleys." I informed him that he had a lot more learnin' yet to go. He and I chartered a Piper Tri-Pacer to fly from Des Moines, Iowa to a manufacturing plant in Walnut Ridge, Arkansas. Along the way, we ran into stronger headwinds than anticipated, and our pilot being a cautious soul, and bless him for it, got concerned about the fuel supply and decided to set down on a rather nondescript air strip in south Missouri to replenish his gas supply.

We landed without hitting any cattle or hogs, and then taxied up to a deserted little office, shop and hanger. The pilot decided to go one way looking for an attendant while my boss went the other way down a road where he could see a house. After about 15 minutes my boss returned and said he had found a guy who had assured him he would be there "dreckly." John looked at me and asked, "What does dreckly mean?" I responded that it most likely meant the man was engaged in some activity, which he planned to finish before tackling anything else, but he would come directly to us after

188

finishing his current task. John appeared a little doubtful and skeptical, but in about twenty minutes, here came the attendant, and he refueled our aircraft. We arrived an hour late at Walnut Ridge, but John had acquired a new expression for story telling, especially when in my presence.

"Like buying a pig in a poke," might be heard in many parts of the United States, but in our neighborhood, a paper or cloth bag was a "poke," pig or not. Many people were reticent to say bag because bag was a synonym for scrotum. How this came about is debatable, but the connotation has diminished over the past century. A burlap type bag was called a tow sack, gunny sack or grass sack.

Some farmers owned weighing devices that are defined as steelyard scales. They were long steel beams with graduations in pounds, and designed to hang from a hook or rod, so they would be balanced when a sliding weight was set at zero on the scale arm.

The object or material to be weighed was suspended from the end of the beam opposite to the scale and pivot point, and then the sliding weight was moved along the graduated scale beam till the beam was again in balance. Supplementary calibrated weights could be hung on the end of the graduated beam to weigh heavier items. These weighing devices were referred to as "stillards" or "stillyerds," depending on the individual articulation. Such definitions are still common today, and just recently I saw an ad in the Rolla Daily News, listing a "stillard" scale for sale.

I seen her "wrench" the dishes in the "zink". The word saw was not used to express visual acuity, except by those who had been drilled in school by a grammar-conscious teacher. One individualistic and interesting older lady always said, "I seed." Many who used seen instead of saw laughed at her, but only behind her back. Clothes were not rinsed, they got "wrenched", and for those fortunate enough to have a sink, they were happy to show you their "zink". How the last word developed is a mystery, unless one conjectures that some early zinc-plated or galvanized sinks induced it.

Not many folks could afford a veterinarian to spay their female dogs, but most were aware of the procedure, and would declare, "Too many curs around here now, that un ought to be "spaded". I think, "spaded" evolved through conversational transfer between people who did not read much, and may not have seen the word spay in print. I never heard the word neuter until I was grown. Our male animals would be "cut" or "fixed."

You're liable to "ketch" a cold if "youens" go "pooshin" through them "booshes" on a day like this. Grammatically, some people would enunciate push and bush correctly, but "ketch" and "youens" were universal translations of catch, and you, where you is meant to be plural.

We heered them comin' from a "fur" piece away. In our early days, this was very acceptable grammar, and amenable to great articulation. Nobody in our community needed a dictionary to understand the language of their neighbors.

A special expression was used to cast judgment on persons, especially women, when certain individuals were deemed to be haughty, stuck-up, snooty or condescending. "She thinks she is something on a stick." It was not always clear as to what subtle condemnations of character were intended or inferred, but the elocution was notably pungent and acrimonious at times.

When men told ribald jokes, and used lewd or sexy language in the presence of women, some women said the men were "blackguarding." I do not know the origin and derivation of this word, but the meaning and intent of its application was clear to everyone in our community. Today, this allegory would be defined as sexual harassment, and lawyers would swarm like wild honey bees in a hollow tree.

My first two daughters were just four and two years old, and had not tidied up their play area as directed by me. I walked up to them and announced in a grouchy and stentorian voice that I intended to "clean somebody's plow," if conditions didn't improve. Terry, the oldest, promptly remonstrated, "Don't keen my plow, keen Penny's plow." It is something to chuckle about yet today, though fifty years in the past. Terry had grasped the general intent of this Ozarkian threat without hesitation. She had already been indoctrinated by her grandfather's stories.

Ozark men often developed conversational bywords. Today, it is rare to hear anyone under the age of fifty using bywords. Maybe some will occasionally say "by golly" or "by gosh", but not on a habitual basis. My grandfather Malone always inserted "I jollies" at propitious places in his conversations for punctuation, emphasis, accentuation, and embellishment. "I jollies, they'll get the best of us if we don't vote 'em out." And "I jollies", he was sure right about that. Great Uncle Willie Malone's byword was "by swanser", and he might say, "I swanser, that horse is gonna kill me yet." One of his riding horses kicked him in the stomach, and he was stove up for a couple of months. Other memorable bywords: by cracky, I grannies, I juxner, by dingies, by George, by gum, by doggies and one inimitable character used "sugar" frequently. "Sugar, you cain't git blood out of a turnip." "Sugar, that ain't no way to act."

Elocution by those old timers with the inclusion of bywords was better and a lot more charming and interesting than listening to the babble of many politicians, business executives, city and PhD school administrators who rattle continuously, but with ands, buts, ahs and uhs inserted between every two or three words. And then there is the unbearable blather mouth who has to take a very audible sucking breath every three or four words, but will run his or her mouth at full throttle as long as there is a captive audience.

Individual rounds of firearms ammunition are normally called cartridges. Our hill country hunters and shooters pronounced this word in a delightful way. They might say, "I ain't got ary catridge left after my last squirrel hunt." "Catridge" just seems to have better definition and ring to it, compared to the harsh sounding cartridge. And they might use "nary" instead of "ary; in either case meaning they don't have a single one of the subject identified. Also, they may iterate, "There ain't nary a 'chanct' I'll get my corn in before

May first." Others would say chance, but come down real hard with a long A emphasis. And often, a long A highlighted the "chanct" pronunciation.

Face-to-face greetings were usually "howdy" or "hi", and sometimes followed by queries as to the well being of the greeters. Rarely did anyone respond with the often dishonest "great, great" one hears today. We might say jocularly, "fit as a fiddle" or simply declare "fine." And then there are those persons who are so occupied and indifferent they will ask you how you are and if you answered my wife died last night and I think I will die too, they may well say fine, fine. If a youngster said "fine" an adult might counter with "fine as frog hair?" and followed by "split four ways?" if the child had previously answered yeah or yep.

Other responses to "how are you" were "fair –to-middlin'" and "tolerable" though the latter rolled off the tongue of my paternal grandfather as "jist tolable."

Many of the folks in our area were of Appalachian stock and of lineage dating back to the immigrants from the Elizabethan era of England, but few made any big to-do about ethnic origin. Many didn't know much about their genealogy before settling in Missouri. I never heard St. Patrick mentioned until I attended school at the Missouri School of Mines and Metallurgy at Rolla. Irish was pronounced "arsh."

Previously mentioned euphemisms for death were adhered to but a more exclamatory "deader than a doornail" was used to describe a discharged battery or a battery-operated tool such as a flashlight. People were "laid out" when they had been prepared for display at a wake. Other usage was prominent, such as "she laid out her clothes for the party," or he "laid out" his tools to fix the wagon, and if a gladiator knocked an opponent out or unconscious, he might brag, "I laid him out."

Nobody enunciated fire or queer. "Quare" and "far" reigned instead. One might say, "It was mighty quare how that far got started, and if it had gone another "eench" it would have got my barn. Give him and eench and he'll take a "maal." Gone was often enunciated with a very long and emphasized O.

"Backbiting" was ascribed to uncomplimentary talk about someone behind his or her back, and is mentioned in Psalm 15 of the Bible. Hill people considered it a sin against a neighbor, along with other sins enumerated in Psalm 15.

Most folks planted potatoes and garden peas as early in the spring as possible because these crops didn't do well in mid-summer heat. After a long winter with nothing left to prevent scurvy and rickets except pickles, home canned blackberries and plums we welcomed a mess of new green peas and savored a mix of peas creamed with small new potatoes that were dug before maturity. A standard exposition of the adults as they devoured this dish was, "Boy, I could eat every potato and pea in the bowl." As we kids matured, we would glance at each other and quietly soliloquize, "Oh no, not again." And then there were dissidents who complained, "I'd druther have my peas without the taters." "Druther" was almost universally a synonym for rather.

In isolated cases a person with lack of taste for peas might be criticized and denigrated with "He is the 'quarest' person I ever seen—don't like peas."

When one of our hill men said his paints had "turned up missin'" he wasn't a budding artist or house painter, but had lost or misplaced his trousers. "Britches" was also a common definition for pants or trousers.

The conglomerated pronoun, "You-all" as notably used in southern parts of the United States was not common to our community. Rather you could hear and still can hear in some families, "You-uns come see us," or "What do you-uns think about that?" Possessive words such as ourn, yourn, hisn, hern and theirn were not uncommon to our vocabularies.

One of our former pastors used "nekked as a jaybird", and very appropriately, in a sermon. He is not a native and I'm almost certain that he lifted the expression from some publication or heard it used by natives. He is a learned person and a voracious reader. When I quizzed him with

"Nekked as a jaybird, eh?" he just grinned and said, "Yeah." Literate or not, if you were naked in our community you indubitably were "nekked."

I "brung" everything we needed "fur fixin" the fence. If anything was brought it was "brung" in our neck of the woods. And linguistically, the phonetics of fixin' established the meaning, i.e. everyone understood that the statement, "I'm fixin to go to town," meant that the speaker was preparing for a journey to town. And if an argument between persons generated a comment such as "I'm a fixin to fix your wagon," then somebody better get ready to fight or offer conciliation.

An interesting expression that I have heard only in the Ozarks and common yet today: "I think a lot of him," or the object of the preposition could be her, them or other designated person. The speaker means he likes and respects the person a lot. I think this could confound or stump many linguists and exegetes.

Well, I reckon it's purt near time to omega this chapter. A professor at MSM who taught some of my engineering classes, and not a native of Missouri, frequently introduced "purt near" into his lecturing and counseling—"You purt near flunked that exam." It was a common Ozark expression, meaning almost, about or very close—this professor had lived in Rolla a long time and also used other colloquialisms of the area.

Our people were disdainful of arrogance, hypocrisy, pontification and influence peddling. They might not have the elocution of the Bible but they would agree with Colossians 2:8, "See that no one takes you captive through philosophy and empty deception, according to the tradition of men, according to the elementary principles of the world." They also would think like John Ruskin who said, "Any one wrapped up in himself makes a pretty small package.

15/ High School Walk

My older brother Wilbert (Wib) graduated from high school in the spring of 1937 at age16. He started grade school (first grade) a year early, and also had been allowed to skip a grade.

High school graduates were allowed to teach the lower grades one through eight in rural schools. However, state regulations required high school grads to pursue a college education through certified correspondence courses and summer college sessions, in order to maintain eligibility to teach. "Wib" matriculated in the summer at the University of Missouri in Rolla and Columbia. He obtained a teaching contract with the rural Elk Prairie School District, and beginning in the fall of 1937 taught there each year until he was inducted into military service in 1942.

Wib attended rural Hawkins Bank High School during his freshman and sophomore years. It was a small two-room operation and located about four miles from Seaton as the crow flies. He rode our horse or walked to and from school on a route similar to that a crow might have flown. Only the first two years of high school were offered, and in later years this school was closed.

Wib completed junior and senior years of high school at St. James High. A private school bus operator had established a route to haul rural high school students from our area and other locations along the roads leading to St. James. He walked to highway 68 to catch the bus. Later, Earl Malone took over the bus route, and Wib didn't have to walk as far, and during inclement weather, Earl came to Seaton to pick him up. Riders paid a monthly stipend for their transportation.

I began high school in the fall of 1937. By that time the school bus operator and route had changed, and I had to catch the bus three miles from home on highway 68. The road was improved considerably from that of the early thirties, but still a gravel surfaced route. The route operator owned his bus. He received some subsidy from the St. James school district, but much of his income was derived from monthly fees paid by the student riders. I paid three dollars per month during my first year, but by the time I graduated, the fare was up to five dollars per month. My friends, that was a right smart amount of money in those days, and I still had to walk three miles going and coming. Now and then, I was lucky enough to hitch a ride, and in bad weather Dad hauled me to the pickup point. While a freshman, I sometimes walked another quarter mile, down highway 68 and then caught the bus from Aunt Mary and Uncle Fred's store at Clinton Bank.

During my first two high school years, the bus was a converted van and about 18 teenagers were crammed into it. Willie Gravatt was the operator and owner during all my high school time and for several years thereafter. He was a good driver and maintained control of the gang. The vehicle was heated for winter driving, but distribution of heated air from the front was poor. Actually, we were jammed together so much that there was enough communal body heat to avoid any major suffering from the cold. Warm fall and spring weather caused more discomfiture because there was no air conditioning other than wind through the windows. And then, we had to endure the dust from the graveled roads.

One morning during my sophomore year, a pickup truck pulled out of a driveway in front of our bus—Bill managed to swerve enough to mostly sideswipe, and though we slid into the road ditch, no one was injured. With some fender straightening we were able to drive out of the ditch and continue to St. James. Damage to the pickup was greater. Anyway, we got an extra charge of adrenalin to start the day.

The worst day of my life on a school bus occurred because of physical misery. Shortly after leaving school an intestinal bellyache hit me, and I didn't think I would make it to my drop-off point without succumbing to number two. Not only was the griping eating at my innards with fury, but also my mind was in turmoil with the potential for crushing embarrassment. Luckily, my sphincter held tight, and scrambling off the bus at my drop-off place, I dashed gingerly (it is possible, believe me.) to a nearby abandoned iron ore mine site, and let go with as much physical relief as I've ever experienced.

Also, as a sophomore I had developed an ingrown nail on a big toe, and walking with shoes on caused the toe to bleed, and pain increased with each step, so after disembarking from the bus I shucked my shoes and walked home barefoot. I did this until cold weather, and by that time the condition of the toenail had improved. I cured the ingrowing by shaving and scraping the middle of the toenail with my pocket knife during the evenings, until the curvature of the nail changed and grew out to where it did not turn into the side of the toe. My Dad coached me during this treatment process since it had been successful for him when he was a boy.

Great Uncle Willie Malone's house was only a half-mile from where I caught the bus, and one day he hollered at me as I was walking by while headed home, and asked me to come up to his house. He introduced me to a granddaughter and her mother Clara (nee Ellis) who was married to their son, Cage. She was a lovely little girl of seven who with her mother was staying with Uncle Willie and Aunt Jennie until Cage got settled in a new job too far away for commuting. Until they could move to Cage's location, the girl would attend school at Clinton Bank, which was just a quarter mile down Highway 68 from where I normally caught my bus.

I was asked if I would let the little gal walk with me in the morning so she would be safe. I said sure, and would even take her to the Clinton Bank School where I could catch my bus. Our travel went well until we hit the long hill before reaching the highway, and then she didn't have the stamina to keep pace with me. Finally, with concern that I might miss the bus, I told her to hold on to my belt and I practically dragged her huffing and puffing for the remainder of the trip. I already had to get up quite early in the morning to get chores done and leave home in time to catch the bus, so I didn't want to change my schedule. Consequently, it just became routine to let the little girl hang on as I kept a normal pace. They moved in a couple of months, and I rather missed the tyke. I cannot recall her name and wish that I could see her now to ask her if she remembered those trips. I never saw her again after they left Uncle Willie's.

For four years of high school my routine included getting out of bed at 5:00 a.m., starting a fire in the cook stove for my mother to make breakfast, dressing for chores, to the barn to milk three or four cows, back to the house to wash up, change clothes, eat breakfast, then head out at about 7:10 to walk three miles to catch the school bus at 7:50 to 8:00 a.m. About 45 minutes of walking at a brisk pace was required.

In the winter it was dark until after breakfast, and I carried a kerosene lantern to the barn for illumination while milking and feeding the cows.

Before going to the barn, I also started or revived fires in our wood burning heating stoves. When adequate coals remained overnight in the heating stoves, I removed a small shovel full of coals to the cook-stove firebox as a fire starter for kindling and firewood. Otherwise, coal oil (kerosene) was poured on wood kindling and paper, and then lit with a match to get a fire going.

My mother made biscuits from scratch every morning, and with biscuits, meat and gravy in my gut, I was substantially prepared to sally forth. Lunch was a brown bag affair or vittles wrapped in a newspaper. Once in a while my lunch was stolen from the shelf in the locker room, and I went without eats until supper. Maybe the thief was hungrier than I. I was never able to catch a culprit.

On January 17, 1939, my younger brother, was born. Searching for a name, my parents finally settled on Gilbert, so a trio of Berts came into being. As they cogitated about selecting a middle name I suggested Bryan, and that was it. I don't know if Gilbert (Gib) is aware of the origin of his middle name, and I have not mentioned it because some people have an aversion to their middle names. A middle name or middle initial is requisite to a military career. Woe unto those warriors who have neither. They will be harassed until one or the other is adopted, or they will be directed to forever insert N.M. I. instead of a middle initial.

It was interesting to have a baby among teenage siblings, and we pitched in to help our mother with her added responsibilities. We got along okay and continued with our schooling without any interruptions. About four years later, after Wib and I were serving in the armed forces, we were fortunate to be home on furlough together for a few days. Our mother had sewn a uniform similar to ours for Gib, and he proudly stood with us as she took pictures. Some 15 years later, he too would serve in the armed forces.

In my junior year at high school, my sister Kathleen was a freshman, and it was nice to have company on the trek to and from busing. The bus route was expanded, and Bill Gravatt had purchased a custom built bus of orthodox design and yellow color, though it was a short wheelbase unit with a capacity of only about 30 passengers. Vision, seating and almost everything else was a big improvement over the van.

After my graduation, Bill got a larger orthodox school bus with dual wheel rear drive and extended his route to Seaton, so Kathleen didn't have to walk three miles anymore to catch a bus. By that time there were other students from the Seaton area that caught the bus including Kathleen's best friend Ilean Shoemate.

Though an overflow concrete slab had been installed in Norman creek where the road to Seaton crossed, the creek could not be forded during severe flooding. However, the larger school bus with higher clearance could cross most of the time, even with significant stream flow.

During my high school tenure, St. James did not indulge in varsity football or track—just softball and basketball. Logistics prevented me from participating in those varsity activities, plus I was small in physical stature, and likely could not have made the teams anyway. However, there were intramural programs for both basketball and softball, and I entered into those activities.

A spring softball league was partly sponsored by Pepsi Cola and participants were awarded Pepsi pins for exemplary play. I was the pitcher for one of the teams, which was coached and captained by Bill Morrison. In the playoffs we almost had the tournament won until I threw a changeup off-speed pitch that was blasted out of the field with two on base. Ed Potter was school coach, and he grinned at me and said, "You picked the wrong batter to throw that pitch to." At that embarrassing point, he didn't tell me anything I didn't know or wanted to hear. Bill was disappointed but didn't chastise me, and I still got a Pepsi pin.

You don't hear much about intramural sports in our schools today, and the lack of such programs runs counter to what education is all about. Varsity sports at both the high school and college levels are emphasized at the expense of the average student, and from my viewpoint is a condemnation of our school systems and parents who allow this carnage of physical training opportunities for their children. Every kid that aspires to participate in a sport, which is supported by public taxes, should have that opportunity. If the American Civil Liberties Union wants to do something credible, they should soak their feet in this pot of discrimination.

For a small high school, St. James fielded a pretty fair concert and marching band. I started with elementary music studies and then decided to try the trumpet or cornet. After scraping together enough money, I acquired a low cost cornet, and after some practice was accepted as a band member. Later I bought a used cornet of better quality and my playing ability increased. However, two crooked front teeth bothered my upper lip when playing, and handling higher notes was difficult. Ray Dull, music instructor and bandmaster, had warned me that I could have problems with the cornet, and had suggested the clarinet as an alternate. Then, after I persisted with the cornet, he accused me of not practicing enough. Actually, I probably practiced more than the average band member. At times, my parents made me leave the house to practice. I probably frustrated all the hoot owls, and if coyotes had been around then I'm sure they would have howled at more than the moon.

I hung in there and played with the band till graduation, though I continued to have lip trouble. Not everyone liked Ray Dull, but he was a good director and knew his music and instruments. He took us to regional and state band competitions, and we usually ranked well. Once I played a solo, but I was nervous and pummeled some notes. Needless to say, I didn't win any ribbons, and Ray didn't schedule me for any more solos. Ray fancied himself a singer and entertained an assembly of students with a rendition of "On the Road to Mandalay." I was not qualified to critique singers, but somebody must have felt qualified because Ray didn't sing for us again.

I still have that cornet in its battered case. Now and then, I will attempt to play it, but my lips don't want to get in shape to perform respectably, even though the two crooked front teeth became abscessed and were removed many years ago (see "Dental Dents" in Chapter 12).

John F. Hodge was Superintendent of the St. James school system during my high school years. The kids had nicknamed him "Snort" because of his manner of speaking. We didn't have much contact with him, but he was well respected, and in later years the expanded high school was renamed as The John F. Hodge High School.

Louis Donati taught math and world history. We liked Louie, as he was known, but even he had difficulty inculcating a bunch of inattentive teenagers with the importance of world history. Louie went on to become Superintendent of the St. James schools, and for many years has been recognized throughout Missouri as an outstanding educator. Mr. and Mrs. Donati attended the fiftieth year reunion of my high school class in 1991.Mr. Donati passed away a short while after I had prepared the first draft of this manuscript.

Several boys in my senior class took the typing course, including myself. I didn't have any problems learning the keyboard touch system, but my stubby, cow-milking fingers were not designed for speed. Nevertheless, typing was one of the most beneficial abilities acquired in high school, and here I am, applying, applying, though carpal syndrome may be on the horizon and my abilities have not improved.

Only one boy beside myself enrolled in the shorthand course. He claimed it would help him when he went on to study and practice law. I've dealt with many legal beagles since then and have not known one that recognized a Gregg squiggle. I took to the Gregg system like a duck to water, and here again, it was one of the more beneficial skills that I learned in high school.

The ability to take notes in shorthand during my college classes and military training classes was very helpful. Most men don't know any Gregg shorthand, so it could be applied surreptitiously. Today, I don't remember enough shorthand for practical application.

Earlier, I indicated that I learned to drive an auto at age eleven. At that time Missouri did not require driver's licenses, but later, legislation was enacted to license all drivers, but written or driving tests were not required.

A license was effective for two years and the minimum age for license eligibility was sixteen. A parent or other acceptable sponsor was required, in the presence of the licensing agent, to vouch for the driving ability of a sixteen year old before a license could be issued. My first driver's license was issued on March 25, 1940—the fee was 25 cents. I still have this original license. I must develop the temerity to proffer this to a gendarme who may stop me because of an infraction of traffic rules.

Occasionally Dad was too busy to go to town for supplies, and he let me drive the pickup to town. I parked the truck at Uncle Robey's farm store, and they loaded the list of supplies while I was in school. I liked to drive, and welcomed a vacation from riding the bus. I tried to schedule my travel so at some point I could pass the school bus and honk at student passengers who recognized me. Later Dad traded for a 1 ½ ton dually truck, and to wheel it around was more

202

exciting yet. In the driver's seat I rode up higher than in a car or pickup and felt like the king-of-the-road, especially if I could meet or pass the school bus.

I practiced "double clutching", seeking perfection in manipulation of gear changes so I could shift at higher speeds without clashing gears, and also worked on timing of speeds and shifts so I could hit the hills under optimum conditions to get up and over in the higher gears, which resulted in better engine efficiency and lower fuel consumption.

Dad never double-clutched. He raked the gears without a flinch, while I cringed, fearing he might rip out the gearbox. Otherwise, he was an excellent driver, and never experienced a traffic accident with his trucks, though he drove many thousands of miles on old U.S. Route 66 and in some of the worst of St. Louis traffic.

On one trip, Dad and I sat for fifteen minutes waiting to cross a busy St. Louis street where there was no traffic light or cop. Traffic didn't let up in either direction of flow, just one vehicle after another, and almost bumper-to-bumper. Finally, Dad said, "I'm tard of this," and he ripped across, while brakes squealed on both sides of us. He had calculated he could make it if their brakes held, and he timed it precisely.

In those days, much of Route 66 paving was narrow gauge of only eight or nine feet width per driving lane. Dad would not let me have the wheel to drive on 66 while loaded with cattle or while in St. Louis. Now and then, he let me drive on 66 as we headed home. I was prone to drive on the curb of the pavement when meeting large trucks. Dad would stipulate, "Stay on your lane, don't let them hog the road, they won' hit you," and they didn't hit me, yet I was concerned—it seemed at times that the distance between us was little more than the thickness of a Sears Roebuck catalog.

Vehicle wrecks were common on Route 66. The worst one I witnessed occurred in the three-lane section near

Eureka, Missouri. Two cars collided head on—traveling in opposite directions; both tried to pass at the same time.

In Chapter 9, the ford at Norman creek was mentioned in regard to crossing during high water flows. The approaches on either side could wash and erode, causing difficulties when entering or exiting the creek. Also, holes could be scoured out in the creek bottom, and the high level of flow and the roily condition of the floodwaters would obscure large rocks and other debris deposited in the ford.

We studied the creek flow, looking for new riffles and unusual points of turbulence in the fording area, and if potential obstructions were indicated we deferred crossing until the water level dropped to a point where we could make a more precise evaluation of potential hazards to traffic.

One day late in the afternoon, Dad and I approached the creek as we headed for home and noted the water flow was at a level higher than what was normally acceptable for a safe crossing, even with our higher clearance dual-wheeled 1940 Chevy truck, but anxious to get home after being away all day, Dad said, "Let's try something." We removed a tarpaulin off the truck rack and draped it over the front and hood to prevent water from flowing directly into the engine compartment. With rope we tied the tarpaulin down at crucial points, and then I straddled the hood to help hold the tarp in place. Dad put the truck drive in "granny" gear (lowest), eased into the edge of the water, and then opened the throttle all the way as he plowed into and through the creek. Water washed all over the hood and me, but we didn't hit any big rocks or washouts, and the engine never sputtered. After crossing, we stopped to give thanks and to remove the tarp.

That 1940 Chevy was a mighty fine truck. Dad drove it hard, and into the 1950s until he quit long distance trucking. He continued to use it for short hauls to and from local towns. He sold Phillips 66 gasoline and oils at his store, and always used Phillips' number 10 weight "Troparctic" brand oil in the venerable straight-six Chevy engine. It didn't have an oil filter, but we changed oil every 1000 miles or so.

Engines are smoother and more efficient today, but they don't make them a lot better.

Our high school class of '41 was not noted for theatrical talent, and if any graduate went on to thespian greatness, I haven't heard about it, but we did put on a fair three-act play in our senior year.

St. James high school was noted for its "cracker box" gymnasium. Dimensions were pitifully small, spectator seating very limited and the ceiling was so low that shooters of long basketball shots had to effect a very shallow arced trajectory if they hoped to make a basket.

Eventually, the moribund cracker box was retired after the school district residents approved bonding to fund the addition of a new gymnasium. Along with the new gym a new stage was added for theatrical and musical productions. Our senior play provided the occasion to christen the new stage. The gym was completed in time to host some varsity basketball games during the latter part of our senior year, and also in time to host a regional basketball tournament.

During my high school years, Wib was teaching at the rural Elk Prairie one-room schoolhouse. In 1937 and 1938 he boarded with Alma and Alex Simily, and Dad drove over to bring him home for weekends. In 1939 Wib bought a 1935 standard model Chevy car. It was a smooth running little car for that era, and he could come and go as he pleased. He was good to me, and on one occasion let me drive his car to St. James-Rolla to participate in a regional band competition. Having a car to drive while in high school was then like what kids today might call "awesome."

We attended pie suppers at Elk Prairie, and one year Wib allowed me to recite a monologue that I had authored—either it was a lousy concoction or the residents of that area just didn't want to recognize and acclaim a budding poet laureate. At another Elk Prairie pie supper a guy that had purchased a pie gave it to me. The owner of the pie turned out to be an old lady, and she had prepared the worst imitation of pumpkin pie ever created. I managed to consume a very small portion, and the lady was offended at my reticence to dutifully suffer more. Anyway, my behavior did not appear to adversely affect Wib's standing in the community. Obviously, the guy that bought the pie was better informed about the culinary and baking abilities of area residents than I.

Somehow, enough money was scraped together to buy a class ring and a new suit for my graduation. I rode to St. Louis with Dad and Uncle Raymond Malone to select a suit. While Dad was picking up supplies at wholesale grocers and hardware dealers, Uncle Raymond and I visited two large men's clothing stores for me to examine suits. Though prices and fittings were satisfactory in many available suits, I didn't like any of them. I liked a tweed I had seen in Bishop's store at St. James, so bought it after returning home.

My class ring was nice, but after the novelty wore off it was not of much interest to me and eventually I gave it to my mother. Rings annoy me. I wore a gold wedding band for many years until I mustered the courage to ask LauraBelle if she minded my not wearing it. She said no but with reticence, I think. I shucked it and she had it reduced in size to fit on her finger along with her grandmother Williams' ring.

In the spring of 1941 I graduated from high school in the company of 54 classmates. I was class valedictorian, and my family was pleased, but the honor did not mean a lot to me, because even at age seventeen, I was cognizant of my limitations, which would be driven home to me as I pursued advanced education.

A huge bureaucracy of pseudo-education has inexorably developed in our country, and continues to proliferate unabatedly under the aegis of teacher's unions and extraneous coteries of administrators, who are more interested in self-aggrandizement and socialization than concerned about the future of our children. Their malfeasance has often been aided and abetted by "politically correct" and hypocritical politicians, who would sell their souls to get elected or reelected to public offices.

Unless a rock floor of morality, ethics, discipline, stewardship, courtesy and an expanded basics curriculum is restored to our educational systems, the future of our country is grim. The history of the rise and fall of the Roman Empire is legion. Such evidence for sure should be daily medicine for instructors and students alike, and until the shifting sands of educational institutions are stabilized with rock and cement.

There are no plausible reasons why a kid of average intelligence needs twelve years of confinement in classrooms to achieve a level of learning sufficient to enter the collegiate sphere. And kindergarten is little more than a giant baby sitting operation, engendered by a coalition of irresponsible parents and self-serving administratively dominated school systems—a redundant, wasteful exercise that should be abolished; yet there are advocates for extending this public-supported baby sitting to an all-day hoorah on a national level. Many schools are already on such a schedule. Meanwhile, drug and alcohol abuse runs rampant in the secondary and high schools.

Unctuous perpetrators will take umbrage at my words, but "feelings are often hurt on the sharp edges of the truth." (Author unknown).

16/   Priming the Pump

Upon graduation from high school I was offered a small scholarship to a business school in Missouri. Ed Potter, athletics coach and student counselor, recommended that I take the scholarship and become a certified public accountant. I demurred, because I really did not know what I wanted to do. In my mind there was somewhat of a hankering for a shot at further education on a collegiate level.

Oscar Glen, who was the Chevy dealer in St. James, came out to Seaton and asked me to work for him and train to be his parts and service manager. His offer was not appealing to me, and as the summer wore on I began to evaluate the possibilities of attending the Missouri School of Mines and Metallurgy (MSM) at Rolla.

As fall registration time at MSM rolled around I had accumulated just barely enough money for tuition and registration fees, and I needed to find a source of income to pay living expenses. Part-time jobs in Rolla were hard to come by without a mentor or family connection to assist, and I did not know many people in Rolla. The Federal government sponsored a work program named The National Youth Assistance Agency (NYA) that was funded by the government and administered by universities and business organizations, which employed youths part time within their operations. I applied for NYA assistance and was approved for work with the MSM bookbindery under the management of Mrs. Elizabeth Southgate.

My memory is a little bit hazy about this, but I believe we were paid 35 cents per hour, and limited to only 10 hours each week. Four students were assigned to Mrs. Southgate's care, but due to different classroom schedules, all did not work at the same time. Occasionally, we would see everyone together for an hour's work. My freshman year Mrs. Southgate's crew consisted of a sophomore, junior and senior in addition to myself. I endured some teasing but no hazing, and I liked all my fellow workers and we got along well.

Mrs. Southgate loved her "boys", but was also a taskmaster and supervised us closely to see that we took our work seriously. She was proud of her bindery products, and would not release a rebound or repaired book before it had passed her thorough inspection. Whenever possible she assigned jobs based on her evaluation of individual proficiencies. Most high quality hardback bindings were sewn to hold the pages together, and I liked to do that job. However, she preferred the senior's handiwork for sewing, and he did most of the sewing jobs unless a rush job evolved and he was not available—then I might be allowed to sew. I worked for her until I was called to active duty from the Army Air Force Reserves in February 1943. Later, while on military leave, I stopped to visit with Mrs. Southgate and she was tickled to see me.

Mrs. Southgate did a special binding for Dean Curtis Wilson's daughter, and I was her personal courier to deliver the finished book to the Dean's residence. I was pleased that she chose me but a bit shy about the assignment. When I rang the doorbell the daughter (about 14 or 15 if I estimated correctly) answered the door with a smile, and noting the book, quickly assessed my mission. She invited me inside and introduced me to her mother. Both were nice, and after a brief chat I departed. It was the only time I was in the Dean's residence.

My NYA work provided enough income to pay my board and room of $3.00 per week with Aunt Mary and Uncle Fred Castleman who lived at 707 E. 7th St. in Rolla. They were good to me, knowing that it was a rough row for me to hoe financially, and I did go home during the weekends and holidays. Becoming oriented as a freshman at MSM was tough for me. It was the first time I had been pretty much on my own and I didn't indoctrinate very well.

Hazing of freshmen wasn't in full swing for a month or so, but I could never accept hazing as of any merit whatsoever—redundant and repulsive to me and I eluded the tormentors as much as possible. When the sophs and upperclassmen pulled the old get-acquainted charade out at the school mine area during an evening, I stayed just long enough to answer roll call, and then faded into the woods away from the bonfire to let the darkness envelop me. I had night hunted enough to know how to navigate in the dark, and had no problem finding my way back to town and to my bed for a good night's sleep—while a lot of those poor freshmen suckers were wandering around lost, and dragging in to town naked or half-naked in the wee hours of the morning.

The big muddy tug-of-war hazing event was held during daylight hours and I was in the thick of that. Though it was supposed to be a freshman-sophomore contest, there was no pretense of honoring any rules and juniors and seniors piled on. Outnumbered by two to one, the freshmen lost of course. Thereafter, we were herded and hounded around and through various abusive and humiliating harassing activities. They steered us down the storm drainage ditch from Jackling Field to the east of the campus where there was a large catch basin filled with water and whatever. They doused us in the wet stuff and as we emerged two stationed upper classmen forced each dousee to take a chew of twist tobacco. Were those bastards surprised when I grabbed a twist from their hands, took a big chew, and stood there momentarily chewing it like an old cow chewing her cud. I said, "That's damn good stuff," and before they could recover their composure, I took off like a bat out of Hades.

I had learned to chew tobacco when seven years old (though Dad did not know until after I left home) and had acquired immunity to green-faced sickness at an early age. However, twist tobacco such as "Old Kentucky," which they gave us, is very potent stuff, and I spit the chew out after gaining distance from the tormentors. Some guys would get sick from the chew almost immediately—turning white, and then green followed by puking.

All freshmen were supposed to get very short butch hair-cuts and wear a little green stub-billed beanie cap along with green suspenders. I got a cap and suspenders and wore them, but did not get a butch cut. Finally, they caught me and two held me while another with a pair of hand clippers sheared a band down the middle of my head to near the skin, and front to back. I didn't know the shearer but I studied his face intently, so I could remember him, for I fully intended to beat the crap out of him at the first propitious moment, but if I saw him again I did not recognize his mug. Still, I did not get a butch cut—just combed the hair across the gap as best I could until the hair grew out. No one bothered me again. The battered beany cap is still in my possession. I really don't know why I've kept this icon of an era that was anathema to me.

At mid-term I was academically stressed, but by the end of the semester I had recovered to end up without any I's or F's and had earned one S.

The MSM letter grading system was based as follows: E for excellent, and rating three grade points per hour of course credit; S for superior, and rating two grade points per hour of course credit; M for median, and rating one grade point per hour of course credit; I for inferior with no grade point credits, and F for failure. If I remember correctly, a student could not graduate unless his or her overall grade point average was 0.80 or more.

I did not have enough money to pay tuition and fees for the second semester, so I asked Uncle Robey Malone for a loan of $100.00. He forthrightly responded, "What do you want it for?" and I told him. He replied without hesitation that he would wire the funds to the Rolla State Bank, and the money would be there when I needed it, and it was. He asked no more questions and made no conditions for the loan—not even a cursory comment such as, "Pay me back when you can." Fifty years later I was chatting with him one day and I asked, "Do you remember loaning $100 to me so I could go to school at MSM?" He grinned just a little and replied,

"Sure you paid it back?" That was a sample of his dry wit and humor, I think.

A standard school year at MSM consisted of two semesters of 18 weeks each. 160 hours of course work including twelve hours of Reserve Officers Training Corp (ROTC) Credits was required to obtain a Bachelor of Science degree in engineering.

MSM was chartered under auspices of the Federal Land Grant Act, which specifies that a participating college must provide ROTC training for every able bodied student during the first two years of undergraduate work. Today, ROTC training is not required, but is optional for those students who choose to participate in a four-year program that culminates with the awarding of a reserve commission in the U. S. Air Force. In my day and for several years after, a four-year ROTC training was also optional, but all graduates were commissioned as Second Lieutenants in the Army Engineers Corp.

So, to graduate in four years of normal matriculation, one must carry an average of 20 course hours per semester, and very few students could coast through that kind of regimen. Things are not the same today. Many changes, some good, some bad, and at this point I'm referring to academics. Otherwise, I'll not comment—I would not want to expand this chapter to book length.

With funds from Uncle Robey's loan I enrolled for the second semester, but did not select a major course of study. I liked freshman chemistry though my grade for the first semester was not exemplary. K. Kerschner held forth as chief lecturer for frosh chemistry and graded on a curve. On one test I received a grade of 66 per cent, which was superior by his curve. On the front of my exam paper he had drawn two large sixes with little faces sketched inside the prominent rounded sections of the sixes. He was tough, impartial and fair with a dry humor that often shown forth during lectures and grading.

I joined the MSM rifle club for a while and enjoyed shooting the excellent .22 caliber target rifles. I learned a lot about shooting and was doing well, but dropped out after deciding that I wouldn't be able to participate in all the shooting events necessary to be an effective component of the team. I liked to get home on the weekends too much to invest a bunch of time in extracurricular activities. Moreover, I didn't have funds for such. No one asked me to join a fraternity, but I had no interest in them anyway.

My grades improved during the spring semester, and I was looking forward to continuing at MSM for the next fall semester.

It was May 1942, and since the Pearl Harbor debacle the U.S. industrial war effort had shifted into high gear. A lot of industrial operations were concentrated in the Wood River, Illinois area, and I had relatives there, so I headed that way to look for a summer job. I applied at the International Shoe Company tannery in Hartford, and was called to work the next day.

Tannery management did not attempt to train me for any particular job, because they knew that I would likely return to school in the fall. There was lots of room on the extra board for me, where workers were assigned to any section that needed assistance. Consequently, in a period of three and a half months I worked in just about every department at one time or another.

The tanning process involves a lot of chemistry and was interesting from many viewpoints. I learned a lot about people, machinery and manufacturing.

There was a step in the finishing process for some leather where the hides went through a station named the "tack house." The operation was composed of three stations where hides were fastened with special steel clips to a heavy steel mesh framing, so the hides would be stretched for a short length of time, while air was blown through and across the frames. A frame of tacked hides was completed every hour, and women did all the tacking or attachment of clips to the hides. Apparently, women were more adept at this activity. During the installation and removal of the hides a lot of clips fell through the retaining mesh to a floor below.

For about a week I was assigned to collect the fallen clips, and I had to do this while the women were tacking, because the adjoining stations were under air draft and heating. As a young, innocent and redheaded male, the women sitting above me subjected me to continuous ribbing and harassment. I learned words and acquired information of which I was not previously aware. It was somewhat of a precursor to what I would later learn about contemporary language in military basic training.

One week I helped unload railroad hopper cars filled with raw materials and coal used for firing the steam generators. I worked with some guys who didn't know much more than I about the job, and it was a wonder we didn't inadvertently unload something into the wrong storage bin. We didn't have a switch engine, and moved the cars with hand-operated lever jacks. It was real labor.

This factory job was my first experience with punching a time clock and contending with union representatives and recruiters. The union rep had a ready spiel for each encounter, but I stood my ground and refused to join. The rep knew I would be going back to school, but he didn't give a hoot— the union was after every cent they could extort in dues, and the statistics of higher membership enrollment.

Starting wages for laborers was 42 cents per hour, and increased to 45 cents after two weeks probation. Many of the machine operators and other specialty jobs paid much better, and wages for some jobs were based on piecework rates.

Night shift personnel commanded a five-cent premium per hour of work. My cousin, Herman Malone, and I boarded with our Aunt Lizzie Rigsbey while working at the tannery. We decided to go on the night shift in order to increase our earnings. Uncle Robert Rigsbey also worked at the tannery, but on the day shift. Aunt Lizzie wasn't too happy about our going and coming at different hours, but she understood our needs, and arranged things so Herman and I could fix our lunches to take to work.

Cousins Bobby and Evelyn Rigsbey, children of Robert and Lizzie, were younger than I, and both had bicycles. I learned to ride a bicycle using their rigs—had never been on one before.

Also, I rode electric rail cars for the first time. A trolley line ran from St. Louis to Alton, Illinois, with frequent stops in between. For a one-way fare of ten cents, we could ride anywhere the trolley went.

Gasoline and tires were rationed during World War II, so those people with cars and trucks and ration cards were courted and favored by those without auto transportation. Uncle Elmer Malone also had come to Hartford to work, and boarded with Aunt Lizzie, adding up to a full house. When possible he liked to get home to Missouri to see his family on the weekends. One weekend he arranged a ride to Missouri with a friend who had a car, and I went with him. However, we had to find another source of transportation to return to Illinois. A neighbor of Uncle Elmer owned a 1934 Chevy and Elmer convinced him to drive to Illinois to visit relatives and to take us along to Hartford. We headed out on Sunday evening and had to fix a flat tire in St. James. By the time we hit St. Louis it was past midnight, and then the brakes went out. Uncle Elmer was familiar with St. Louis streets, and took the wheel to navigate us through St. Louis without the benefit of brakes. It was fortuitous that at the late hour traffic was very light, and we made our way through the traffic lights and across the Mississippi River bridge without incident. Then we could breathe easier for the remainder of the journey to Hartford. With that experience under my belt I decided I would not try such a trip again unless more reliable transportation was arranged.

Uncle Robert had saved enough gasoline ration coupons to fuel a trip to Missouri, so one weekend they headed that way to visit relatives, and I rode with them. He owned a reliable 1936 four door Chevy with decent tires, and we didn't have any vehicle problems. However, Uncle Robert found a good buy in potatoes at Dad's store, and decided to haul a 100-pound bag back to Hartford. He placed the bag on a board mounted across the front bumper supports.

Everything was hunky dory until somewhere near St. Clair on old Route 66, we heard an unusual noise as we were going up a long gentle grade, and looking back, we saw potatoes rolling down the highway for 200 yards. Bob stopped to take stock, and found only three or four potatoes left in the sack. With all the motion and vibration of the car, a rough spot on the bumper had worn a hole in the burlap bag, and the hole enlarged quickly to disgorge the contents. Though it was wartime there was still plenty of traffic on 66, and some vehicles slowed as they approached the avalanche of spuds, other drivers continued to barrel along and whiz by us. Uncle Bob watched the traffic for a short while, then chuckled philosophically and announced, "Reckon that takes care of our spuds," and climbed back in the car and drove on to Hartford.

My earnings for the summer of 1942, including as many extra work days and overtime as I could get, was more than enough to pay my $100 debt to Uncle Robey and finance my matriculation for the fall semester at MSM.

Fall classes started off well, and I was becoming more acclimated to the pace of MSM. Even got an S grade for differential calculus. Hazing was still in vogue, but not as intensive as the previous year. As a lofty sophomore, I refused to participate in this archaic, childish and sometimes fiendish ritual.

Dutifully, I had registered with the local Rolla (Phelps County) draft board. Anticipating they would soon point a finger at me, I began investigating alternatives more acceptable to my ideas for joining the fray. I was interested in the Navy V-12 program, which would have allowed me to complete my engineering education while preparing for flight training, but at that time, anyone under the age of nineteen required signature approvals of both parents. Dad would not sign my application—he didn't sanction the flying bit.

In October 1942, a recruiting team from the Army Air Forces hit MSM, and I went to talk to them. They informed me that one parental signature would be sufficient. After my pleading, cajoling and begging, Mom signed; but I knew she would worry whether she had done the right thing, so I impressed on her that I did not intend to let the draft board use me to fill their quotas, and I would join something military, come hell or high water—that seemed to ease her conscience somewhat.

The major in charge of the recruiting crew told me I would have to get a release from my draft board, so off I go to their office on Pine Street. The bossy, arrogant woman in charge informed me very curtly and in no uncertain terms that I couldn't have a release, so back to the major I trot to report results of my safari.

The major frowned, pulled out a sheet of official paper and started writing. It was a big desk and I was never good at reading upside down script, so I don't know what he conveyed to the draft board woman. He put the missile in an envelope, sealed it, handed it to me and said, "Give this to her and be assured she will give you a damn release."

Almost running, I rushed back downtown to the draft board office, handed the letter to the obstreperous female tyrant and smirking, announced, "Greetings from the major." She opened the envelope, read the note, visibly paled a bit, and then without comment wrote out my release and handed it to me. I winked at her, but did not say thanks. It was a glorious moment—I still wonder what the major wrote. Anyway, after a lot of fol-de-rol, I had become a member of the Army Air Force Reserves.

I knew that it was only a matter of time until call-up for active duty, and I was well into the second semester at MSM when the official notification arrived in mid February 1943. Under the tutelage of Professor Erkelitian, integral calculus was a problem for me, so I was almost relieved to get the orders and be on my way to fight for Uncle Sam.

Uncle Sam didn't mess around, and only about a week was allowed for me to get my affairs in order and report for induction. I immediately hit the business office of MSM and got a partial refund for tuition and fees, which was enough to launch me into a most broadening experience, to say the least.

From the time I was six years old, I thought I wanted to be a flyer. Johnny Ketchum, a farmer who lived a half mile south of Seaton, always liked me, but he also enjoyed teasing me. One day, Johnny had stirred me up, and sassily I informed him, "When I grow up, I'm going to be a pilot, and I'll fly over your place and s--- on you." Johnny and family never forgot about that pontifical and scatological proclamation from their six-year-old neighbor.

In Chapter 14 I wrote about my boss and I chartering a flight to Arkansas from Des Moines, Iowa in 1955. On our way back from Arkansas to Iowa, our flight course placed us close to Seaton. I showed the pilot the Seaton location on his map and mentioned that my parents lived there. Knowing I was a former Air Force navigator, he told me to do the ground pilotage navigation and he would fly over Seaton. I directed him so there was time to reduce altitude for a near tree top fly by, and Seaton was buzzed twice. I could see Dad at the gas pumps waving, and he told me later that he knew I was in that aircraft.

While turning to make his second pass, the pilot flew low right over Johnny Ketchum's house, and Dad said the Ketchums asked him if I was in that plane, and they wondered if I intended to fulfill my threat of thirty years before.

Author in "beanie" and green suspenders
as a freshman at MSM

Resident			Rolla Address 707 E. 7th St. Phone 900-W	

Resident		
Non-Resident		
Reciprocal Tuition		
Registration, Hospital & Library	36	00
Laboratory	10	00
Contingent Deposit	15	00
General Lectures	1	00
Student Activity	5	00
Missouri Miner		75
Rollamo	3	50
Repeat		

Rolla Address 707 E. 7th St. Phone 900-W

High School St. James   Date of Graduation 1941

Home Address Seaton, Missouri

MISSOURI SCHOOL OF MINES & METALLURGY
Fee and Tuition Bill

FALL SEMESTER
1942-1943   Date 9/7/42

Cashier's Notation:

Received: _____ Dollars

the sum indicated in payment on fees and tuitions shown on margin.

Money Order $_____ Check $_____ Cash $ 75

Remarks:

PAID
MISSOURI SCHOOL
OF MINES & METALLURGY

Bill for tuition and fees at MSM in 1942

Off We Go

...All Present and Accounted For...

My induction orders were a foretaste of the inscrutable manner in which the U.S. Army often operates. I was instructed to report to Omaha, Nebraska, along with a long list of other reservists called to arms. I noted that I was the only person from Missouri on this list of 150 names. Most of the other reservists were from the Dakotas, Nebraska, Iowa and Minnesota. And that was the way it would be throughout my military service—I never served with a Missourian at any station.

After a long and circuitous train ride from Rolla, I checked in at the recruiting center at Omaha late in the afternoon on February 24, 1943. A clerk looked at my orders, registered my name and assigned me a bunk in the National Guard Armory for the night. Other reservists were arriving and by morning most of the contingent had reported. After we had wolfed down a skimpy buffet breakfast, the whole kit-and-caboodle was marshaled, and then hustled to the railroad station to be transported to Jefferson Barracks, Missouri for official induction into the Army Air Forces.

What a fiasco from my viewpoint. I was backtracking. It was a quick and dirty lesson that the Army's convenience is first and foremost--much simpler for them to attach my name to a general order than cut separate papers to send me directly to the Barracks at south St. Louis.

A disheveled gang disembarked at the Barracks. My older brother had been inducted into the Army Air Forces about nine months before, and was based at the barracks with the administrative unit. He had seen the orders for my assignment and knew I was headed for the Barracks. Apparently, he had informed some buddies that his brother would be arriving, and a gawking contingent of onlookers was there to check out another Seatonite. I thought they appeared both surprised and bemused as we sorry looking souls were herded into the reception hall. By that time, after a long train ride in coach cars of not the best quality, I was dirty, tired, hungry, bewildered and did not whimper—just glad an electric cattle prod wasn't used on us.

We arrived in early evening, and after roll call, quarters were assigned and bedding issued. We were lucky not to be billeted in pyramidal tents. Instead, we were assigned to pyramidal huts! Each hut contained five double bunk beds and all were filled.

Next morning we were introduced to a G.I. mess hall. After breakfast, we were shuffled around the horn to receive G.I. uniforms and orientation. Following a hectic day, we wearily trudged to our castle huts. Luckily, I received clothing that fit fairly decently, even the shoes. The weather was chilly, and we dropped the long horizontal shutters, which covered windows that were filled only with screens— no glass panes or insulation. Just as we sat down on our bunks to rest, in comes a tempestuous corporal yelling, "Get those f------ shutters up, you need some air in here." Dutifully, we obeyed, but down the shutters went again as soon as the corporal was out of sight. Any potential punishment for disobedience could not be more discomfiting than shivering in the cold that seemed to be intensified by the cold drafts from the nearby Mississippi River.

Sidewalls of the huts were simply constructed of planks abutted horizontally against each other, edge-to-edge and nailed to vertical studs. Cracks were in evidence where there were irregularities in boards, and the wind whistled through. Knotholes and cracks were usually stuffed with paper—no insulation or inside surfacing of the walls or ceilings. The hut was floored with wooden planks.

A round sheet metal stove with a conical top piece was positioned in the center of each hut, and its exhaust pipe went straight up and out the pyramidal roof at the apex. The hut was quite crowded with ten guys, a stove in the middle plus gear stashed around the walls and bunks. We had coal for fuel, and with some paper and kindling we got a good fire going for the evening. Next morning the stove was full of red hot coals when a soldier came by knocking on doors with a club to awaken everyone. When he hit our door, one of the guys jumped out of bed, and not being used to the place, knocked the stove over, and hot coals flew all over the floor and out the door. The "knocker" saw the coals (black as pitch outside at 5 p.m.) and heard the ruckus. He stuck his head in the door and ejaculated, "My God, did I do that?"

...Reveille and Mud...

Reveille harkened at 5:15 a.m., and we had only about ten minutes after the door banging to dress and fall out for roll call. We lined up bleary eyed in front of our huts, and the sergeant in charge that day would inspect the troops, while a helper with the ubiquitous clipboard called the roll. I'll never forget the raunchy little garrulous buck sergeant ranting and spouting from both sides of his mouth, then shouting, "Don't stand there like a stale, cold bottle of piss." My vocabulary was expanding beyond my expectations. Apparently, vulgarity was part and parcel of the program for indoctrination by the shock troops.

Chow was mediocre three times a day. I never knew there was so much sour and bitter grapefruit juice in the world. I became acquainted with s--- on a shingle, which to the uninitiated means creamed chipped beef on toast. The quartermaster must have bought up the world stocks of prunes. And the coffee was like a verse of the Quartermaster marching song, "The coffee that they gave us was very fine, good for cuts and bruises and tastes like iodine."

Latrine was added to my repertoire of words, and I was fascinated with the sight of so many urinals and toilet bowls lined up in rows in one building. It was strictly communal, and what an atmosphere on a day when half the camp was suffering diarrhea. I longed to be home in the brush.

In a few days we had been shot (vaccinated) several times, physically and dentally examined, dosed with army indoctrination in rules, codes, regulations and bureaucracy. We were treated to a movie, which graphically illustrated the perils of the social venereal diseases, gonorrhea and syphilis.

I was so naïve and docile as a puppy. During the physical exam, my examining doctor handed some papers to me, and told me to give them to the sergeant, which I did as ordered. The sergeant looked at the papers, oh so seriously, signed them, and then in a studious and low confidential-like voice said, "Tell the doctor to send me the cannon report." I dutifully hustled back to the doctor and repeated the sergeant's request. As I spoke, I realized how duped I was, but too late. The doctor looked at me with disgust, and didn't say a word, but with a resigned attitude of "Oh Lord, how many more times and I could strangle that sergeant."

One of those dreaded Missouri late-winter-early-spring wet snowstorms dropped six inches of the heavy white stuff one night, and come morning they had us out in the mess going through formation drilling. Soaking wet feet were the order of the day until after noontime chow, and then, amazingly, enough of the buckle type high top overshoes were found to shoe most of us sad sacks, though sizing was more or less hypothetical with the assumption that if your G.I. shod feet could be inserted into the overshoes, it was a suitable fit. Next day the snow was melting; the terra firma turned to mush and we kept slogging, though I almost lost my oversized overshoes to the tenacious, sticky clay mud of the drill field.

The weather improved, but spring was reticent about making an appearance. I survived five weeks of the Barracks hassle, and then rumors got foundation legs as announcements came from our sergeants that orders of transfer were being posted.

I was in a group of about 100 that was being shipped out to Superior, Wisconsin. The Army Air Forces had developed a program named College Training Detachment (CTD), which was designed for training flight cadet candidates who did not have a college education. I was one of the few with some college credits. My brother, Wib, had seen our orders, and came down to see me off to the troop train, which accessed directly into the campgrounds. One thing I knew for sure, it was good to be leaving Jefferson Barracks.

…Polishing the Fledglings…

Our destination in Superior was the Superior State Teacher's College and we arrived on the 30th of March. Snow was still piled up along the streets and sidewalks. We were lucky and didn't get any major amount of snow after our arrival.

We were housed in a large student dormitory, and quarters were sumptuous in comparison to our dwellings at Jefferson Barracks, yet we still slept in the old standard army double bunk beds.

Food was fair-to-middlin', and we ate from china type plates in a more conventional dining room, which was a welcome diversion from the clanging and often wet metal trays used in regular army camps. We ate family style and scraped residues from plates and utensils into garbage cans. The cooks were ladies, and brought dishes of food to the tables.

A captain was in command of our group, and his staff consisted of two first lieutenants, one shave tail, a staff sergeant, a buck sergeant and a couple of corporals. They handled all administrative, management and military training, while the staff of the college conducted academic studies.

At first our command staff performed as if we were already cadets, and were quite rigorous with all the old gung ho, spit and polish. But finally they realized we were hardly removed from basic training, and began to relax and mellow somewhat.

The college initiated their programs by giving aptitude and I.Q. tests. Most of the course work was so rudimentary that I was eminently bored. The Dean called me to his office to discuss my test scores and visit with me. He did not, of course, have any records of my MSM background, but he had reviewed my scores for their tests. After we talked he understood why I had done so well on their tests. He told me that I didn't belong there, but he could not do anything about that. The course work was so elementary that I could have reversed roles with the instructors.

One redeeming feature of the CTD program was our exposure to ten hours of flight instruction in Piper Cubs at a local airport. I was sometimes tense at the controls, but thought I did well with takeoffs and landings. We were not allowed to solo, but at the completion of the ten hours of flying the owner and chief test pilot of the civilian flying school subjected us to a check flight. He was a crusty son-of-a-gun and didn't like to repeat any comments or instructions. During all of my physicals in the Army Air Forces, I never had any notations of flaws in my hearing, but I always had problems with hearing some voices when loud background noises were present. This was the case the day of my check flight.

As I was on my takeoff run, I had just lifted the tail preparatory to the final acceleration to takeoff, when he yelled at me, and I thought he said, "Cut her back." As I started to reduce the throttle, His hand shot out like a snake striking and rammed the throttle back to full bore, and we proceeded to take off. He was livid, and yelled some more after we had cleared the runway. After that harangue he didn't say anything further other than to direct me to do certain maneuvers. They didn't give us their recorded evaluations of our flying, but I suspected his writings and verdict was influential in my ultimate classification as a navigator trainee.

Today, I still have problems with some sound wave lengths and frequencies when background noises are present. My darling wife heckled me to go to a hearing specialist and I refused. I notice a lot of people who are discretionary about how well they hear, and more often than not, it's not the hearing, but the listening that may be faulted. To further buttress my resistance to being suckered for $2000 of ultra sound amplifiers, I considered my hearing quite adequate when I could detect a turkey gobble a mile away on a good day that is absent the roar of jets overhead and booming trucks hitting the hills on highway 72. Nonetheless, my wife prevailed and today I wear hearing aids and though helpful during normal conversations they are almost worthless when heavy background noises are present.

While at Superior, some bigwigs from Washington, D.C. arrived to celebrate the umpteenth christening of a liberty ship at the Duluth, Minnesota shipyards, which were just across the bay from Superior. Our contingent marched to the yards and did a lot of standing around in formation while the ceremonies proceeded—not very exciting to say the least.

During my tenure at Superior I was down with the flu for a week. Only two other guys in our group were infected, and the source of infection remained a mystery, though I speculated that there was contact with a carrier through food handling. We were not allowed out on the town while there, though we did have one party when young ladies of the college and city were invited to attend. I was miserably sick from the flu, and got one of the officers up during the night to check me. He gave me some sulfa pills, and the next morning my condition had improved. He stopped to see me and remarked, "You thought you were going to die last night, didn't you?" and I responded, "You're doggone tootin', and I might have if I hadn't gotten you over here with some medicine."

My fling with the CTD program lasted only six weeks, and in mid-May we embarked on a troop train headed for the Army Air Force cadet classification center in Santa Ana, California. Nobody grieved at taking leave of Superior. Most were anxious to get on with more meaningful training.

Superior, Wisconsin to Santa Ana, California was the longest train ride in my life. Some of the passenger railcars were so old that they exhibited signs of warning, "Don't shoot buffalo from the train," and though we had electrical lighting, vestiges of the original gas lighting system remained along with the deteriorated furnishings.

We traveled day and night, and if I remember correctly, we were on the tracks for four nights. We were fortunate to have old Pullman cars with porters, so sleeping was not too much of a problem once I was accustomed to the clackity clack of the trucks on the tracks. Before World War II I had been in only one state besides Missouri, and already within a period of less than three months, I had been in nine more states. We were exposed to a lot of scenery, and occasionally during stops we were allowed to get off the train for a few minutes. Chow was tolerable and varied as dining cars were switched in and out—mostly short order, sandwiches and snack type fare.

When the scenery became boring there were card games. It was my first experience playing poker, but fortunately, I had the presence of mind to gain learning in the lower-stakes or penny ante games. Actually, there was not a lot of money on the whole train, at least not on the troops.

The train made a stop at Barstow, California in the deserts northeast of Los Angeles, and the ambient temperature was 115 degrees Fahrenheit. We were allowed to get off the train, to test us I think, but we climbed right back on to get out of the blistering sun, even though the temperatures in the cars were also near 115 degrees. Passing through the hot belts was the most uncomfortable portions of the trip—all windows had to be opened for ventilation, and as a result, we endured soot, cinders, dust and insects.

Approximately 100 miles after leaving Barstow, we reached our destination, the Santa Ana AAF Base, and the climate change was heartily embraced.

We had arrived at the Army Air Forces' Cadet Classification Center, where we would be run through a battery of intensive and extensive physical and mental tests. This establishment must have been the birthplace and progenitor for the psychobabble mentality that has invaded and proliferated within the halls of many contemporary universities—an incipient attempt to analyze the vagaries of our minds with testing and verbal examinations. The roles of tester and tested should be reversed in many cases.

The eye, ears and reflexive tests were comprehensive, thorough and well done. I have always had some minor problems with depth perception, and their tests were corroborative. This fact coupled with my frazzle with the Piper Cub check ride may have strongly influenced my classification as a navigational training cadet.

My session with a psychologist was a bit interesting, but almost worthless from my standpoint. I had gone into the session psyched up from stories related by compatriots who had already experienced the tête-à-tête with the head knocker, and the pow wow was a letdown. At one point I was asked if I thought our country had anything to fear from Stalin and the communists during the war, and I gave him the answer he wanted, "No", but I was lying through my teeth. He smiled big, and shortly ended the session. Later, I wondered if he was a pinky sympathizer or rather not very well informed—perhaps believing our U.S. Administration "brain washing." Roosevelt and a liberal media had bamboozled a lot of people with the "good old Joe" crap.

Our stay at Santa Ana lasted only three weeks, but during that short time, in addition to all the tests and examinations, marching drills and calisthenics were frequent.

A group of P-38 fighter pilots were in training at the Santa Ana airfield, and they frequently maneuvered right over our parade field. It was a thrill to watch a '38 dive, and then pull out and climb straight up.

After classification as cadets and assigned for navigation training, the whole dang gang of potential navigators was scheduled for preflight training at Ellington Field, just outside of Houston, Texas. We wondered why not preflight in California, but we were destined for another long train ride.

...Preflight and Hurricanes...

We rolled into Ellington Field, near Houston, Texas and for the first time I would be billeted in one of the large two-storied type of barracks. However, we still slept in the standard army bunk beds and conventional army mattresses and bedding. I was glad to draw a bunk on the ground floor of the barracks, and to sleep in the lower deck—my bunk-mate preferred the upper level.

Our clothing had remained as standard G.I. issue from time of induction at Jefferson Barracks, but billed type dress caps were issued to cadets for wear on special occasions, and we wore cadet wings insignia on caps, shirts and blouses.

We arrived at Ellington in early June, and that spelled hot weather in Texas. Moreover, humidity in Houston and the Gulf Coast area is horrendous during the summer resulting in very uncomfortable heat indexes.

We wore a summer uniform of cotton khaki, but were required to wear ties in classes and during special marching formations. We were subjected to frequent massive parade formations on a large drill field, and on the hotter days some cadets would collapse because of heat stress, to be carried off the field by standby ambulances and medics. That is when I learned that by slightly flexing my knees occasionally (just enough so the drillmaster would not notice) that the stress of standing in one spot for a long time could be reduced.

With all the sweating and dust, it was a challenge to maintain a presentable uniform, and we stood at inspection at least once each day, except on Sunday. Most of us bought extra summer khakis with our own money, so we could have clean uniforms between laundry trips—and we paid for our laundering too.

Cadet lieutenants, appointed for each barracks, were responsible for organizing us into formations to march to our classes and to field drills, parades and calisthenics. We were encouraged to sing marching songs, and I learned some ditties that would have been frowned upon in polite society.

One evening after chow there was a lot of daylight left, and a group of us were out throwing and kicking a football around in the area at the back of our barracks. A good buddy was out playing in nothing but his shorts. We were supposed to wear at least a tee shirt in addition to shorts while exercising outside. My buddy was endowed with black hair in profusion on his body, and probably resembled a gorilla from a distance, as he dashed back and forth in his boxer under shorts and barefoot.

I heard a vehicle's brakes squeal, and looking to the street in front of our barracks, saw a convertible come to a screeching halt. Inside sat a blonde and an officer. The officer jumped out of the auto, and headed our way. Old Buck, my friend (a native born Texan), sized up the situation pronto, and tore off for our barracks at full throttle, went in the back door and kept going to the front and out. Then, he crossed to another barracks and entered. The officer saw Buck enter our barracks and went in after him, but didn't know he had exited, and did not locate him. The officer came out irate and threatening, but then shut up and strode back to his car and woman who appeared immensely amused. He was Captain Yates, previously a Hollywood actor, but we didn't recognize the gal though we saw her with him again. We figured that his show of authority and indignation at Buck's exposure was nothing more than a typical case of Hollywood false modesty and hypocrisy.

The academically oriented classes were rather elementary from my standpoint. Classes that I liked most were hands-on and skills acquisition types, such as Morse code and aircraft identification. We also studied ships and watercraft identification. After studying pictures and characteristics of the various ships and aircraft, including enemy vessels and equipment, we were tested for our identification abilities by watching flashes of their pictures on a movie screen. It was fun and I did well with those exercises.

I enjoyed learning Morse code, and though I excelled in its receiving and transmission, today I probably could not transmit S.O.S. Our code classes were organized so that when students were able to pass standard sending and receiving tests, they were allowed to skip the remaining sessions. Three of us out of a class of 40 finished two weeks ahead of schedule. I can't remember anything commendable or extraordinary I might have accomplished during the spare time unless it was writing to my mother.

During the first five weeks at Ellington I was served the best food ever in my entire time in military service. The mess hall was conventionally designed with picnic type combination benches-tables, and the service was cafeteria style. We ate from G.I. metal trays, and discarded residues to a garbage can after eating. However, the fare was abundant, well prepared, tasty and attractive. For breakfast we had the choice of three or four juices, three or four fresh fruits, eggs to taste, ham, bacon, sausage, toast, French toast and pancakes. For lunch there were three meat entrees, choice of several vegetables and usually three different desserts. Fresh milk was always available. Supper was similar to lunch, but on a larger scale and diversity—almost like being on a cruise ship today I would think.

Table fare was certainly terrific, but alas, the cornucopia of goodies would come to a screeching halt after a hurricane ripped up the base.

Storm warnings were flying in the Gulf and off the coast at Galveston, just forty miles south of us. A hurricane was predicted to come inland, but no one was sure as to how strong it would be or where it would make landfall. Winds began to pick up at our base in the early afternoon, and by dusk shingles and other camp debris was flying in the air and rain was drenching us.

About 8:00 p.m. a command went out for all cadets to get out of the barracks and go to the flight lines to help hold down AT-6 flight training aircraft. Ellington Field was not only a preflight training center, but was a base for advanced flight training in the single engine AT-6. Those planes were tied down with cables, and we were instructed to hang on to the cables to relieve some of the snapping surges caused by powerful wind gusts. It was a dangerous and fruitless activity, and the officer who ordered us out to attempt this strategy should have been court martialed. Several planes broke loose and a bunch of cadets were injured. One sustained a broken back.

The base commander, a colonel, was reprimanded, and later purportedly transferred because he hadn't flown the planes out before the hurricane hit.

The morning after, the base was a mess. Litter and debris everywhere, windows shattered, roofs torn away and general havoc. Classes were postponed for a couple of days until some semblance of order could be restored. Much equipment and facilities were damaged and out of commission. Several days were required to restore electrical power to all operations, and there was concern about contamination of water supplies. Mess halls were operated like field stations for about ten days. We had to wash, rinse and disinfect our mess kits, and the food was worse than most field rations—the cooks and mess people just were not experienced in coping with such conditions. Four weeks later when I left Ellington, the grub was not even close to being back to normal. In fact, the food was lousy, like the difference between daylight and dark and we had difficulty coping.

Houston was a benevolent city for servicemen, but passes to go there were few and far between for us. The commandants could always trump up a reason for restricting us to the base. Inspections of barracks and uniforms were frequently picayunish, and unfairly gauged to provide disciplinary excuses to withhold passes. Likely they believed that fewer cadets in Houston meant fewer problems in general with control and disciplining of the troops. Peripatetic officers were notable for making surprise visits to barracks during off hours, and they didn't have to look far to find some minor violation of rules to gig us enough for restriction to the base. A few autocrats even pulled the old notorious "white glove" caper where a swipe of the white-gloved hand could indubitably display some minor evidence of dust or soiling.

After nine weeks of preflight with a hurricane to boot, we were anxious to get into navigation school, but it was not yet to be. We were scheduled next for aerial gunnery school in Harlingen, Texas.

For the historical record, my preflight class was Class 43-19N, which meant that my class was the 19th contingent of navigation cadets to matriculate at Ellington in 1943. A new group of cadets would arrive about every ten days to begin preflight classes. My group was 19N, and I was assigned to Flight two of four flights in Squadron E.

18/   Into the Wild Blue Yonder

...Aerial Gunnery—Is It loaded?...

We arrived by train in Harlingen, Texas, during mid August, and found the climate just as warm and humid as in Houston. Harlingen lies northwest of Brownsville about 25 miles, and Brownsville is located at the very southern tip of Texas, and across the Rio Grande River from the border town of Matamoras, Mexico.

We were thrust into training quite promptly, and I must say that I enjoyed most of the gunnery school training per se. We were schooled in ballistics and the armory we would be exposed to in the Army Air Forces. We were taken step-by-step, from air guns up and through the .50 caliber machine guns. And we fired everything under variable conditions.

There was a huge arena where many types of aircraft gunnery turrets were mounted on stands to simulate firing positions on airplanes, and air guns shooting BB pellets were installed in them. First we fired from the turrets toward stationary targets, and then proceeded to moving targets.

We shot from nose, top, tail and ball turrets. The ball turret was an exceptional challenge to everyone, and few could manipulate it effectively and I was no exception.

We progressed from air guns to shotguns, beginning with trap and skeet shooting. I had never seen trap or skeet setups before, but scored decently because of my experience with handling shotguns while bird hunting. I liked skeet best, but consistently had scoring problems with the number eight position. I didn't score as well with trap.

Then there was a track layout where low and high boxes were laid out on both sides of a road. Four shooters were placed in the back of an open racked army 6x6 truck with an instructor-monitor. The trucks were driven at a moderate speed along the roads while one shooter on each side of the truck bed fired at the offerings from the clay pigeon throwers. Then, the truck would repeat the round, allowing the remaining two shooters to get their practice. It was exciting shooting, but scores were low. The jostling of the platform as the truck traveled over bumps and irregularities of the road compounded the difficulty of hitting a moving target from a moving platform.

All shotguns were twelve gauge, and most were semi-auto actions, though some pump action guns were used. Considering all the wear and tear caused by amateurs and neophytes, the guns functioned well and with a minimum of maintenance problems. Most instructors were competent and safety was emphasized.

After trap and skeet, we returned to the turrets, but this time shotguns were mounted in the machine gun positions. These turrets were mobile, being mounted on flat bed trucks, so they could be moved from station to station or driven on the track layout of clay pigeon throwing stations. Operating power was supplied to turrets from either electrical generators or hydraulic pumps, depending on the design of the turrets, which in turn were driven by transmission of power from engines on the truck. Top, nose, tail and ball turrets were designed to accommodate the various bombers, and both electrical and hydraulically powered turrets were installed on some bombers such as the B-24 Liberator. Its top turret was electric while the nose, ball and tail units were hydraulic in the later models.

At fixed turret ground stations, targets were presented at various speeds of travel on elevated tracks or from suspended cables that could be manipulated by ground operators to rapidly change positions. Coordination of eyes, hands and timing was the name of the game, and a real challenge to maneuver the turrets to make hits with the shotguns. Tough shooting and more misses than hits—doubly compounded when firing from units on moving trucks.

The gunnery student's first contact with machine guns took place in the shops, where they were studied piece by piece through takedown and reassembly. Repetitively, forward and back we worked until we could completely disassemble and reassemble the .50 caliber gun while blindfolded. Then and only then were we readied to shoot these guns from pedestal mounts on a range equipped with both fixed and moving targets.

First we fired the .30 caliber machine guns, and then advanced to the .50 caliber. The fifty was massive in size compared to the thirty. Of course, ballistics were much different and the contrasting energy delivered to the target was cogent when firing. These guns were attached to pedestal stands with a swiveling connector, so the gun muzzle could be moved laterally and vertically. The .50 caliber was quite a handful and had to be grasped firmly with both hands to maintain stability when firing. An instructor was always close by, and frequently admonished shooters to fire only when they were in firm control of the weapon. If someone lost his cool, and let a firing gun get away from him when a proximity stop failed, it could swing around to bring others on the line under fire, and it happened once while I was there. Luckily no one was injured or killed.

Twenty gun mounts were stationed on line and about eight feet apart at the machine gun range. The area of firing was hard surfaced with asphalt to facilitate maintenance and cleanup of ejected brass. If I remember correctly, the targets were about 5 x 10 feet, and were mounted on a carriage that ran on a track across the range at a distance of 200 yards from the firing line.

Cartridges were fed to the guns by belts and the pointed full metal-jacketed bullets were tipped with a soft paint. By using different paint colors, several gunners could fire at the same target as it made a pass across the range. The bullets passing through the white cloth target left a residue of color, and the individual gunner's score could be counted based on his assigned ammunition color. We didn't have to clean the guns, so never saw the effects of the coloring material on the bores of the barrels. I don't recall any one mentioning or questioning about the possibilities of adverse effects. I liked to shoot the big fifty. It was exhilarating to feel and hear the heavy chatter and thumps as it was fired.

One day we were preparing to fire the fifties, and as we waited for the target to start moving and a signal to begin firing, a coyote trotted on to the range about 100 yards out. The instructor ran up to my station and excitedly yelled, "Let me have it." He jacked in the first cartridge and began automatic firing at the varmint. That old coyote switched on his afterburners and not a bullet touched him.

Our gunnery training was concluded by firing the .30 caliber machine gun from the back seat of an AT-6 advanced training plane. The gun was mounted so I had to stand almost erect to fire at the target towed by another AT-6. The tow plane kept their targets trailing at a good fifty yards behind them, and well they should, considering the manner in which some guys handled those guns. The ride was very choppy, and it was almost impossible to maintain a steady aim on a target at about 150 yards. The pilots were not happy with their assignments, and they hustled through the firing exercises without a lot of consideration for the gunner. A safety cable linked between our seat frame and parachute harness was used during firing, and I'm sure it saved more than one gunner from being ejected.

A radio aerial was strung on the AT-6 from a post in front of the pilot back to a post toward the tail. One day after an aerial firing sortie, we noted an AT-6 taxiing to the apron without a viable radio aerial. When the cadet-gunner disembarked, we got the sad story—he had shot the aerial apart with his trusty .30 caliber machine gun. The disgusted pilot walked away while the chagrined cadet told us about his ineptitude. However, disciplinary action was relatively mild, consisting of a verbal reaming and reprimand from our squadron commander.

Harlingen's mess was conventional G.I., but completely staffed and operated by WACS (Women's Auxiliary Corps), with the exception of the male mess officer. I thought I had acquired quite a bawdry vocabulary from working in a tannery and duty at Jefferson Barracks, but the WACS at

Harlingen added some polish and finesse. We cadets may have been the vanguard of the reverse sexual harassment syndrome. If there were any good cooks in the mess crew, their talents were not demonstrated. Chow was mediocre at best.

The general atmosphere at the Harlingen base was more laid back than previous stations, and the administration treated us more like army personnel than Air Force cadets. We had to do calisthenics, but drilling and marching were held to a minimum.

We were allowed considerable freedom on the weekends, and passes to visit Harlingen or other nearby areas were routinely dispensed. However, there was little to do in Harlingen. At that time the population of the city was only about 8000 and dominated by Chicano people. The Mexican girls gave us a wide birth, which was fortuitous for us, since we were not interested in stirring up any conflicts or promoting a knife blade between our ribs.

The Harlingen liquor stores didn't have any Bourbon whiskeys, but stocked plenty of scotch whiskey, and at a fair price. Why this commercial anomaly, I don't know, for in other parts of the U.S. scotch was scarce. Anyway, a buddy and I were in town for a steak, and then with little else to do, decided to buy a pint of scotch. After a small swig my buddy eschewed any more scotch. A thrifty soul, I drank the remainder of the bottle's contents on our meander back to the base since I was afraid to try to sneak any liquor past the guard at the gate. I was drunk as a hoot owl, but fortunately, upchucked later, and survived with only a headache and queasy stomach the next morning.

A special pass was required to cross the U.S.-Mexico border into Matamoras, Mexico, which lay just across the Rio Grande River from Brownsville, Texas. One Saturday I went across with other cadets, and my experience forever wiped away any desire to visit Matamoras again.

Most street surfaces were composed of dirt, and that day it rained enough to convert the dirt to mud and puddles. A couple of bars catered to soldiers and were focal points from which brothels radiated, one after the other, mostly as individual operations in one or two rooms—abutting against each other along both sides of the streets. Kids plied the muddy streets, pimping for sisters and whoever.

In addition to the plethora of bordellos, there were establishments that catered to the prurient minds and lascivious nature of many army pilgrims—putting on demonstrations of perverted sexual acts and sexual aberrations for fees.

While in Matamoras, I drank nothing but a couple of bottles of American beer, where I could observe the caps pulled off, and then I drank from the bottle. I visited an open market, which was in better physical condition than the rest of the town, but yet revealing a distressing lack of cleanliness and sanitation. I was deterred from buying anything to eat such as fruit.

I soon had more than my fill of Matamoras, and ready to depart, asked the cadets I had arrived with if they were interested in leaving, and with their demurral, I took off solo. I had concluded I wasn't about to be gallavantin' in Mexico after sundown. I crossed the bridge back into Texas, and since there was no bus scheduled for Harlingen in the next two hours, I began hitchhiking, and soon caught a ride on a farmer's flat bed truck. The farmer had already picked up three G.I.s who had been scrounging in Matamoras, and I listened to their stories. One chap left an indelible impression on my mind with his descriptions of forays into the bordellos, and his boasting that he never paid over fifty cents for an encounter involving copulation. After inquiring about some of the intimate details, I was convinced that this guy had not been impressed by the Army films about sexually transmitted diseases, which were compulsory viewing for each and every military person.

Gunnery school was most certainly an interesting interlude in my quest for flight training, but eight weeks had sated my appetite for throwing lead, and I was ready when my assignment to navigation school finally evolved.

...Before GPS...

After completing our training at Harlingen, about a week elapsed before we received orders for our new assignment. Navigation schools were located at Hondo and San Marcos, Texas, Monroe, Louisiana, and one in California. Guys would be going to locations all over the U.S. since both navigator and bombardier cadets had taken the gunnery courses. I drew Hondo, which is located about 40 miles west of San Antonio, and the majority of the navigator candidates were assigned to Hondo. It was a sad parting—we would not see some buddies again.

I entered navigation training on October 24, 1943. Our quarters were located in single story wood framed buildings, and we had individual bunks with conventional G.I. type bedding of mattress, sheets, blankets, comforter and pillows. Space was reserved in each barracks for tables and chairs that could be used for writing and reading. There was room near our bunks to hang outer clothing. Underwear and other personal items could be stored in footlockers or a nightstand by our bunk.

The mess hall was similar to previous Army facilities, except for longer tables and folding type chairs. We still ate from metal trays and food was served cafeteria style. Quality of chow was only fair, and far removed from satisfying any epicurean tastes.

The organization structure of a class at Hondo was similar to that at pre flight. A navigation class graduated every three weeks, and consisted of a group, which was divided into three or four squadrons of four flights each. The complement of each flight varied from ten to twenty cadets.

At Hondo, two flights were quartered in each barracks, and they marched in flight formations to chow and to classes. Aviation cadet (A/C) lieutenants were appointed for each flight with responsibilities for organizing and leading the flight during all marching and similar activities.

Within the first six weeks of training, we were taught the basics of the four navigation systems: Pilotage, dead reckoning, radio compass and celestial; and the use of instruments and tools of the profession. Then, we began to apply this knowledge on practice flight missions while continuing with ground school refinements and enhancements of navigation skills and knowledge.

Texas is a real big patch, and much of our flight navigation training was conducted over areas of the state. However, longer flights were required for night celestial navigation. I was on flights to Phoenix, Arizona and to Wichita, Kansas, and in each case, we flew in, stayed overnight, then flew back to base, scheduling the flying hours so there was both night and day hours to use the sextant to take stars and sun readings, respectively. Also, we satisfied over-water navigation requirements by a flight to Biloxi, Mississippi—by doglegging into the Gulf of Mexico, and then into the Biloxi airport. After an overnight stay, we returned to home base by a similar flight over water.

Most of our in-flight training was accrued in the small twin-engine AT-7 with small twin tail rudders—an excellent aircraft with two 450 horsepower radial engines, but nonetheless, it didn't take a lot of turbulent weather for the AT-7 to shake and bump enough to severely exacerbate problems with reading instruments, calculating and recording data.

The AT-7 had room for three navigation stations with observation windows, and each fixed seat was furnished with a fold-down writing platform. A fold-down seat was available for an extra passenger-observer. Instructors flew with us on all training missions, and since the AT-7 didn't require a co-pilot on most flights, the navigation instructor rode in the co-pilot seat. That position was much more comfortable than the fold-down jump seat, and better for pilotage navigation, since vision was better and of wider span than from our side windows.

On our trip to Phoenix, we flew in the C-60, an adaptation of the Lockheed Lodestar that could accommodate more navigator trainees. The population of Phoenix at that time was only about 100,000, and today it is one million or more.

Phoenix was a lovely city then. After flying in during the early evening we located a covey of gals and had a real nice party during the evening.

As I remember, Wichita was a city of 80,000 population and rather blasé though we did find a little nightlife—enough that I had a bursting headache next day trying to practice navigation in a wind buffeted AT-7 on our way back to Hondo. Today, Wichita's population is over 300,000.

We flew into El Paso one hot day, and did not find it very exciting, but were not there at night—population of El Paso then and now, respectively, 80,000 and 500,000 plus.

Flying at night we could always recognize Waco, Texas, because of its mercury arc street lighting. The distinctive glow of its lights was even discernible through light cloud cover, and offered a reliable navigation checkpoint.

...Break in the Action...

On Christmas Eve at about 9 p.m., 1943, I received a telegram telling me that my Grandmother Malone was critically ill, and to come at once. The base was half deserted because many cadets, officers and staff were on pass and off the post for two or three days for the holiday. One green officer-of-the-day was on administrative duty for our group, and I legged it over to his office to show him the telegram. Early on we had been informed that we could not get a leave except for death or certified imminence of death in our immediate family, but I thought, why not give it a shot. The bleary eyed O.D. thought a while, then drawled, "Well, I don't know what I should do, and there is no other command available, so I guess I ought to give you a leave." So, he sat down and typed out papers authorizing a ten-day emergency leave. He arranged for a ride into Hondo, and I was lucky to catch a train out that night.

The telegram had been sent by a cagey Uncle Raymond Malone, who had also sent the same telegraphed message to his son Charles, who was in the navy at Bremerton, Washington. Uncle Raymond had worked at the Fort Leonard Wood Army base in the Rolla, Missouri area, and was astute about learning the ways of people in the Army. He reckoned that by timing his telegrams, he could take advantage of an undermanned and lesser-experienced station command during the holiday lull, and his maneuver worked. I was home within two days, and Charles arrived a few hours after I. He had hitched a ride on an Army Air Force B-25 to Kansas City, and then caught a train to Rolla.

Our grandmother was very seriously ill, though death was not imminent. She lingered for several months before death, and it was the last time we saw her alive. We loved our grandmother and were thankful to have this last opportunity to visit with her.

It was great to be home and visit with family and friends. Furlough time passed quickly, and too soon I was on the trains back to Hondo.

...Pinning on the Wings...

I was anxious to get back into navigation training. Having missed ten days of training with my class, I was reassigned to the following class, 44-4, which was three weeks behind my original class. Consequently I repeated a few days of previously covered class work.

I liked the instructors of my new class better than my old group, particularly the first lieutenant who was my special monitor and mentor. His name was C. D. Trail, and a veteran of the real old horse cavalry before switching to the Army Air Forces. He encouraged and disciplined me. Once, while we were undergoing daily inspection before class work, he stopped behind me as I stood at attention in formation, and in his clipped Texas drawl expostulated, "Malone, a man who would shine the toes of his shoes and not the heels, would do number two and not wipe." And he did not say number two, but rather used a common scatological word. He knew how to get your attention, and sure motivated me to spend more time on maintenance of shoes, uniforms and other personal items.

Lieutenant Trail preferred that his students be exposed to organizational leadership, and he took the initiative to have me appointed cadet lieutenant for my flight. Some of my classmates were not all that impressed with my assigned authority, but somehow we managed to get along, and I was able to maintain some sense of orderliness in our formations as we marched to classes and other functions. Also, I was responsible for leadership in the maintenance of our barracks in a state of order and cleanliness, which was no small task.

As school progressed, we were increasingly occupied with navigation training in flight, and some of our more interesting trips were described under "Before GPS (Global Positioning System)." At that time we could not have begun to imagine anything like GPS as a pinpoint navigational system based on satellite transmissions. Now, anyone with good sense and a reasonable knowledge of topography can be a competent navigator by using adequate maps and a small handheld satellite receiver. Such instruments are available from sporting goods stores, and are touted for use by deer and elk hunters operating in remote areas. Recently, I have read reports about some numbskulls who have taken these units into woods and mountains, but without maps of the areas they are traversing. Topographical maps are absolutely essential unless the more expensive units, which can be preprogrammed to display specific topographical areas, are used. Even so, batteries can run down or equipment can malfunction—then adequate maps become lifesavers. Of course, in any case, one must be capable of map reading and interpretation. Many of the earlier models of handheld GPS units and some of the lower cost models simply produce readouts of positions in relation to longitude and latitude, and they are perfectly acceptable and more economical, but maps are mandatory accessories for efficacy and safety.

GPS units on today's aircraft and ocean-going ships are much more sophisticated with automated assimilation, recording, display and transmission of data, all based on route maps preprogrammed into the computerized data system.

Later in the World War II European theatre of operations, I would see and use some of the precursors to modern electronic systems for navigation, and they will be discussed in a subsequent chapter.

I logged 115 hours of flying time during fifteen weeks of navigational training, and 33 hours were night flying time. Our pilots were very competent and friendly. They never made any miscues during my sashays, unless a jolt at El Paso could be designated as such. We were in takeoff mode, and the wheels had just lifted from the runway, when bang, we dropped back to the runway with quite a jolt, but we bounced back into the air and kept going. The day was very hot and the asphalt runway had heated to cause localized ground thermals that had dropped us.

Hondo was a small town in ranching country with about 1000 population. I would not have expected it to grow, but my current road map atlas lists its population at 6000. Due to Hondo's proximity to the airbase, it sported a tailor shop, and I bought my first officer uniforms there. Hondo, Texas derives its name from the Spanish word "Hondo", meaning "grommet," or the reinforced inner surface of the cowhand's lariat loop. Hondo, or also listed as "Honshu," is the mainland or largest island of Japan. Hondo-to-Hondo by the Great Circle course, a route of 5130.5 nautical miles, was a simulated exercise by the navigation cadets.

John Nance Garner, Vice President of the U.S. during President Franklin D. Roosevelt's first term, was a native of the Hondo area and owned a ranch just west of Hondo.

Occasionally we were allowed weekend passes, which could begin after Saturday morning inspections, and we were supposed to be back on base by midnight Sunday. If you passed through the gate after midnight, you would be placed on report, and as a disciplinary action, would not be allowed passes for a month. Some cadets would simply skirt the gate when they knew a route through or over the fencing. Most everyone went to San Antonio, or San Antone as we dubbed it, for outside recreation. Action was limited in comparison to Houston, which was considered a soldier's type of town. We all felt compelled to visit the Alamo, but it didn't provide a lot of inspiration for me.

I graduated from Aviation Cadet Navigation School, and was commissioned a second lieutenant on March 18, 1944— one year and 18 days from the time I was called up from the Reserves. Some graduates were married—some even with kids, and when their wives could make it to graduation and commissioning ceremonies they pinned navigator wings on their hubbies. A few mothers of graduates attended and did the pinning of wings while some guys' girlfriends did the honor. Most of the new shave tails including me, pinned the wings on our new officer's blouses with our own fumbling fingers.

A few graduates were appointed flight officers rather than commissioned lieutenants; they were guys who somewhere along the way in training had goofed up enough to blemish their record but not enough to wash them out of school. This happened more often in pilot training than in navigation or bombardier training. Most flight officers would eventually be commissioned second lieutenants after they had proved themselves in service. Insignia bars that flight officers wore on the shoulders of their blouses, hats and shirt collars, were composed of blue enameled ends separated by a gold lacquered center section. I thought they were prettier than my gold bars.

A twelve day leave, including travel time, was granted to all graduates, and each had orders of assignment and travel to various Air Force commands in different parts of the United States, where we would receive physical and documents checkups before subsequent assignment to transitional training in the airships that we would be navigating.

...Furlough and Reception...

I was packed and ready to go before graduation ceremonies, and didn't delay after commissioning with getting into San Antonio to catch a train to Missouri. It was an exciting day, and in new blouse and trouser "pinks" for the first time, I became a bit careless. Dashing from the Air Force truck that had transported us to San Antone, and starting to cross the street, I stepped close enough to a moving auto that its fender clipped my left knee as I jumped back. The driver was a G.I., all concerned that he had hit an officer. My knee hurt a bit, but I knew it wasn't cracked, so I told the driver to go on, that I was okay. I was anxious to get on with my journey home and headed toward final training.

My knee did not bother me until I was in Northern Ireland some four months later, and then for three or four days in a spell of damp weather it ached. I should have gone to the medics about it, but never did. Today, my left knee will trouble me occasionally when there is a major barometric pressure shift. Gee, could probably have finagled a ten or twenty percent disability pension if I had gotten the problem on my medical records. It would have been as legitimate as some feigned injuries that garnered disability pay.

Everyone at home in Missouri was glad to see me again, but not as impressed as I with my new lieutenant's insignia, but they were pleased I had made it so far. Mom was already worrying about the next leg of my odyssey. Dad and I were in Rolla one day and met a G.I. on the street who snapped a salute at me. I recognized him as a friend and spoke his name. Then he stopped to visit. I was more embarrassed than he about the salute.

Dad was trucking quite a lot during wartime, and while on leave, I went with him one evening to take a load of cattle to St. Louis. We were coming back late at night, about two a.m., and I was driving when we saw a flare ahead. I slowed and Dad told me to pull over on the shoulder and stop since we saw there had been an accident.

I had seen some bad accidents on old Route 66, but this was one of the worst. We were first on the scene, and glad to see a deputy sheriff pull up soon after we stopped. A large single axle truck and a two-door 1940 Chevrolet had collided almost head on. The truck driver's leg was broken, but his passenger in the cab was only scratched and had put out the flares and gotten notice to the sheriff.

Five Negro second lieutenants, apparently bound for Fort Leonard Wood west of Rolla, had been in the car, and all were dead as far as we could ascertain. It was a gruesome scene. Two had been thrown from the car, and one was hanging head down with a foot caught between the driver's side door and the roof of the car. The sheriff summoned ambulances and tow trucks, and then we left. I let Dad finish the drive home.

Too soon my leave was over, and I was catching a train at Rolla to head east to Springfield, Massachusetts.

New officers were paid eight cents per mile travel allowances from station to station, by the shortest route, except where the rail line was on government land grant right-of-ways, then three cents per mile were deducted!... Screwy but a fact. The allowance pretty well covered my transportation and other costs from Hondo to Missouri, and then to Massachusetts. However, we did not receive the payment for expenses until arrival at our next duty station.

I arrived at Westover Field, an Army Air Forces base and the First Bomber Command's Reception Center, on the first of April, and was there for about three weeks. My time at Westover in the Reception Center was scheduled for checking physical and training records preparatory to assignment at a base engaged in transitional bomber flight and ground school training. Ordinarily, only a few days were necessary before assignments to bomber crews and bases were made, and the crews would remain at Westover for B-24 transition or be sent to other transition bases in the First Bomber Command.

Lo and behold, though I had previously passed the high altitude low-pressure chamber test during classification, they could not find records of my test. Certification of the test was required, no ifs or buts about it. They would not crank up the test chamber just for me, so there were a few days delay before I was tested. In the meantime, the roster of new pilots, bombardiers and navigators had been assigned to crews and training bases, leaving a few others and me in limbo, but only for a short while.

I liked Westover and preferred to stay for a later assignment to a crew in B-24 training, but in a few days I was transferred to Chatham Field, Georgia and placed on an extra board for navigators. The train ride was uneventful, and I arrived at Chatham around April 21.

...Banding the Big Birds...

Chatham Field was a transitional base where crews were trained to fly in the B-24 Liberator bomber—a four engine aircraft with large twin-rudder tail, and classified as a heavy bomber. The training agenda was set up for complete crews, consisting of pilot, co-pilot, navigator, bombardier, engineer-crew chief and top turret gunner, tail turret gunner, radio operator, nose turret gunner and two waist gunners, one of whom was the armorer. Ground school and flight training was oriented toward strategic bombing, and these crews remained together until assignment to a combat zone of operation. Pilots had been trained and checked out in B-24s before arrival at transitional training.

Due to the foul-up at Westover, I was still between classes, and I was placed on standby status, subject to assignment to a crew that might lose their navigator because of illness or other reasons. I was entered into a ground school class already in progress while I waited for a flight crew.

Waiting wasn't all bad. A motley bunch of five officers, including two pilots, needed a navigator to make an excursion flight to Cuba, and I got the nod. Over-water flights of significant distance required a navigator to be on board according to First Bomber Command regulations.

We flew into Batista Field, near Havana, one day and returned to Chatham Field the next day. We bunked at Batista Field in U.S. Army Air Force operated facilities, but went into Havana for a night on the town. Nothing was hinted to me about the purpose of the flight, but I always figured we were rumrunners. I tended to my navigation, which was good experience, and enjoyed the sights of Havana.

In the company of three of the officers on the trip I saw some of the nightlife. One officer was a captain in administration at Chatham—a grandfatherly type; he took me under his wing and frequently remonstrated with me to not do this or that. His admonishments were well taken and we got along fine. A little blonde entertainer at one of the clubs was not pleased when the captain cajoled me away from her clutches.

I purchased a ladies handbag made of alligator leather for my mother, and she used it for many years until worn out. I bought some other souvenirs for my mother including a pair of castanets fashioned from gourds that are hanging in our home now.

Shortly after my Havana trip, a crew lost their navigator to illness, and I took his place. The crew was already about half way through training, so I missed some flying time, but even so, I flew fifty hours in a period of about three weeks. A one thousand mile over water flight was a navigational training requirement, so this was fulfilled by using a flight plan that took us out over the Atlantic Ocean, then doglegging to Havana, Cuba as our final destination. It was nice to get another trip to Cuba, and to again have another night to see more of Havana. Quite a contrast, I'm sure, to what it is like now after decades of Castroism.

On my first high altitude flight we were climbing, and at about 16000 feet there was a sudden release of fluid into my oxygen mask. There was no pain in my head, just a feeling of pressure relief. I dropped my mask from my face and it was full of a gooey-like green fluid. My sinuses had apparently cleared through my nose and mouth as a result of the atmospheric pressure reduction. I quickly cleaned the mask so I could get oxygen-enriched air again, and I never experienced any similar problems during later flying at any altitudes. However, I have sinus problems today that began a few years after my military flying days.

Our quarters at Chatham Field were little better than at basic training in Jefferson Barracks, and I was back to upper and lower bunk beds. I took the top bunk because my navigator roommate was a carouser, and I wanted him in the lower bunk when he returned from his frequent nocturnal escapades off the base. He came down with gonorrhea (colloquially designated "the clap"), and I was glad to be rid of him. I never saw him again after he went to the infirmary, but I suppose he was reassigned to a crew after treatment.

Chatham Field was located near Savannah, which was a nice town, but not very lively. Nice beaches were close by, and we hit them now and then. I saw some pretty southern girls, but didn't become romantically attached to any—there was a lot of competition.

The officer's mess was sub-par, and I don't remember any real good meals. The weather was hot, humid and sultry. On arrival at Chatham, I had to purchase regulation cotton khaki shirts and trousers for summer wear. Thankfully, blouses were not required for evening wear, though some of the command and administrative types wore tan blouses at the officer's club and at officiations. I did buy a "50 mission crush" billed type hat, fabricated from tan summer cloth, to wear for a photo that my mother had requested. My wife still displays that photo on her bureau in our bedroom. Also, the billed cap with large frontal officer insignia seemed to impress the girls more than the small foldable hat with just a gold bar insignia.

At completion of transitional training, we were issued B-4 bags that were large zippered traveling bags with large side pockets, and the bag opened up so dress clothes in the inside compartments could be hung while in the bag. I was also issued a smaller reinforced canvas bag with many zippered compartments for containment of navigational maps and gear. I already owned a modified type of duffel bag that I had used previously for travel. Yes, we were being prepared for departure from Chatham and thenceforth to routing and further marshalling for overseas duty.

Ab, Wib and Gib – furlough
Christmas, 1943

Ab and Wib
March 1944

...Checklist...

Our crew left Chatham Field by train on June 12, 1944, and arrived at Mitchell Field on June 13, 1944. Mitchell Field was located on the eastern end of Long Island, New York, and was an Army Air Forces staging base.

Mitchell was our last step before heading overseas, and all our records were thoroughly checked and brought up-to-date. We were briefed on flight routes and issued all necessary maps. A sextant, chronometer and other navigational gear, which was required to navigate a B-24 bomber anywhere was issued to me, and this equipment would remain under my custodial care as long as I was on active combat flying status. A B-24J aircraft was assigned to us, and we would ferry it to Great Britain by flying the North Atlantic route to the British Isles.

On the 18th of June we ground checked, and then flew the B-24J for two hours in the Long Island area, and our pilot pronounced her airworthy. This aircraft had been flown directly from the factory with a bottom ball turret installed, but when such aircraft reached England and the Eighth Air Force, the ball turrets were removed—you would have thought that these planes could have been manufactured specifically for the 8th without the ball, but things didn't work that way in the military-industrial alliance.

The balls were prone to maintenance problems, not many gunners could handle them well, and they added a significant amount of weight to the aircraft. In the B-24 Second Division of the 8th there was consensus that the tail turret gunner and waist gunners could pretty well cover the attack areas that the ball turret might handle. The B-17 was quite a different bomber, and they stuck with their ball turrets.

While at Mitchell we were free in the evenings. We usually completed daily assignments and meetings early in the afternoon and then took the commuter train into New York City (it was not called the "Big Apple" then) for sight seeing, stage shows and some night clubbing. I'll always remember one joke told by a nightclub comedian that went like this: My buddy and I were walking down 5th Avenue and met this good looking babe—as we passed, I said to my buddy, "Wasn't that Hortense?" and he replied, "Nah, she looked perfectly relaxed to me."

I was exposed to television for the first time, and watched myself talking on a demonstration unit in Radio Center. I wasn't enthralled with the "Big Apple" then, and during subsequent visits years later my opinion didn't change a lot.

The last item on the Mitchell Field checklist was a "short arm" inspection (to the uninitiated, a physical check for social diseases), just before embarking on our B-24J to leave the Island to head out on our scheduled overseas route.

Our departure was delayed two days because the co-pilot came down with strep throat, and a replacement pilot had to be flown in to Mitchell to complete our crew. I liked the original co-pilot, but his successor was okay too. We departed Long Island on June 23rd bound for Dow Field, Bangor, Maine Air Force base.

...Crossing the Deep...

Our flight time to Bangor was only two hours and forty minutes, and we arrived in early afternoon. The normal cruising speed of the B-24 without bomb load was 175 miles per hour (151 knots). We normally used nautical miles and knots in our navigation calculations because one nautical mile is equal to one sixtieth degree or one second of longitude at the equator, and our charts and maps were drawn in topographical terms of the earth as defined by global longitude and latitude measurements. I also recorded our air speed in statute miles per hour on my log, but all charting was done in nautical units. Our air speed indicators displayed miles per hour, so conversions were constantly necessary, but easily and quickly done with a hand-held slide rule type calculator, especially developed for Air Force navigators and designated the E-6B.

Indicated air speeds were determined by pitot tube type instrumentation mounted on the planes, and because of variations in air densities and temperatures at different altitudes, the true air speed is usually more than the indicated. For example, at zero degrees Centigrade (32 degrees Fahrenheit) and 1200 feet of altitude (corrected for barometric pressure) the indicated air speed would equal the true air speed, but at 25,000 feet altitude and minus 50 degrees Centigrade (-58 degrees F), which was not unusual during bombing missions over Europe in the winter, the true air speed is 240 miles per hour when the indicated air speed is only 165 m.p.h. Of course, higher speeds were advantageous for avoiding anti-aircraft fire, but extra fuel was required to climb to the higher altitudes. Today's jet powered aircraft fly at much higher altitudes where they actually gain fuel efficiency by taking advantage of favorable jet stream winds.

Ground speed was the really critical factor, for if you were heading directly into a 100 m.p.h. wind while flying at a true air speed of 240 m.p.h., you actually would be traveling over the earth at a ground speed of only 140 m.p.h. Inadvertently, this could happen on bomb runs if winds shifted or winds had not been correctly predicted. Effects of wind direction and velocity on ground speed were also calculated with the E-6B. Of course, the navigator had to determine the wind characteristics by establishing checkpoints by pilotage, radio or other instrumentation such as radar.

At Bangor we were again briefed on routes and procedures for flying the Atlantic. Also, our personnel records were reviewed, and the aircraft ground checked again. We received brief physical exams, including a "short arm" inspection. We were stabled at Bangor for three days and underwent two more short arm checks—one exam just before departure from the base. No one was allowed to leave the base. Bomber Command did not want anyone to get a venereal disease before leaving the continent, and demanded daily checks to eliminate anyone who might be coming down with a social disease such as gonorrhea or syphilis.

Many years later when employed in the northeast I took business trips by auto that routed me through Bangor. On each pass through I could not help but remember our brief stay there during World War II. And I almost expected someone to tell me I would have to take a short arm exam. At that time Bangor was home to the largest and best dinner buffet that I have ever experienced. Sorry, I can't recall its name or explicit location.

We took off from Bangor at 1:00 p.m. on June 27th, bound for Goose Bay, Labrador. Flying was visual and smooth until near Goose, and I enjoyed the scenery, especially the St. Lawrence Gulf and Anticosti Island in the Gulf—this island being renowned for its large whitetail deer population. If you want a trophy, it is the place to go. We crossed New Brunswick, the Gaspe Peninsula of Quebec, and then crossed the Gulf into Quebec again, and on to Labrador, which is part of spread-out New Foundland.

We landed at Goose Bay late in the afternoon after a four hour and 40 minutes flight from Bangor. At the time I originally drafted this manuscript, I heard on TV that former President George Bush was on a fishing trip in Labrador while also being interviewed about current politics. But he wasn't where we landed almost six decades ago—but likely in the western area around the Twin Falls or Churchill Falls locations.

Goose Bay lies at the head of Melville Lake, which exits to the Labrador Sea and the Atlantic Ocean. The area looked desolate. Air base facilities were limited to refueling and briefings on our continuing route, weather reports and emergency procedures. Some supper was provided, and then we went to bed. We were up early for breakfast and an update on the weather, and then we were off to Iceland. The cooks packed a lunch for us, but I don't remember the fare.

We flew just a few miles south of the southern tip of Greenland. An outpost air base was located near the tip in a long narrow fjord, but we had been warned that it was a tricky place to land in good weather, and almost impossible in bad weather. This base was socked in at the time of our passing, but radio contact was maintained as long as possible in case an emergency developed. The area where the WW II B-17 bombers and P-38 fighters went down on the ice is several miles east of this emergency base. Those aircraft immediately began sinking into the ice and have continued sinking farther every day since. Not long ago one of the P-38s was recovered from the depths of the ice after several years of laborious and very difficult work. It is not expected that any more will be recovered.

Once we had reached my calculated point of no return, I told our pilot to forget about Greenland, and that Iceland was our only chance if trouble developed. Our total flight time from Goose to Iceland was nine hours, and the pilots were on instruments half of that time due to cloud formations, but generally the flight was smooth with little turbulence.

We plowed through some rain about half way to Iceland, and then burst out into bright sunlight, and I began shooting the sun with my sextant to determine lines of position (LOP). The sun was at a high angle and toward 90 degrees of our flight course. That sun position gave sextant readings that provided LOPs more or less paralleling our flight path. The LOPs checked well with my dead reckoning navigation, which I was using with Mercator charts from the time of departure from Goose Bay. Estimated winds from Goose briefings had been applied to the dead reckoning, and after we broke into the clear at about 4000 feet altitude above the ocean, I then estimated wind direction and speeds by studying the waves on the ocean surface. The aircraft was equipped with a small drift meter with a viewing glass calibrated with lines so you could align wave directions with the lines and read out the angle of flow in degrees. At best it was an approximation and as reliable as the observer's experience. Estimating the wind velocity from observation of waves was an art and accuracy again very dependent on abilities of the individual to interpret the effect of wind velocity and direction at varying altitudes.

This was the first and last time that I would use my sextant after graduating from navigation school. It was not practical for our type of bombing operations in the European Theatre of Operations.

At one point during our flight to Iceland the pilot got to worrying about fuel supply, so with his fuel consumption readings I did some calculations, and then assured him the supply should be ample, unless the weather and winds changed drastically, which did not happen.

We arrived in Reykjavik, capitol of Iceland, on course and close to my estimated time of arrival (E.T.A.). At about 200 miles out we had confirmed the accuracy of my dead reckoning with the radio compass as signals were picked up from Iceland transmissions.

It was a sort of early dusk when we touched down at Meeks Field, U.S. Air Force Base at Reykjavik on June 28, 1944, and darkness never really fell. From the air Iceland appeared rather bleak to me. We didn't get an opportunity to mingle with the residents, and I slept restlessly during that less than dark night. We were rousted early for breakfast, received briefings on the latest weather reports, and then took off on our final leg, headed for Prestwick, Scotland.

About two hours out of Iceland the pilot called me on the intercom and said there was a B-24 off to our left that he could not identify, and the craft didn't respond to his radio inquiries. He asked me if we were on the right course because the other B-24 was headed in a direction different to us—actually more in the direction of Norway from my observations. No other B-24s were supposed to be in our vicinity at this time, and I assured the pilot we were headed correctly. The B-24 stranger could have been a weather ship monitoring the area because they often flew incognito, or possibly it may have been a captured B-24 with a German crew, flying for the express purpose of deceiving us into changing course and flying into hostile territory. We had received reports of the latter occurrences, and German interference with our radio frequencies. Our pilot was worried and not satisfied until he later made radio contact with the Hebrides Islands and northern Scotland when he then decided we were not lost.

Other than the vagrant B-24, the flight was uneventful, and after six and one half hours in the air on June 29, 1944, we were approaching Prestwick.

As we neared our destination, I broke into a rough rendition of "Loch Lomond" on the intercom and everyone cheered—or I thought so anyway.

We landed safely and parked the aircraft as directed. An Army Air Force four-by-four truck rolled up and we were told to unload our baggage, and they would take care of it and send it to our quarters. Then we were hauled off in a separate truck. We had premonitions that there was afore-thought and scheming in this mode of separating personnel from their gear. To confirm our fears, when our bags were delivered to our quarters, they were lighter by the bottles of whiskey that we had stashed in our B-4 bags. The game was apparently old hat to them, and well organized to fleece the unwary pilgrims fresh from the States. Good liquors and whiskey were scarce in the United Kingdom. By regulations we were not supposed to bring in spirits, so they had us by the gonads—we couldn't file a complaint. The day was June 29th, 1944, and we were glad to be on the ground, even though our whiskey had been stolen.

…Irish Eyes…

We were expecting to be sent to a combat air base in England, but it was not yet to be. After a night at Prestwick, on June 30th we were trucked to Stone, England near Warrington. We were there until July 10, 1944, when we were loaded on a small ship and taken to Northern Ireland.

Prestwick is located on the west coast of Scotland, about 40 miles southeast of Glasgow. We shipped down the Firth of Clyde and across the North Channel to the coast of Northern Ireland. We were taken inland by truck for about 40 miles into the northern part of Northern Ireland to what appeared to be an old army station, which had been rented to the U.S. A. F.

We were given indoctrination in English customs, operations of the U.S.A..F.in England, and information as to potential assignments and responsibilities. We lolled around quite a bit, and I was beginning to wonder if the 8th Bomber Command knew which end was up.

We were near a small village—Cluntoe, if I remember right, and were allowed to visit there, but the natives were not all that friendly, and seemed reticent to converse with us. They certainly lacked any characteristics of loquaciousness.

I tried to pump a young man about any Malones who might be living in the area—he said he didn't know any, and without adieu straddled his bicycle and pedaled off. Maybe I didn't want to trace my lineage that far anyway. For all I know, the Malones may have been the leaders of the opposition to the British Protectorate. I do believe that I have some revolutionary blood.

We were not allowed to go to Belfast. Probably the English figured they had enough problems with Northern Ireland and greater Ireland, without some half-assed American airmen running around stirring the pot.

The station was not equipped with an organized physical recreation program, so we got some needed exercise by running and playing games. I fell while running a race and sprained my left wrist. I didn't report the injury to the medics, and I still have some problems with that wrist if it is stressed. At the time I didn't want anything to further delay my advancement to a bomber group.

After twelve days of a rather lackadaisical and lackluster interlude, we were flown back to Warrington on July 22, and then entrained for our operating base in England at Hethel.

...East Anglia...

English trains were nothing like American trains, except both ran on steel tracks, and they were no more or less comfortable. The English trains were slower, partly because of high population concentration and congestion. Consequently, it was a long day's ride from northern England down to Norwich, England. Norwich was a city of over 100,000 population, and located in East Anglia, which is a sizeable area of England with a lot of coastal regions and thrusting out to the North Sea.

We were trucked from Norwich for about ten miles to Hethel air base, the home of the 389th Bomb Group, Second Division, Eighth Air Force. Hethel, per se, was a small crossroads village with a few residences and surrounded by farms. We were assigned to the 566th Squadron, and this was my home until I had completed my combat missions.

Most of the A.A.F. bases in England had been hurriedly built, or prepared from civilian airports, and then leased to the United States. Yes, we were not just guests in England—we paid our way in a big way. The touted lend-lease program was pretty much a one-way street.

The English maintained the runways and auxiliary roads and other areas. They calmly worked right along taxi strips as the 24s rolled by with outboard props spinning. Tea times were observed on schedule, no matter what. The perennial story told was that the prop of a passing B-24 clipped a Limey worker and the crew of the guilty ship painted a teacup on the nose area of the plane where it was customary to paint a small bomb to tally each bombing mission. Then of course, the Commandant made them remove the cup. I can believe the story.

The countryside around Hethel was generally agricultural with frequent clusters of crossroads residences or farm buildings, and the landscape was pretty. A small forest of three or four acres grew in the middle of our base, and a surfaced path ran through it, whereby we walked or biked from quarters to flight headquarters and the flight lines. Frequently we saw pheasants there.

Bicycles were a major means of personal transportation in England during the war, and a lot of airmen used them on our base. New bikes were unavailable, so you waited until a transferred airman had a used one to sell. I bought one, and it was the first bicycle I had ever owned. I rode it frequently, and sometimes took jaunts around the countryside. Then one day I collided with another airman biker on the base. Both were traveling at a fast clip and my front wheel and fork were damaged so badly that I didn't try to fix it. His bike was badly damaged too, and he limped as he carried his wrecked machine away. We were both negligent and there were no hard feelings.

The English had used steel framing with concrete and mortar type sidewall construction for a lot of the operation buildings and many of the living quarters. Roofs were tiled or sheet metal. My first quarters were in a building divided into rooms with two officers in each. Cot type bunks were provided with sheets, two G.I.wool blankets and a comforter for colder weather. Everything was spartan.

There was a separate communal building for toiletry and showers. Management made a stab at having hot water in the morning for shaving and cursory washing, but you couldn't rely on a supply of hot water. The fustest to the latrine and wash facilities got the mostest, or the early bird got the hot or warm water. Fuel (coal or coke) was rationed to a daily allotment, and we had to be quick and nimble to get hot water for a shower before fuel for the heater was exhausted. There was quite a bit of intra-base pilferage of coal by enterprising airmen who would themselves crank up the water heater when they could latch on to fuel. The caretakers padlocked the utilities room, but furtive, agile and nimble fingered airmen picked the locks to gain access.

Officer's mess at Hethel was literally that—absolutely the worst excuse for food that I encountered at any station on my Air Force tour. Powdered eggs, even in those days, could be fixed decently with only a modicum of cooking talent if the effort was made, but our servings were as a matter of course, ugly greenish unsavory messes. The quality of powdered milk was not all that great in 1944 as compared to now, but nonetheless, with some concerned attention it was amenable to conversion to a palatable drink. Ours tasted like chalk water. If you could take it, you at least got some needed dietary calcium.

About the only fresh fruit we got were a few oranges now and then. Cooked prunes were served fairly often, but it is difficult to ruin prunes unless there is malice aforethought. The canned grapefruit juice was worse than that served at Jefferson Barracks—I had thought that impossible.

Fresh salads materials were scarce, and even the pickles were sub-standard. It's a wonder someone didn't come down with scurvy.

Desserts were usually cake or English cookies and crumpets. Our cooks (and in this case I use the term loosely) could not bake a decent cake with commercial sized prepared mixes that were in limited supply.

The proud announcement went out that we would have steaks for Christmas dinner. We did have meat, but as sure as the legs I stand on, I know horsemeat was served, and admittedly, though tough it could have been worse. Some old farmer's nag had been taken to the "knacker", who in turn had sold the butchered remains to an intermediary, who then sold the meat to our mess sergeant. Anyway, that's what I thought. Field rations would have been a significant improvement, but then again, even that grub has to be prepared properly to be appetizing.

Enlisted airmen would remind us fairly often, "We had fresh eggs for breakfast this morning," and there were reminders of other servings that made my mouth water. All the competent and conscientious cooks and mess sergeants must have had a vendetta against officer airmen of the 389th Group or our superiors were not on the ball.

A building had been designated as the officer's club, but it was not even a facsimile of one in the States. You had to get there early in the evening if you hoped to get a drink of rationed whiskey. The supply of the ubiquitous English mild and stout beers was usually plentiful, and to give it some due, it was better than no beer at all. I never tasted any that was cold, and I've always wondered if it would have been tastier cold. The club featured decent toilets and wash facilities, and usually sported hot water—officers often shaved there when they could elbow up to one of the washbasins.

I liked the pubs in Norwich and visited them occasionally. However, we were cautioned not to go without signing in with squadron headquarters. Trucks were furnished for transportation to and from Norwich and you had better be on that return truck if you were scheduled to fly the next day. Rarely were we informed of flight schedules before the eve of bombing missions, and we were obligated to check the bulletin boards late in the afternoons or early evenings every day. And schedules could change overnight and you wouldn't know you were flying until someone awakened you in the early morning hours. Even when schedules were posted, someone from operations came around to arouse all flyers for preflight meetings and preparations.

Much depended on the vagaries of the weather, and I was awakened as early as 2:30 a.m. more than once to prepare for takeoff at dawn. All of our bombing was done in daylight, and an early start was desirable, particularly if the mission was long and weather predictions were unfavorable for the return home. No one wanted to fly home in the dark—Luftwaffe fighter planes could slip in undetected at low altitudes and pounce on individual aircraft after they broke formations to make approaches to the airports for landings.

Mission planning and preparation was an involved procedure. After wakeup we could stop at the mess hall on our way to operations and eat if we wished. We walked to the operations building where there was first a general assembly and briefing of all crews. The Group Commander or other high ranking officer would stand in front of a huge wall map of Europe and the British Isles, which displayed a colored string that marked and outlined the route to the target area. He identified the actual target and provided general operational information, and then concluded by wishing us luck.

An operations officer read off all the crews by pilot name and their formation positions by element, squadron and group. Then he described the size of the effort and named the groups and wings that were participating in the raid.

An element consisted of three B-24s—four elements to a standard full squadron—three to four squadrons to a group and three to four groups in a wing. There were four wings in the 8th Air Force 2nd Division. The first and third divisions of the 8th were composed of B-17s. Hence, for an all-out effort the mighty 8th could mount an assault of 1000 to 1500 bombers for one sortie, though different targets would likely be assigned to each division. I rarely flew on a mission composed of less than one wing. Often the whole division was engaged. There were times when not enough planes were available or in condition to mount a major effort.

Good and tight formation flying was critical to protection from enemy fighter planes, and to orderly and accurate bombing. Formations were stacked and staggered. Each element had a lead ship with two wingmen. Then the elements were stacked and aligned as lead, low left, high right and the fourth element in the slot or bucket, which was lower in the middle of the squadron and trailing. A low right, high left squadron formation might be used depending on the positioning of squadron, group and wing formations. A trained lead crew was placed in the lead ship of the leading element of each squadron, and a deputy lead crew flew as a wing ship to the lead ship.

An initial point (I.P.) was always established to identify the location for beginning the bomb run to target, and the lead bombardiers should have everything set at that point so only fine tuning of bombsight settings needed to be made on the bomb run. Before the I. P. there was dissolution of the master formation so squadrons were lined up to bomb individually. There was a lot to this game and good planning and leadership was essential to be successful. Big decisions were incumbent with people similar to myself, who wouldn't turn 21 until December 29, 1944.

Back to briefings and ground preparations. After general briefing, the pilots, navigators, bombardiers, crew chiefs and radio operators were briefed as groups, and provided more detailed information: signals, radio codes, maps, weather, flak maps, secondary target locations, points for chaff distribution and flare colors of the day. If during flight there was reason to believe some of the initial codes had been deciphered by the enemy, the radio codes and flare signals would be changed as the mission progressed.

The latest weather information for the mission routes was again reviewed and estimations of locations and concentrations of anti-aircraft gun batteries were provided.

Our next step was to assemble our gear to take to the flight lines. We dressed to the best of our ability to match the predicted weather conditions. We had individual lockers for storage of cold weather boots, jackets and headgear, but if we wanted to wear electrically heated suits, we had to check them out each mission—these suits then were not always reliable, and were just skeleton rigs similar to early bed electric blankets, and had to be worn under substantial outer clothing. They were energized by plugging into 24-volt outlets at stations on the plane. Most of the time I tried to get along with long underwear, a pair of wool pants and coveralls, plus and extra wool shirt under my bomber jacket with artificial type fleece lining. I have observed outside temperature readings of minus 50 degrees centigrade (-58 degrees Fahrenheit) at an altitude of 25,000 feet, and it was not a lot warmer in the nose of the B-24. If predicted temperatures were in that range I would wear the heated suits. There were always some air leaks around the nose turret to keep my rear end cool.

On each mission we were required to check out both a "Mae West" life preserver and a parachute. We were encouraged to wear a flak jacket and steel helmet when flying in anti-aircraft gunnery zones. These items also had to be checked out the morning of the mission. The shrapnel protection equipment was heavy and cumbersome, and I wore the jacket and steel helmet only when I could see shell bursts in our immediate flight zone. The jackets were made of over lapping steel plates and sewn into cloth layers to give some flexibility—nothing like today's much lighter police armor made with "Kevlar" plastic as the projectile stopper.

Each B-24 was supposed to be equipped with two emergency medical kits, and the crew chief was responsible for checking them out for each combat flight. They contained morphine and the smart chiefs checked the kits for morphine in front of the supply clerks at the checkout counter—the clerks were not above suspicion. The clerks for sure checked the kits when returned after missions. The crew chief (also designated the engineer) was the curator of the signal flare cartridges, and it was his job to get the necessary colors for the two Very pistols (flare firing guns) assigned to each B-24 that flew in England and the combat zones.

The chaplains usually came in to the dressing rooms while the crews were putting on flight clothes and getting gear together. They were available for counseling and prayers. The protestant chaplain was normally reserved and quiet, waiting for the airmen to take the initiative. But Father Beck was a corker—an irascible character, who would say, "O.K., all you fish eaters, get over here."

All combat flyers were issued a Model 1911 Colt type .45 ACP caliber semi-auto pistol, and it was an individual decision to carry or not carry on combat missions. I chose to carry, and I chose the leather shoulder holster. I estimate that about half carried. Some took the guns on the aircraft because they were concerned about theft if they left them in their quarters. Some didn't want to be bothered with the extra baggage, and others thought the gun could get them into more trouble than it would help if captured by the enemy. The guns were manufactured for the military by several companies, but I had one of Colt origin, and I wish I could have kept it, but had to turn it in when I left England to return to the States. Some guys lied, and said their pistols had been lost or stolen, then sneaked them home.

It was recommended that each airman also check out an "Escape Kit" that would be turned in after the flight if he made it back. Several small items were packaged into this small cloth kit that could be beneficial to anyone who might survive a bailout and escape from the enemy on the ground. A small booklet containing key words in German translated into English and neatly folded silk maps of France, Germany and Spain were included as basics. I retained a set of the silk maps when I returned to the States and today I display them to students in our Junior High school when doing oral history presentations about my military experience. Of course I have to tell the girls that all the silk was being used for our maps and not available for silk stockings during WWII.

After the crews were assembled with their gear, we were hauled in trucks to our B-24s, which were dispersed all around the airfield and parked on "hardstands" (concrete surfaced areas) where they also were serviced and repaired.

The maintenance chief for each bomber who was usually a tech or master sergeant would be waiting for the crew's arrival, and had already prepared the plane for flight. He might have just finished some engine work and run the engines through to see that they were ready to go. The pilot would talk with the maintenance chief, and then make any ground preflight checks that he desired. If the pilot was satisfied, he would announce, "O.K., let's go," and we would board. Most of the crew had already stowed equipment at their stations. The pilots would crank the engines, and then run them up and do other flight checks as we were taxiing, lining up and marshalling for the takeoff.

My first 15 missions were flown in both H & J models of B-24s, but my last 15 missions were in Js only—as a navigator, I don't remember any significant differences. I believe that both were fitted with the magnificent Pratt & Whitney R-1830 radial engines that with two-stage superchargers and using 100-octane gasoline were rated at 1200 horsepower at 2700 rpm. Many veterans of the Eighth Air Force Second Division have much detailed knowledge of the history, design and performance of the B-24's engines and structure. A source of information may be The Second Air Division Association that publishes a Journal and its address is; Second Air Division Association, Eighth Air Force, P.O. Box 484, Elkhorn, WI 53121-0484. Also several books have been written about the B-24. "B-24 Liberator in action" by Squadron Signal Publications, Inc, Aircraft Number 80, details the origination and design of the 24 and through the evolution of each model of the aircraft and its equipment as flown in both the Pacific and European theatres of operation.

After takeoff, the first major task was assembly and getting into formation as the planes were circling and gaining altitude over England. Each group had their own special tail markings for identification and large individual letters for the squadrons. The wing leaders assembled above and around a ground radio beacon called a "buncher", and announced when their groups were in formation and ready to depart the buncher area. Group leaders would shoot certain flare color combinations to identify their positions, and were talking back and forth on the VHF radio with lead pilots of their squadrons.

Often, a special painted and marked B-24 ship would fly as a formation starter and then return to the base. Our formation assembly ship of the 389th Bomb Group was named the "Green Dragon" and was an old model D without a nose turret. Most of the group assembly ships were model Ds that had been retired from combat use.

Before the coasts of France, Belgium and the Netherlands were secured by the Allied Expeditionary Forces, the mission commanders tried to get the formations to an altitude of 20,000 feet or more before making landfall, in order to reduce damage from coastal anti-aircraft gun batteries. With the advancement of Allied armies into those areas, we could hit the coast at lesser altitudes, and save fuel used to gain altitude over England and the channel or North Sea.

The 389th bomb group was composed of the 564th 565th, 566th and 567th squadrons. Personnel living quarters were separated by squadrons, but in areas not far apart. Each squadron had an operations office for administration, and most of the administrative officers were also active combat flyers though scheduled less frequently for missions. The quarters for officers and enlisted men were separated. Also, as mentioned earlier they had separate mess halls. However, everyone was free to intermingle and visit at will. Generally, relationships were informal.

...Tune Up...

We arrived at Hethel on July 22, 1944, but it would be a while yet before we flew a combat mission. Again, there was a lot of indoctrination and getting acquainted with facilities and systems of a bomber group.

The British had developed a navigation system called "GEE" and based on radio waves transmission similar to television. I learned to use it by flying eight hours or more over England while also becoming acquainted with other navigational aids.

GEE was a very effective and accurate positioning system, but was limited to short range use and not effective much beyond 100 miles even during favorable transmission conditions. The Germans would jam the transmissions to the English coast at times. However, it was a tremendous aid for navigating over England, and I relied on it heavily.

The volume of air traffic over England was almost unbelievable, and flying safety was complicated; not only by the congestion, but there were many restricted areas off-limits to over flight. England was protected by many anti-aircraft batteries plus fighter patrols. If you deviated from your assigned route or flight pattern you could be in much trouble.

Once when we were coming back solo from a mission and approaching the Dover coastal area, without warning a battery laid a couple of shells close to us. We had clearance to make this approach, but some gunner didn't get the message or misidentified us. Possibly, they may have just been warning us.

Anyway GEE was a blessing, and over England, I had my nose in its CRT screen lining up the blips half of my flight time. We were provided special maps and charts for plotting our positions based on GEE readings. When the system was performing well you could almost pinpoint your location. Much depended on the distance from the radio stations and weather conditions.

We blasted off on our virgin combat mission on August 1, 1944. Our target was a strategic railroad bridge at Nogent-Sur-Seine, France, about 60 miles southwest of Paris, and behind enemy lines. Three squadrons of the 389th group were scheduled to hit the bridge, but nobody connected. I don't think the lead bombardier ever picked up the target in time to get set up properly. Conditions were good for visual bombing, but the bridge was located in rural wooded terrain, and checkpoints were not easy to pick up.

Our squadron dropped its bombs from 19,600 feet altitude, and the only explosions I observed were in plowed fields. Our total flying time for the mission was seven hours because we followed a rambling, deceptive course to avoid anti-aircraft batteries, and to keep the enemy guessing, plus we lost a half hour or more as the formation made a 360 degree circle and doglegs trying to find the target.

Next day we hustle back to Nogent-Sur-Seine, and our bombing altitude was lowered to 17,400 feet. But to no avail, our squadron missed, and I saw only a few bombs strike near one end of the bridge after the 567th let go.

During those first two missions our bombardier was on training assignments, and I dropped the bombs via a toggle switch, just at the moment when bombs exited the bomb bay of the squadron leader—all in accordance with plans and orders. Even if our bombardier had been flying with us, he would have toggled the bombs on the leader's drop just the same as I. This was standard operating procedure (s.o.p.) for squadron bombing. However, I knew that our lead bombardier was not on the target, and so stated at debriefing when questioned about the drop. On the learning curve that was one of my first mistakes

Debriefings always followed each mission, and a light colonel got all the squadron navigators together and chewed us up one side and down the other. Possibly the lead navigator was at fault and had not provided adequate information to the bombardier, but the fact that most wing crews didn't have bombardiers and their navigators were directed to drop on the lead crew drop, did not cut any ice with this hotshot. But so much for my honesty and desire to be helpful under difficult circumstances. Thereafter, I had genuine hate for that officer, and vowed that if I got back to civilian life and met up with him, I'd take him down a peg or two, then and there. Strangely, I never saw the bird again, and I wondered if there was an intrepid whistle blower in our group or if he might have gotten a dose of his own medicine.

We flew again on August 3rd, and our target was an oil dump near Paris, France. Orders called for bombing from 23,600 feet altitude. When we arrived at the target area, we could not perform visual bombing because of excessive cloud cover, and radar directed saturation bombing tactics were forbidden because we were too close to some icons of Paris. Radar was not accurate enough for concentrated spot bombing, and if used, may have resulted in a splattering of bombs over a much wider area than the selected target. The mission was recalled, but we received credit for a combat mission because we penetrated to the target area. Anti-aircraft fire (flak) was heavy in spots, but our ship (The Little Gramper Jr.) was not hit.

I saw my first aircraft (a B-17 bomber) go down in flames—it was two or three thousand feet below us, and only two parachutes emerged. I don't know what their target had been, but the flak, enemy fighters or weather must have been rough on them because we saw other B-17s scattered and headed toward England.

...Getting in the Groove...

We flew our fourth mission on August 11th. It was a "No-ball" mission, meaning it was an easy go. Bombs were dropped from an altitude of 20,300 feet on a tactical target just inside Germany. Flak was light and not accurate. Our bombardier had returned to the crew, and crawled into the nose before the I.P. point so he could toggle the switch that released the bombs. We really didn't need a bombardier since we simply dropped our bombs when the lead ship dropped their bombs, so he spent much of his time on the pilot's flight deck, or roaming the ship, and I was glad because he got in my way in the nose area which was cramped with both of us and the Norden bombsight that was used for visual bombing.

The Norden sight was a complicated piece of machinery, but a very precise instrument when working properly in the hands of a competent bombardier, and with accurate inputs from the navigator such as groundspeed, wind speeds and wind directions. Altitude and temperature corrected data was also fed into the instrument. A drift gauge was imposed on the view plate of the telescopic lens, and the bombardier could use it to make corrections for wind drift changes on the bomb run.

The German anti-aircraft marksmen were testing us more with each foray into enemy territory, and on our fifth mission to northeast France near Anizy, we ran into some very accurate flak. Several craft suffered damage from shrapnel holes but no planes were lost from our group.

I was rapidly acquiring much respect for the skill of German anti-aircraft gunners. They accosted us with both 88 millimeter (mm) and 105 mm guns. In some areas a large concentration of gun batteries put up barrages of shells, but with foreknowledge of their locations we charted our flight courses to by-pass them, so they were not effective unless they could surprise us with a freshly installed set up. We most feared those mobile and stationary units who operated sophisticated tracking instrumentation that allowed them to fire on individual planes and elements. Of course they had become familiar with the cruising speeds of the B-24s and B-17s and had weather services for reporting wind speeds and directions aloft at our elevations, and this data was cranked into their control systems. The experienced crews usually tracked the lead elements, and often times with great accuracy. With accurate range finding equipment they timed their shells to explode at our altitudes.

When possible we changed altitudes to avoid altitude-timed charges, but that strategy did not foil the gunners for long because they could recalculate trajectories rather quickly. They also were quite aware that once on the bomb run we could not horse around with flight changes, and flak damage was most rampant on the run. Hence, I.P. selection and approach courses were planned very carefully to minimize flak concentration, volume and accuracy. Obviously, there were some targets so heavily protected that you just had to plan to take it, no matter how ferocious the fire.

When you could see fire in the middle of the black ball from the explosion and bursting (flak) of the shells you knew they were darn close. When you heard rattles and bangs like large hail on a sheet metal roof, or stones hitting sheet metal, you knew the anti-aircraft gunners were on target, and it was "cuttin' bullet patchin'" time. Civil War soldiers coined this latter expression when fear caused their lower sphincter to contract and grab the crotch of their drawers, hence in hyperbole and exaggeration, cutting out patches. In those days, cloth patches enclosed the lead round balls that were rammed down the bores of the muzzleloaders—making a gas seal to increase pressure and consequently higher velocity of the bullet as the expanding gases from burning powder pushes the bullet down the bore.

Shrapnel from the shells could be devastating to the fuselage, wings and tails of the B-24 or any other aircraft. Small pieces pierced the relatively light aluminum alloy skins easily and large shell fragments tore holes large enough for an airman to crawl through. Some projectile pieces would cut the aluminum structural members and equipment with the ease of a shop shearing press. Few ships survived a direct hit in the main fuselage though it was not uncommon for shells to pass cleanly through some part of an aircraft without detonation.

Our sixth mission was a run to an airfield at Zwischenahner, Germany, near the Netherlands's eastern border. We bombed from an altitude of 23,300 feet in light flak, but without any damage from shrapnel.

It was standard procedure to disperse "chaff" (strands or narrow ribbons of metal foil similar to Christmas tree tinsel) to promote interference with radar transmissions of the anti-aircraft gun control systems. Waist gunners tossed the chaff out of the B-24 waist windows where their .50 caliber hand manipulated machine guns were mounted. Distribution of chaff began at the I.P. or about 15 minutes before reaching the target and continued until a few minutes after bombs away, or until flak had diminished. Chaff might also be dispensed at other times when unexpected anti-aircraft fire was encountered. Chaff was effective if all ships in the formations cooperated to produce a continuing trailing blanket of the foil strips.

The use of chaff was especially important on the bomb run when a steady course had to be maintained so the bombardier could set up and make final adjustments to the bombsight. The Norden sight was linked to the aircraft's automatic pilot so the bombardier could make flight path changes or corrections directly with the bombsight controls. In a fashion he was flying the plane.

Railroad marshalling yards at Dessau, Germany were the target of our seventh mission. We bombed from 21, 700 feet, and flak was intensive, but luckily for us, not too accurate. However, I observed one 24 shot down from another group. I saw parachutes open but couldn't get a count as the plane slowly spiraled down.

On mission number eight we trekked to Metz, France, which is located in northeast France about 25 miles from the German Border. We bombed railroad marshalling yards from a relatively low altitude of 18,500 feet. Chaff was dispersed during the bomb run, but flak was light, and we had no problems returning home.

...Winging It...

On August 24th we headed for Brunswick, Germany to strike a munitions manufacturing complex. The weather was clear and we had no problems with bombing the target from an altitude of 21,700 feet. Barrage flak was much in evidence, but we didn't take any shrapnel damage. However, seven minutes after bombs away and on course back to England the number two engine failed and our pilot feathered the prop and informed everyone we could have a problem.

Our pilot worked to stay in formation by cutting corners and switching into positions with following groups. We were okay until just one hour after losing number two engine power the number one engine quit.

We were at 18,000 feet elevation and approaching the Zuider Zee of Holland. With two engines out on one side of a B-24 you lose altitude at a significant rate, even at full power on the remaining two engines.

On the intercom the pilot and I discussed our options, which included heading for still enemy occupied Belgium and eastern France, with the potential of being shot down or crash landing, or trying to reach England over water across the North Sea. The pilot would not make a decision (as aircraft and crew commander, his responsibility), so I told him to briefly hold a steady course across the Zuider Zee at full power so I could calculate our rate of descent in relation to distance traveled. My subsequent analysis showed that we could reach the coast of England with 1000 feet of altitude remaining if the engines held up while running continuously at full power. If the engines failed or even if one engine faltered we would be in the drink, and few people survived a B-24 ditching, though all members of the crew wore life vests and the ship carried two inflatable life rafts.

Our pilot still would not make a decision, and asked me to decide. Statistically, I made the wrong decision, and Doc Woodin, Chairman of the Physics Department at MSM, would not have been proud of me, but I did not hanker to go down in flames, die in a smashup, become a prisoner of war or worse. Moreover, I was always a home boy, so I chose the higher risk shot at making it over the cold briny deep to jolly old England. All crew members had been listening on the intercom, but not one joined in the discussion of options other than the engineer-crew chief who volunteered that from his observations the remaining engines were performing well. I can only surmise that they had confidence in my calculations and optimism and prayed that it was the right decision for all.

By God's grace we made it. Air-Sea-Rescue was contacted at about 100 miles out, and at about 60 miles from the English coast a P-47 fighter plane appeared to escort us. It was encouraging and comforting to see the smiling pilot's face off our wing. Soon after, I got out of the nose position and stayed on the pilot's deck (which would have been my ditching station), smoking cigarettes and praying.

Our pilots were operating the two starboard engines at maximum rpm and manifold pressure as we neared the coast of England, on course and at 1000 feet altitude as I had estimated. The P-47 pilot directed us to a fighter plane air strip right ahead at the coast, and our pilot made an almost straight-in approach to a beautiful landing. He had completed a masterful piece of flying.

During the harrowing flight, we had tossed overboard anything on the ship that was not permanently fastened down or essential to the ship's operation—flak jackets and helmets, all machine guns and ammunition. The crew chief even hacked off heavy transformers and motors on the electrically operated top turret, and then threw out the fire ax he used to do the chopping. Reducing the plane's load may have gained us an extra 500 feet or more of altitude, so we truly were cutting it close.

We were trucked back to our base at Hethel, and scheduled for another mission on August 27th. Meanwhile, our squadron commander and operations officer took mechanics to the airbase on the coast where we landed and fixed number two engine. Then they started engine number one without any fixing, and emphatically said there was nothing wrong with it. They flew the plane back to Hethel, and then summoned our pilot to their offices and grilled him about the number one engine. Apparently it was an angry confrontation, and our pilot averred the engine had malfunctioned. More about this later.

...Bane & Nemesis...

I flew on two more missions in August. On the 27th we went deep into Germany and almost reached Berlin, but the target was so obscured by cloud cover that we had to turn back. The tops of the cumulus clouds were at 25,000 feet and the command lead had skirted us around for a while looking for possible breaks in the cloud cover. Flak was moderate, and we didn't lose any planes from our group. Plans were made to jettison our bomb loads and I had calculated distance and time to the jettison point in the North Sea. Then we were informed not to jettison. We received credit for a mission because we had penetrated to the target area.

On August 30th we flew a milk run to Fluery, France and struck a communications and transportation center of the German armies with a mixture of fragmentation and 250-pound utility bombs.

During August we had flown on 18 days—eleven missions and seven recalls or abortions. Some of the aborted flights were as time consuming and harrowing as completed missions and mostly caused by weather problems.

Weather was the bane of our life. The weather over England and Europe was monitored on a 24 hour basis by ground stations and weather aircraft, but weather is a fickle beast, and we encountered unpredicted conditions that upset plans, delayed missions, and caused cancellations of missions on the ground and in the air.

Some missions were cancelled while far into Germany, and even at the target area as noted above. With a full bomb and gasoline loading the B-24 altitude limitation was 26,000 to 27,000 feet, and for that reason there were times we couldn't climb above the clouds so visual contact could be maintained for formation flying. Fog or solid cloud cover from the ground up to 10,000 feet or more often socked in England. Competent pilots could take off in the soup on instrumentation but none could land under zero visibility in England at that time. It was rough for the Air Force weather forecasters who were often alternately praised and castigated.

During my early combat era our bombing missions were escorted by P-51, P-47 and P-38 fighter planes. They did not have fuel capacity to fly on the longer bomber flights and return to England, so bombers could be without escort at times when they were most susceptible to attack by enemy fighters. Later, the P-51s were equipped with disposable wing tanks and except for deep penetrations of Germany, they could escort us into and away from the targets before they had to turn back to head for England. In any case it was imperative that crews remain on alert for enemy stealth fighters who lay in waiting to pounce on stragglers or isolated groups of bombers.

As the ground troops advanced through France, most of the escort P-47s and P-38s were reassigned to ground strafing and bombing in troop support and destruction of enemy transportation, storage facilities and supply lines.

Enemy fighter aircraft attacks remained a constant threat, but nevertheless, anti-aircraft fire was our worst nemesis. The heavily industrialized areas of Germany were ringed by thousands of anti-aircraft batteries. You could not invade the air space over the Ruhr valley complex of cities and industries without losing planes to flak. And then in some places, just a few batteries existed, yet their shooting could be exceptionally deadly accurate. One such target existed in the Karlsruhe area of southern Germany where in one raid we lost four ships from our group to flak. It was a long haul to boot.

All crews were instructed and warned to not land with bombs aboard without prior approval. Jettison points were assigned in the North Sea or other waters for disposal of bombs when a mission was recalled. There is a humongous number of unexploded bombs in a couple of special areas of the North Sea.

Bombs were not armed until we were ready to begin the bomb runs to the target. One of the waist gunners was also the armorer, and it was his job to pull the pins so the small turbine in the nose of the bomb would be released to turn as the bomb dropped through the air, and thereby actuate the fuse that was set to detonate the bomb on impact. If the bomb cargo was composed of several small bombs, the crew chief or other crewmember might help the armorer expedite the arming process. Also, there were timed fuses that could be set to detonate the bomb in the air at prescribed altitudes, and other type fuses that were designed to detonate the bombs after they had penetrated the earth or reinforced concrete structures.

An assortment of 250, 500, 1000 and 2000 pounds bombs were available, and were selected for use in relation to tactics and the characteristics of the target. The 250-pound fragmentation bombs were used to create widespread damage to above ground structures and equipment. The 500 pounders were great for destruction and disabling of airfields and marshalling yards. 1000 and 2000 pounders were selected for increased penetration and maximum concentrated explosive forces to destroy concrete structures and other massive installations. Bomb weights and types were often varied by squadron loadings to provide diversified attacks on certain targets. The larger bombs were charged with a highly shock sensitive explosives powder called RDX, and that was the primary reason we were directed to not land with bombs in the racks unless cleared by mission command.

On one mission a B-24 could not induce a 2000-pound bomb to release from the racks. The crew worked on it all the way back from the target, and at the designated jettison point it was still hung up. Low on fuel, the pilot in desperation rejected the tower's directives, and landed at his home base. When his ship hit the runway the bomb broke loose from its hangers, dropped through the bomb bay doors and went skidding down the runway, and then headed toward the control tower. The control tower evacuated in no time flat, but the bomb didn't explode. The pilot received a severe reprimand because he could have ordered the crew to bail out over England, and then set the plane on autopilot to fly out over the North Sea to ditch when fuel was exhausted. However, this tactic could have caused loss of life too, and as often said, "All's well that ends well."

On the first and third of September we participated in two recall missions that consumed respectively, five hours and fifteen minutes and four hours of flight time. Also, on the third of September we flight checked an overhaul job on a squadron B-24. On the latter type of flights only the pilot, co-pilot, navigator and engineer were required.

On September 8th we flew mission number twelve. The target was near Karlsruhe, Germany, and bombs were dropped from 24,000 feet altitude. The target was well hit, and I could see tremendous smoke and damage as the bombs exploded, but we paid a high price for our success. The AA gunners tracked us in and out on the bomb run, laying their exploding shells on the noses of all three squadrons of our 389th group—flak was intense and accurate. I could hear the shrapnel rattle as it struck our aluminum shell, but our ship weathered the firestorm without losing any engines or controls. However, our 389th group lost four ships including one from our 566th squadron, and I watched all ten of the crew members bail out of the 566th victim. We were not all that far from Switzerland, and the weather was nice on the ground, so maybe some of them made it to that neutral country.

A high school classmate of mine bailed out of a disabled B-17 over Germany and escaped into Switzerland. Ultimately, he was repatriated home. He has a great story that ought to be published.

After the Karlsruhe sortie we received a four-day pass, and off to London we went to do the town.

...Big Ben & Piccadilly Circus...

London's Piccadilly Circus is aptly named—a sort of circus at night. Total blackout didn't hamper the street operations of the prostitutes, and vendors were hawking their wares with frequent loud calls of, "condoms, condoms." It took a while for me to comprehend some of the conversations and solicitations because of the hodgepodge of Limey accents. A cacophony of sounds and noises permeated the air, and the hustle and bustle of foot traffic was pressing all over the circle and square. I came, I saw, and conquered my temptations, "Don't you know old chap, I say."

In London I was treated to my first exposure to the "Jerry" "buzz bombs." Our bombardier and I were having dinner with two English gals in a third floor dining room of a hotel. I heard an unusual continuous roaring, rumbling and chortling-like buzzing sound in the night air outside, and noticed the girl's eyes enlarge and they began to shake and quiver. They were almost terrified as the buzz (V-1) bomb approached, and the noise was getting louder all the while. At our level above the streets we could hear the distinctive buzzy, puttering sound of the bomb carrier's engine quite well, and we knew it was close by. It passed along our street just above the top of our building and struck buildings about two blocks over. Our companions were so disturbed and upset that they just wanted to go home, so we obliged and escorted them to the "underground" (subway) by which they could readily reach their homes.

There was no question that the unpredictability of the buzz bomb's track and range struck fear and consternation into the hearts and minds of many London citizens and residents of other English cities. As I was waiting at the train station to catch a train back to Norwich and Hethel, a buzz bomb exploded near the station. Some of our crew arrived shortly thereafter with wide eyes and shocked faces—they had witnessed the destruction and death as they were headed for the station.

The bomb carriers were launched on courses directed toward London and other areas of highly concentrated populations. Flight was maintained by exhaust gas propulsion from a small pulse-jet engine—similar to early aircraft pulse jet engines. Small stubby wings provided lift to carry the bomb laden craft on a glide path after launching. With limited thrust and lift its speed was low and range was only about 100 miles or less. The craft was not flight controlled after launching and the flight path altitude decreased from a relatively low launching elevation to about tree top level before the engine fuel was exhausted and the rig nosed down to crash. When you heard the engine cut out, you knew it would drop quickly and the bomb would explode on impact. Some did not explode and the British recovered parts for study.

The buzz bomb was ineffective as a logistical weapon of destruction, but it certainly had a marked adverse psychological impact on the British civilians.

I witnessed one buzz bomb pass by our base, but it landed and exploded in a nearby farmer's field with no damage other than leaving a hole to be avoided or filled in. The craft didn't have a target guidance system and the Germans just launched them on random courses at times.

During my London outing I was in my hotel room one evening, and about midnight I heard pounding on my door, and then, "Navigator, let us in." I recognized the voices of two of our enlisted crewmen, and let them in. They were out-of-breath from rushing from their room to my room to escape U.S. military police (MPs) that were on their way upstairs. They were two excited and nervous flyers.

The two frolicking airmen had been partying in their room with two English women when one of the gals proudly informed our boys that she had an American Indian boyfriend. Turns out the Indian was an American Negro G.I., and one of the crewman was a southern "Cracker" who immediately bopped the garrulous gal as the light dawned. She had run outside their room and begun screaming for the MPs.

The crewmen stayed in my room for a half hour, and then I reconnoitered to see that the coast was clear, and they departed. We heard nothing further about the incident, and I expect the MPs had seen it all before, and did not make any great effort to find the culprits.

A fairly decent meal could be gotten at London's better restaurants, but the menus were limited, and meats were scarce. Everything was rationed and chefs were more scroungers and connivers than cooks. There was a famous U.S. subsidized mess in London (can't remember the name) where any American military person could eat at reasonable prices, and the food was excellent. They enforced a strict rule that you ate everything you took, and warned you before participation, that if you ignored the rules, you would be fined and reprimanded, and notations of the violations would go in your records.

...Flying for Patton...

Returning from London on the evening of September 12th we found our crew listed on the bulletin board— scheduled for a mission the following morning. We flew our 13th mission on the 13th of September without any qualms on my part, though a couple of crewmen shyly asked if we knew what day it was. Our target was a munitions factory at Ulm, Germany, and we bombed from 22,000 feet altitude. Flak was ubiquitous but moderate in concentration, and I wore my flak jacket and helmet during all periods of flak exposure. Damage to our ship was light, the target was well hit and all in all it was a good day. So much for the 13th of September. Of course it wasn't Friday the 13th.

Activity in the 8th A.F. slowed considerably in September, as General Patton and his army was moving so well and fast that the need for destruction of enemy rail yards and other support facilities was not as important. We logged some flight time by checking out overhauled aircraft. And then suddenly, Patton's charge slowed because he was out running his fuel supply chain, and tanks and armored vehicles were out of gasoline.

The Second Division of the Eighth A.F. cranked up their B-24s to haul some fuel to Patton. Large tanks were installed in the bomb racks area so we could haul 2000 gallons of gasoline.

On September 21st we took off with a load of gasoline under layered but scattered cloud cover. Nearing the Belgian coast we climbed to 8000 feet altitude to avoid small arms fire in some still enemy occupied areas. As we moved into Allied Forces territory we let down to 3000 feet, and then approached our destination at 2000 feet altitude. We landed at a U.S. Air Force fighter plane base close by St.Dizier, France. It was late in the afternoon by the time our cargo of gasoline was unloaded, and we decided to stay over night— sleeping in the B-24 and on the ground near the aircraft.

We walked into St.Dizier that afternoon, and there was some activity at a bar, but not much to drink. It was the first time I had been on French ground. St.Dizier was small with likely only 1500 population before the scarring of war. Street toilets were still operative and the copilot took a picture of me standing inside the toilet enclosure, where only my feet were displayed through the opening around the bottom of the walls.

We were warned to stay out of town after dark. This area, though liberated, was not considered safe at all times because of possible infiltration by the enemy. There were six of us on this journey; pilot, co-pilot, crew chief, radio operator, a first lieutenant from our group intelligence branch who had come along for the ride and observation of the cargo mission and myself, the navigator.

K-rations were provided for the cargo flights, and that is all we got to eat. A P-47 fighter-bomber group was based at the airfield where we delivered the gasoline. Our pilot walked over to their headquarters tent and asked if we could eat with them, and they said no. They probably thought we were fat cats since we were based in England. They offered no explanations or apologies like perhaps they might be short on rations. Little did they know, or would have believed, that our English mess was not equal to their field rations.

I slept pretty well in my clothes and rolled in a blanket on the ground with an extra jacket over me. I could have used another blanket in the cool of the morning hours. I was up early before sunrise. The pilot was sleeping in the nose of the ship with his head on a floor plate window and with legs stretched out in the access alley—probably the best by far of any place to sleep in the plane. I rudely awakened him by thumping on the window from outside, and he greeted me with a snarl, but he didn't go back to sleep. Anyway, we got an early start back to England.

Our return trip was uneventful. We flew at only 2000 to 3000 feet altitude, and the ground was visible most of the route. I could see the vestiges of the old trenches from World War I in France and Belgium, plus glimpses of the remnants of the Maginot line.

We consumed about as much gasoline on the cargo flight as we hauled in to Patton, but efficiency was never a matter of much consideration in the view of the exigencies of war.

...The Kassel Mission...

On the 23rd of September, the day after returning from France, we flew a recall mission. On September 27th we bombed engine and precision tooling factories at Kassel, Germany from an altitude of 22,200 feet. In and out to the target, flak was evident but scattered, and our 389th Group survived without any significant damage. However, German fighter planes struck hard and in force at the 445th Group of our wing and a total of 27 B-24s out of the group of 37 were lost in the air. Three ships crash-landed in Allied territory in

Europe. Only four ships of the 445th got back to their England bases and one crashed near Tibenham. Two reached the RAF emergency landing strip at Manston, England. 236 airmen were missing in action (MIA) and 112 killed in action.

One flight of ME-109s and FW-190s barreled straight through our group in one firing pass, but then went on to join other flights that were clobbering the 445th. They wheeled through our group so quickly that our gunners didn't get off a shot. I saw one derisive daredevil do a snap roll as he bored through the bomber formation. Our P-51 escort fighters heard the bomber distress calls and ultimately got to the battle area to claim at least 18 kills of the German attackers.

The 445th had turned away from the other groups at or near the I.P. and appeared to head toward a different target. They were 40 miles from us when the mass of German fighters hit them. Apparently, there was confusion and errors in target identification or other misinterpretations by the navigators and command pilots. There is yet today debate and contention among survivors and observers about just what happened. It is the most outstanding example of the strategy of the Luftwaffe to strike individual ships or formations that strayed from the cover and defensive power of large and concentrated bomber formations.

It was the highest loss of aircraft and personnel from a single group in one mission during the air wars. Much information is available about this disaster through the Kassel Mission Historical Society (e-mail: kmhs@kasselmission.com).

As we returned to the Second Division area near Norwich we observed flares from B-24s in the air and landing at their bases—signaling for emergency landings and wounded men aboard. It was almost discomfiting to accept the good fortunes of the 389th this day after hearing some of the tragic and gory details of the 445th demise and also damage and grief sustained to a lesser degree by other groups. A 20 mm shell decapitated one co-pilot—I could close my eyes and imagine the blood running down into the navigator's station in the nose.

...R & R...

October opened quietly. On October 2nd we flew a short two-hour night flight over England. We were told it was for practice, but no realistic motive was disclosed. I stuck my nose in the CRT of the GEE box and kept it there most of the flight—taking position fixes one after the other. I sure did not want to get lost or shot down over England by English gladiators.

We were idled until October 9th when we flew our 15th mission. Our primary target was Koblenz, Germany on the Rhine River and towards Wiesbaden. We encountered weather problems and had to bomb the secondary target nearby from an altitude of 22.000 feet. In addition to weather complications, another group had flown through our group, and the confusion had contributed to our bypassing the primary target.

With all the milling around, a lot of AA batteries were quite active, but we didn't think we had taken any serious flak damage. However, after we returned to our base in England and the pilot was on the downwind leg prior to landing approach he put on the flaps, and only one side went down. The other side had been damaged by shrapnel and wouldn't respond. And horror of horrors, the down flap would not respond to the up control.

It was rough flying for a while as the harried pilot wrestled with controls, and the frantic co-pilot radioed emergency conditions and announced preparations for a crash landing. I climbed on the flight deck behind the pilots in readiness for a crash landing while other crewmembers prepared for a big slam. God was with us and the pilot got the down flap up. The pilot landed without flaps at 150 miles m.p.h. The brakes and tires were smoking and we ended up in the grass about 100 feet beyond the runway surfacing without any major damage to the 24. We were thankful that the brakes worked well. We were a bit shook, and kissed the grass.

On the 11th of October, our pilot aborted our plane from a mission because of mechanical problems that in my mind were of questionable nature, and I think squadron operations thought so too. Our operations officers perhaps thought our pilot was getting too edgy. Anyway, we were shuttled off for rest and recreation (R&R).

We spent a week at a place which had been an estate and then converted to R & R use by war-weary airmen. I didn't remember the name of the hostelry but thought it was located Southwest of London. In recent correspondence with Kelsey McMillan, Editor and Group Historian of the 389th Bomb Group News she sent information showing our travel orders stated Moulsford Manor due West of London. The AAF managed the operation with assistance from the Red Cross. It was a nice interlude for a while with great rooms and the only decent food I'd consumed in a long time. Our pilots and crew thought it was just the ticket, but I did not think I really needed such care as yet. And to boot, I got an excruciating toothache one day late in the afternoon, and had to take two aspirins every four hours all night to endure the pain.

Next morning, I was hauled over to an American air base with a resident dentist. The tooth was abscessed and had to be extracted. This bad tooth was jammed against another front upper tooth, which would have to be pulled later in 1948 (see "Dental Dents" in Chapter 12).

After we returned to the 389th. from R & R we found that our squadron and group were flying combat missions, but our crew was not being scheduled. Then, we were assigned to make night flights over England. Strict flight plans were observed as we simply flew from one checkpoint to the other, and I never knew the objectives of our night flying. The pilot claimed he had no knowledge of the administrative objectives and was just following orders. As mentioned earlier, night flying over England was extra hard and stressful work for me. Our pilot never complained and I believed he preferred the night flying to combat missions.

...Change of Venue...

The pilot of our crew and I had not had any personal conflicts until after we started the night flying bit, and even then, our differences had no direct relation to flying. However, he had changed. He told stories of having served in the Army at Casablanca in Africa, and we knew it was fiction. He was in my age bracket and couldn't have fit that experience into his time frame from my assessment.

One evening I mentioned that I needed a shower, but the boiler room was locked, and consequently, no available hot water. Our pilot said he could get me in to start the hot water heater, and showed me a key ring holding several lock picks. I shook my head, no thanks.

My pilot and I wore the same size hat. Around the base we mostly wore the small so-called "cunt" (derivation is likely traceable to the imagination of a World War I G.I. of Ozark or Appalachian lineage—this word is defined in Vance Randolph's "Down in the Holler") hats. He took a liking to my "cunt" hat and offered to trade his for mine. I liked his hat just as well and said, "Sure, why not?" And we swapped hats. I really saw little if any difference in the hats.

Lo and behold, a day later, my pilot confronted me and accused me of stealing his hat! I was astonished and perturbed. I offered to exchange hats, and he vehemently denied having my hat! The situation was bizarre, and he was unfathomable to me. The co-pilot who had witnessed our exchange of hats was present during the confrontation and was not inclined to get involved, and rightly so, but I could see he was aghast.

I was not going to be intimidated, though the pilot was a lanky six-footer, and I informed him he was crazy, and to go fly a kite. He bickered and chastised me for a couple of days until one evening, as I was sitting on the john at the officer's club, he pounded on the door of the stall and threatened me with violence. I told him that as soon as I was done with my defecation, I would be out and knock some out of him if he didn't have sense enough to leave me alone. I warned him that I intended to defend myself vigorously. He was not there when I cautiously exited the stall and I didn't see him in the club. He did not bother me again.

The next day I went to the squadron commander and told him I wanted to be assigned to another crew. Of course, the first response from the major and his operations officer who immediately tuned in, was why? I didn't tell them the weird and sordid story—just said that the pilot and I had become personally incompatible, and I would not fly with him anymore unless ordered to do so. Their eyes lit up, and they wanted to know if it was because of his flying. His relations with the op manager had been frosty since he had testily rebuked the captain for adamantly telling him there was nothing wrong with the number one engine that quit on our harrowing two-engine flight across the North Sea (see "Winging It").

Our pilot had received the Distinguished Flying Cross (DFC) for heroic flying on the foregoing mission. I think squadron operations resented his decoration because they believed there was pilot error involved in the engine conk out, and I believed that myself. Moreover, my suspicions were buttressed by the fact the crew chief got drunk one evening, sought me out and confided that it was possible he had forgotten to switch gas tanks to keep fuel flowing to that engine, and it may have quit simply because of lack of fuel. I don't think the crew chief told anyone else, and neither did I because we had no proof of dereliction of duty. The pilot had not tried to restart the dead engine.

At the same time the crew chief confessed to me that the reason no one heard from him on the intercom while we were in the combat zone was that he couldn't talk—he was too scared. He was about my age and also manned the top gun turret, which was a scary position with its broad expansive view, yet with no way to see action below. I never violated his confidences—I could empathize with him.

I didn't believe our pilot deserved the DFC either, but for a different reason—by his dereliction he forced me to make a critical decision that by odds was wrong, and denied the responsibilities of a ship captain. I did not tell operations about that either, but in retrospect perhaps I was derelict for not doing so. I told them he was a very competent flyer of the B-24 (very true), but we had irrevocable personal differences. I knew they were skeptical, being men of experience in personnel relations under trying circumstances, but they didn't quibble and said, "You are, as of now, off his crew," and they seemed to relish saying so.

Operations promptly slapped my former pilot and crew back on combat status, and scheduled them for a mission the next morning. They did not tell the pilot I was off the crew until that morning. He found out with great surprise and anger when awakened for the mission. When he asked if they had awakened his navigator and bombardier, he heard, "You ain't got no navigator, no more," and almost gleefully, it was reported.

While waiting for reassignment I came down with a miserable head cold, and went to the flight surgeon for some pills to ease the discomfort, and then he confined me to the infirmary for observation, and in spite of my protestations. After three days of fretting and farting around in the infirmary, I convinced the doctor to let me out the next day.

That last day while sitting on my cot and reading before getting my release slip, I heard something unusual, and looking up, saw my former pilot entering the open dormitory-like ward, all disheveled, still wearing his flight helmet with radio cups, and dragging a loosely bundled up parachute.

While assembling over England for a mission, his plane and another B-24 of our group had a mid-air collision, and he was the only survivor from his crew. He said the other plane came up under his left wing, and the first he knew of trouble was when he heard the other plane's props bite into his left wing. He said his left wing fell away, tearing off the canopy on his side of the cockpit. When he reached down to unbuckle his seat belt, he just fell out and then parachuted to safety. He was wearing a backpack parachute.

Only the radio operator and the bombardier of the other plane got out alive. The bombardier was wearing a backpack chute. I went to interview him, and he said he had squeezed through an unbelievably small jagged hole that had been ripped in a bomb bay door by debris from the collision. Then and there, I resolved to always wear a backpack chute when flying, though it was heavy and fatiguing to wear for long hours, especially while standing and moving around in the nose of the B-24.

Previously, like many crewmen, I carried the portable chest pack parachute that had to be snapped to your harness at your chest before jumping. We wore the relatively lightweight harness all the time and stashed the packed chute near our workstation. It worked well and could be quickly snapped on under normal conditions, but if you were in a tumbling, twisting fuselage, it would not be easy to snap on, and retrieval could be difficult or perhaps impossible. I suspect that is what happened to several of the crewmen on the colliding B-24s.

The radio operator managed to get out the top hatch of the aircraft and just in time to open his chute at 300 feet altitude. His story was related in a copy of a formal USAF statement obtained through the courtesy of Shiela Berube of O'Fallon, Missouri who had a cousin on the crew of this ship named "Earthquake McGoon." He said the engineer could not find his snap-on chute and they had planned to both ride his chute but only one could get through the hatch at a time and when he got through the hatch it closed on his foot. As he jerked his foot he fell away.

I prevailed on the doctor to let me out immediately after the mid-air collision event because I knew the co-pilot of my former crew had a brother stationed in England with AAF ground forces, and I wanted to talk to our squadron commander about that. I told the major that I knew the brother and his location. The major immediately picked up the phone and made arrangements with the brother's unit to bring him to our base.

Funerals were held regularly for deceased airmen and other military personnel in England, and within two days I was with a small group headed to the U.S. cemetery at Cambridge, England to attend last rites for a mass burial, which included the casualties from the mid-air collision.

I was riding in the back of a small canvas enclosed truck bed with an intelligence officer who had flown with my previous crew, and a couple of friends of the deceased crew members. Our Protestant chaplain and Father Beck from our base rode in front with the driver. Along the way, M.P.s stopped the driver for some minor infraction, and would have let us be on our way quickly if Father Beck had not jumped out to berate the M.P.s for stopping a funeral procession. I think the M.P.s would have dragged us down to their station if the Protestant chaplain had not intervened by getting Beck back inside the truck cab, and then imploring and begging the M.P.s to let us proceed on our sorrowful journey. They relented, but we barely made it in time for the funeral.

Forty some flag-draped coffins were lined up side-by-side over a large opened graves site. Military rites were conducted with Catholic, Protestant and Jewish clergy participation. Flags were presented to English wives of a few of the deceased.

Later, I arranged for some photos of the Cambridge cemetery and sent them to the mother of my former co-pilot. She and I corresponded for several years after, but I never made it to Redding, California to see her.

After my former pilot entered the infirmary, I saw him on the base only once again, and I heard that later he was reassigned to Stateside, U.S.A. The Christmas after World War II ended, I received a card from him, but I did not respond. Truth is sometimes truly stranger than fiction.

In early November I was assigned to a crew that had a crackerjack bombardier, but needed a navigator to become a lead crew.

Fighting Men

...Leading the Pack...

Sylvester P. Bergman was the pilot of my new crew, and his crew also had flown 15 missions. "Berg" was 26, and a seasoned topnotch pilot—steady, calm, easy going but brooked no nonsense, a fine leader and commander. I don't think we ever exchanged a cross word. Oral Laws was the co-pilot and about my age. He had trained to be a fighter pilot, but had some problems that resulted in his graduating as a flight officer. "Berg" was good for him, and Oral became a very able pilot of the big birds. However, he retained some of the reckless spirit.

We were returning in formation from a mission, and Oral was flying the ship. He and the co-pilot on his right wing decided to see how tight a formation they could fly. I tolerated their jacking around for a while but finally couldn't stand it any more, and then called Oral on the intercom and told him that I hadn't survived German flak so far to have my life jeopardized by slaphappy pilots. Nothing changed, and the wing tips drew closer together, if anything. I came back to him on the intercom and said, "Damn it, cut it out, or I'll report you to operations." It was the only time that I ever chastised or threatened a fellow crewman, but my reaction restored sanity to his flying. All was quiet on the intercom after my blast—I thought most of the crew was glad I intervened. Berg didn't say a word to me, but I'm sure he took charge of the situation, and nothing like that occurred again.

I moved into quarters occupied by Bergman, Laws and our bombardier, Steve Beno, plus similar officers from two other crews, except the other crews didn't have bombardiers, and flew wing only. This barracks was just a building with one open room and a small cast iron stove plump in the middle. Our bunks were portable G.I. fold up canvas cots, and sthe beds were arranged around the inner perimeter, parallel with the sides and ends.

Our bedding added up to a mattress pad, two G.I. wool blankets, a G.I. comforter and sheets, if you could wrangle the latter. The bedding was adequate for the damp, cool and raunchy winter weather until the Battle of the Bulge in Germany when our A.F. command ordered each of us to give up one blanket to be sent to ground troops in Europe. I didn't mind, and when colder weather set in, I spread my dress overcoat over the one blanket and comforter. Fuel was not always available for the stove.

Laws and one of the co-pilots in the room were perennial horse-a-rounders, and one evening they dropped some flare cartridges in the stove while it contained hot coals. When the shells exploded, the stove door blew off, the stove rattled and shook, and red and green fireballs flew around the room along with dust and smoke. With considerable chastising and cussing, the rest of us dampened their spirits for a while.

One night we were all in bed with lights out. My cot was located between Laws and the other playful co-pilot. They got into a lighted match tossing fight, and most of the lighted matches were sailing over and by me. The first time I asked politely for them to cease and desist. The second time I threatened physical harm as the barrage continued. The third and last time I said nothing, but I slipped my Colt Model 1911 forty five from its shoulder holster hanging on the wall beside my cot, racked the slide and then it became so quiet you could have heard a pin drop. Never again did they horse around with me in the middle, and no one ever mentioned the incident to me. And later they nicknamed me "Happy." Perhaps they whispered "flak happy" under their breaths.

All the crew had acquired nicknames: Bergman was "Skipper" or "Pops"; Laws was "Hotte Rocks"; Stephen Beno at age 29 was the grandfather of the crew and dubbed the "Whip"; William C. Robertson, the engineer, answered to "Shorty"; the armorer and waist gunner, Clinton L.

Culley, responded to "Clem"; Thomas D. Hyde, the nose gunner was known as "Old Soljer"; waist gunner George Loeser was appropriately heralded as "Baldy"; Tail gunner Calvin E. Scarbrough rated "Burr Head" and radio operator, Howard W. Jeffrey Jr. was accorded the moniker "Daddy Dit". A great crew indeed. I am much indebted to Howard Jeffrey, also known as "Jeff" and "Bink" for refreshing my memory of these nicknames with his discourses in his "Logge of Ye Old Static Chaser." Actually, I think Jeff was instrumental in the development of some of these nicknames.

The crew had begun training for lead crew status before I joined them because they had been promised a navigator at the time I quit my original crew, and I had been delayed by the hospital stay and funeral arrangements.

I began training with them on November 9, 1944, and we practiced bomb runs. At the close of this practice we ran into icing and landed in a snowstorm. Thereafter, we made practice runs any day the weather was reasonably cooperative through November and in to December.

Then on December 6th the 389th group was called to make a maximum effort and 41 planes were mustered to strike a viaduct at Minden, Germany. We cleared the runway at dawn and flew as deputy lead. We bombed successfully from 23,000 feet, and we were on oxygen for four and one half hours. No flak problems, but it was a long haul, and number four engine cut out on approach to our base because of lack of fuel.

We went back to practicing for lead crew status. Earlier, the squadron navigator (administrative) had recommended me for GH training, and I had taken some ground school GH indoctrination.

GH was an improved type of the English GEE navigation system, but with longer-range capabilities. As the Allied armies had moved forward through France, GH transmission stations had been established in secured positions. GH was so accurate that under favorable receiving conditions, one could pinpoint the aircraft's geographic position, enabling bombing through cloud cover. Previously, any bombing through cloud cover had to be done by radar fixes, and accuracy was poor. Consequently, radar (we called it "Mickey") bombing was used mainly as a saturation bombing technique. However, radar had served well as a means of establishing aircraft position when the ground was obscured by cloud cover and during night flying. Of course it was subject at times to jamming by the enemy.

Before we could get in a GH practice mission we flew with our 389th Group to strike a two-span bridge across the Rhine River at Karlsruhe, Germany. We bombed from 22,000 feet, and the flak was as intense as during my twelfth mission to Karlsruhe. However, 16 squadrons preceded us while on their way to another target in the area, and the chaff they dispersed helped reduce the accuracy of AA guns as we arrived at out target. Our group still lost one ship to flak, but our ship took only one hole in the tail, and the tail turret gunner was unaware that shrapnel almost got him. Karlsruhe was a deep penetration, and we carried 2500 gallons of gasoline at takeoff and two 2000-pound bombs. We were flying the "Little Gramper III." I flew in "Little Gramper Jr." on my first combat mission, so it is obvious that the longevity of B-24s was not too great—the Gramper family had run through four generations in short order.

No rest for the wicked (weary, maybe?) they say, and next morning we took off in the fog on our 18th mission. Our primary target was Hanau, Germany, but instead we hit a railroad marshalling yard at Friedberg from 22,000 feet altitude. The 88mm and 105mm gunners were well tuned and flak was everywhere. It was a Second Wing effort, and one plane was lost from each group (389th, 445th and 453rd). No chutes emerged from the distressed ship of our 389th, and it spiraled down rapidly. We flew deputy lead for the 566th squadron and our flak damage was light.

On December 14th we flew our first GH lead practice, and made seven GH practice bomb runs. When using GH navigation the navigator set up the bomb run and dropped the bombs.

We flew our 19th mission on December 19th! We were scheduled to fly deputy lead, but one engine on our first assigned ship developed an erratic r.p.m, and after changing planes we were delayed getting into formation. So, when we caught up to our squadron formation we had to fly the slot or bucket position. We bombed a railroad marshalling yard at Ehrang, Germany from an altitude of 21,700 feet. Flak was scattered and no planes were lost from our group.

On return to England our base was closed by weather, and we diverted to St. Mawgam, England. Next day we flew to Hethel and landed at 1:30 p.m. while visibility was only 700 yards.

On the 23rd of December we went up for another GH training session. My instructor said I was doing great, but then I took him aside after landing, and began asking him some questions that I had not thought much about before. Would I continue to be a lead navigator with my own crew if I became a GH specialist? The answer was no—I would likely be leading a wing on GH missions, and could be assigned at times to a crew in any one of several groups, either in our wing or loaned to the first or third wings—much depended on how I performed. Then I persisted further, "With all that responsibility will I be eligible for promotion to a captain's rank?" Again, the answer was no.

A navigator could make captain only by serving also as the administrative squadron navigator, and you probably guessed it—that job was handed down from buddy to buddy (politics in all stations of life) and I already knew the anointed one when a replacement came due in our squadron. Moreover, I wouldn't fly as often as a GH leader, and the completion of my allotted 30 missions would be delayed.

As mentioned earlier the Norden bombsight was a marvelous piece of machinery and in the hands of a competent bombardier could do a bang up job of guiding the bombs to the target. Therefore, visual bombing with the Norden was the preferred choice when weather allowed. Ultimately, GH would develop till it was equally worthy.

The upshot of it all was that I said no thanks; I'd rather stay with my own crew. I had been promoted to First Lieutenant, and apparently in today's vernacular, had hit my glass ceiling. That was that and I continued with Bergman and crew as a lead navigator for visual bombing. I never regretted my decision. I never saw any statistics, but I'd wager that more wing and group lead ships were shot down than planes in any other position.

My decision to forego GH lead navigation was fortuitous in another respect. When the Korean War cranked up, Reserve Air Force navigators were being recalled right and left, but only navigators with GH experience. By then, I was married with one child, and with no desire to navigate an attack bomber over Korean battle zones. A chemist at the organization where I worked at this time was a former GH navigator and was called to report for active duty. He seemed quite healthy when we played cribbage during our lunch periods, but somehow he didn't pass his physical at induction time. Later he would reveal how he managed not to pass.

We flew our 20th mission on Christmas Eve day. The 8th AF put up the greatest number of heavies ever, and several targets were involved. Our 389th Group put up 51 planes (normal was 33 to 36), and our target was at Cochen, Germany. However the lead ship screwed up on an attempt at the scheduled bomb run. They claimed that the Norden bombsight had frozen up, but I knew differently—they had not picked up the target because they had taken us off course. So, they called for our crew as the deputy lead to take over the lead and make a run for the secondary target.

I had anticipated what was coming because I knew they were lost, and I was scrambling to pick a checkpoint for a heading to the secondary. On this trip I was sitting at the radar station behind the pilots since it was a better place to work and I had an observation window near me. Snow covered the German landscape, and pilotage navigation was not easy. Later I regretted that I had not stayed in the nose where I had an observation window on both sides of the

304

plane. With all my bustling around, my oxygen hose had become disconnected and I wasn't aware of it until the co-pilot hollered at me. Bergman claimed that when he asked me where we were that I replied, "I don't know and I don't give a damn," but I really don't remember saying that. Oxygen deficiency can quickly discombobulate the mind.

Meanwhile, with all the ruckus, our bombardier, Beno had gotten real nervous while wondering if we would get hit by enemy fighters during our wandering around, and he told Berg that he had located a target, and to switch the ship to automatic pilot so he could take over with the Norden bombsight. The bomb bay doors were opened and Beno was trying to line up on his target of opportunity. Suddenly he corrected course rather violently, and all the elements of our squadron, including our two wingmen, were flopping all over the sky—it's a marvel we didn't precipitate a mid-air collision. We were not stabilized yet when Beno triggered our bombs away, and the other planes in our squadron dropped their bombs as they saw ours released. Beno was trying for railroad marshalling yards in a small German city named Kirn and located in a narrow valley. As bombs dropped from our struggling, heaving formation in disarray and wobbling over the target, they walked up and down the slopes on both sides of the valley and across the city. The unlucky residents of Kirn couldn't have known what direction they should run or hide. It appeared that only a few of the 500 pounders struck the rail yards.

After we landed back at Hethel, two different navigators ran up to me and asked, "What the hell did we bomb?" I wondered what some of the others recorded in their logs.

Operations was disappointed with Beno's bombing, but it really was my fault for the turmoil and poor bombing performance. Nonetheless, operations were suspicious and dubious about the assigned lead crew's story of bombsight freeze up, and their criticism of our poor work was not severe. At least I didn't hear about any denigration.

Our crew celebrated my 21st birthday (December 29th) by flying mission number 21. The only candles I saw were the flashes of fire in shell bursts as we approached our target. Our target was cloud obscured Ulman, Germany, but the lead ship's "Micky" (radar) and GH support malfunctioned, and a target of opportunity, rail yards at Fuesdorf, Germany, were bombed from an altitude of 23,000 feet. Flak was accurate and didn't damage us, we thought, until our approach to landing at our home base, when numbers three and four engines cut out almost simultaneously. After landing, an examination of engine cowling discovered evidence of penetration by small fragments of shrapnel. I never learned what engine components were damaged.

We were right back at it next morning, December 30th, and took off at 6:00 a.m. from an ice-covered runway into ground fog, headed for Euskirchen, Germany. We bombed a viaduct and railroad yards from an altitude of 22,800 feet, and the outside temperature was minus 31 degrees Fahrenheit. No major problems developed over Europe, but on return to England a hydraulic pump failed and Berg had to make two passes to get the wheels down to land at our base.

...Delectable Doris...

B-24 R+ had been assigned to us as our regular ship during lead crew training, but we had been flying other 24s on missions because of repairs and maintenance scheduling for R+. A beautiful painting of a voluptuous nude girl was prominently displayed on the nose of R+. I never knew the very credible artist or the equally adept author of this ship's name, "Delectable Doris." "Doris" was popular and other pilots would vie to fly her.

Doris was back in our custody for our 23rd mission on New Year's Day, 1945. On the flight line before dawn, we didn't get airborne until 8:25 a.m. because of various delays in preparation of other groups for the mission. A railroad viaduct was bombed from an altitude of 22,300 feet and the outside temperature was minus 32 degrees Fahrenheit. The target was near Neuwied, Germany on the Rhine River.

306

Our weather briefings had specifically predicted a tail wind on the bomb run, and the flight course and approach had been designed to take advantage of the added speed to be derived from this wind. However, before reaching the I.P. I had determined that wind velocities were of hurricane caliber and as high as 130 knots—now, that is really whooping it up. We made the bomb run as plotted, and by my calculations our ground speed was only 92 knots (nautical miles, or about 106 statute miles per hour). The weather forecast of wind direction was exactly 180 degrees off! Our bomb run was made into a head wind of 130 knots.

Flak was accurate, and at our low ground speed, the AA gunners quickly honed in on us. Everyone in our group took hits, but fortunately no planes were lost. I could see the fire in the shell bursts and endured some "bullet patchin' cuttin' time" after we took a shrapnel hole in the nose too close to me for comfort.

Bucking the headwinds had caused excess consumption of gasoline, and we landed at a Royal Air Force (British) base at Cambrai-Epinoy, France to refuel. Actually, "Berg" had radioed an R.A.F. base in Belgium just on the border of France, and gotten permission to land! I had given him a heading to that base and then got out of the nose to prepare for landing. It was quite hazy in the area, and he picked up what he thought was the designated Belgium base; but surprise, it was the Cambrai base. I knew we were taking more time than I estimated to reach the Belgium base, but the bases were only a few miles apart. The Cambrai base was certainly surprised, but cordial enough. They refueled us and a bit chagrinned crew promptly took off for England. Jeffrey (radio operator) sent coded messages to Air Watch that we were coming in over the channel to England. To forestall any AA fire the crew fired colors of the day with the Very pistols as we passed near a convoy of ships in the channel.

We took off in "Doris" at dawn in a driving sleet storm to fly our mission number 24. Over Germany the weather cleared, and we bombed a railroad junction and yards at Neustadt from 23,000 feet altitude. The ground was snow covered and our outside temperature was minus 45 degrees Fahrenheit. Conditions were excellent for visual bombing, and we led the low-left squadron with Beno cuddling the Norden bombsight. He made excellent hits on the target, and we received a lead crew commendation.

The trim tabs on "Doris" froze up, and the cables broke as we returned to our base in England. Red flares were fired off to signal preparation for an emergency landing, but "Berg" managed to bring us in without incident.

Much bad weather prevailed in early January. On January 8th after taking off in a snowstorm we got within 40 miles of our target at Neuerberg but had to turn back because the cloud cover extended to over 26,000 feet which was the practical altitude limit for a bomb laden B-24…six hours of laborious flight time wasted.

We didn't fly again until January 14th when we took "Doris" to Brunswick, Germany. Our target was an ultra high priority oil storage depot, and our route in took us across the North Sea, almost to Denmark before turning southeast into Germany, and making a feint toward Berlin. Then we turned west to the I.P. point and got on the bomb run to drop 12 demolition 500 pounders from an altitude of 24,000 feet. Flak was all around us, but we survived without damage to "Doris" or ourselves. At the target we were only 40 miles from Berlin, which was always well defended, not only with AA fire but also by ME-109 and FW-190 fighters (German Messerschmitt and Foche Wulfe fighters).

Enemy fighters didn't hit us on this foray because of great protection for the 2nd Division by six groups of P-51 escort fighters. However, our P-51s had a field day with the would-be attackers, and bagged 190 Jerry fighter craft that were trying to intercept us. The P-51s could range deep into Germany by using disposable wing fuel tanks. Usually, the fuel in the wing tanks was consumed first on the route into Germany, and then the empty tanks were jettisoned before engaging the Jerry fighter planes. Often some of the P-51s would hit the deck and strafe the Jerry airfields before streaking home. They always hoped to catch aircrft in takeoff mode.

The Luftwaffe had been flying some of their ME-163 rocket engine craft and ME-262 jets since November 1944, but those craft were limited to short ranges because of low fuel carrying capacity and high fuel consumption. They waited in seclusion at highly camouflaged airstrips so they could spurt up and jump lagging and crippled bombers, or slip in behind the P-51s. They simply hit and ran. They could easily out-maneuver and out-distance the P-51s for a short while. On two different occasions I saw a ME-262 shoot a P-51down, and then zip away before other P-51s could get near the speedy bandit.

No problems were encountered on our return flight to England, but our briefings included warnings that enemy intruders might follow us back to base, and we were glad to see replacement fighter escort in the air on our return.

The bad weather continued, and we didn't fly again until January 28th when we sallied forth on our 26th mission. It was a "Heller" from the beginning. We took off predawn from an icy runway and into soup, which was solid from the ground up to 10,000 feet. When we broke out of the cloud cover the sun was shining brightly and B-24s were all over the sky trying to get into formation. Half of our 389th Group did not get off the ground, and the remnants still flying joined to form two squadrons.

We invaded the Ruhr Industrial Valley to strike a benzol plant at Dortmund. Our course took us out across the North Sea, then over the Zuider Zee in Holland before heading south into Germany east of the Ruhr. It was a diversionary tactic that wasn't too effective. The industrialized Ruhr Valley contained the heaviest concentration of anti-aircraft batteries in the world, and they were ready for us, as we turned westward to drive to the target. We bombed visually under cloud cover at only 22,400 feet altitude, and 105mm flak was intense, accurate and ate us up.

We flew deputy lead off the right wing of the 566th squadron leader. At bombs away, the lead ship and his left wingman were shot out of the formation and we took over the lead position.

The pilot of the 453rd Group lead was killed by flak, but the co-pilot got the crew home safely. The lead plane of the 445th Group landed on the continent. Tuning into the VHF radio, I could hear myriad laments of many pilots and co-pilots as they battled the controls of shot-up aircraft, took toll of killed and wounded, and in some cases contemplating abandonment of ships.

A direct flak hit took off the end of the right wing of Berthelsen's ship and the crew bailed out. Berthelsen and co-pilot Riggles were berthed in our barracks, and it was a shock for us to come back to empty bunks in our quarters that night. Later, we heard that Berthelsen, Riggles, Winters the tail gunner, Bill Crum the nose gunner, Holorege the radio operator and De Falco the radar operator for counter measures were taken prisoners-of-war, but German civilians killed the rest of the crew with pitchforks.

Our ship suffered holes in numbers one and two engines, hydraulic lines and all over the fuselage, but none of the crew was injured and none of the engines failed.

To cap things off we had to land in a snow shower and on a slippery runway at our base in England.

...Only One in Step...

It was back to Dortmund the very next day—and it would be almost like déjà vu. We were in the air by 7:30 a.m. and on our 27th mission. Our secondary target was at Hamm, located about 30 miles northeast of Dortmund. We flew south and east of Hamm as we entered Germany. After we were 40 miles south of Hamm, we turned north-northeast to make our bomb run. Cloud cover below us was solid cumulus, and the wing and group leads were navigating by "Mickey" (radar) and planned to saturate bomb by radar calculations. We were too far in to use GH because the Germans were jamming it. I could navigate only by dead reckoning, and my plotting showed that the wing leader was heading for the secondary target at Hamm. All at once, our group leader swung us away from the wing formation and we headed for the assigned target at Dortmund in the dreaded Ruhr Valley.

A lot of chatter broke out between the wing commander and group lead pilots. The wing leader said he was on course to Dortmund, but our group lead disagreed. Our group lead pilot said his navigator was right and he was sticking with his navigation.

Our ship was deputy lead, and I told Berg I thought our group lead navigator was correct, though I had no radar for corroboration of my dead reckoning. When we got to the target area at only 22,000 feet altitude, we received confirmation that we were in the Ruhr by our reception from the Jerry AA gunners—they shot the hell out of us again. Meanwhile, the rest of the wing was way off to the East, merrily bombing Hamm, maybe.

Instead of "Doris", which was under repair because of damage on the previous day's mission, we were flying J+, and it was covered with flak holes except for the nose of the fuselage. As I watched the flak bursts it appeared that the shells were bursting right on our nose, and I really expected to be blown off with the nose at any moment. I was mesmerized and at the same time literally paralyzed with fear. I could feel and hear the thumps of the shell bursts and see the fire, but didn't smell the smoke from burning powder. Later, in reflection, I realized that the shrapnel was hitting just back of the nose and consequently, there was no odors of burned powder in my area.

Shells had bored through both left and right rudder structures, leaving big holes, but without exploding. A large piece of shrapnel had penetrated the fuselage between the tail gunner and the waist gunners, leaving a hole big enough for me to crawl through. Angels must have been riding with us. Not a crewmember was injured, and when we landed and saw so much flak damage, we could not believe that no engines had been knocked out, or that there were no gas leaks or failure of controls. God must have listened to me because I sure was praying in the nose, and his grace was with us. Shrapnel cut the tail gunner's oxygen hose, but he managed to patch it together while sipping oxygen from a portable tank.

At one point during the most severe period of the AA fire, I looked over and saw Beno standing stoic-like and apparently staring at nothing. With a second glance I saw white around his oxygen mask and eyes and I touched him and yelled, "What's the trouble, Steve?" He jerked about to face me and pushed his intercom mike button to choke out, "I+ just blew up." I looked out to see I+ falling in two pieces just below us. I+ was flying on our wing, and apparently had taken a direct hit in the middle and the shell explosion had blown it into two pieces. Nobody escaped from either half of the ship, and I watched the pieces dropping as far as they were visible.

Our Group commander and operations officers were waiting for the lead crews and our crew when we landed. As soon as I crawled out of the plane, they wanted to know if I thought we had bombed Dortmund. With my affirmation, they grabbed my log and charts and took off. Radar fixes made by lead planes were transcribed to my dead reckoning charts, and they concluded that our group lead indeed was right, and we had hit the correct target.

I figured the wing lead navigator got his plots to the primary and secondary targets mixed up, or maybe he didn't want to go into the Ruhr flak inferno. Anyway, much royal butt chewing ensued, but our group lead crew was not reprimanded for insubordination. Reconnaissance film taken after the mission showed that we hit the marshalling yards target pretty well, even though our group lead relied on radar fixes.

After a day of rest, we headed for the Goering steel works at Berlin. We made a pre-dawn takeoff on our 28th mission. After taking extra time to get into formation because of much cloud layering over England, we got going, and penetrated well into Germany on the road to Berlin, but then encountered too much cloudiness to maintain formations. We could not get above the clouds, and if we dropped enough to get below the clouds, it would have been tantamount to suicide, offering easy targets for flak and fighter planes. So, the mission was recalled, and we jettisoned our bombs at a designated point in the North Sea.

On return to England all bases in East Anglia had closed because of weather, and we were diverted to the York area of England, about 100 miles north-northwest of Norwich. The weather there was real bad too, and everybody was milling around in the soup, trying to land at one of three or four bases. I was on the deck and I never saw our pilots so busy.

We were flying mostly blind in the clouds, turning and watching for a hole to drop through near a runway, any runway. It was frightening with so many planes in a limited area, and all running low on fuel. Ceiling and visibility were below minimum. Finally, Berg dropped through a hole and saw a runway. He racked the ship around, made a treetop pass, and then set her down—on the wrong runway and wrong direction at Catsfoss, a base that was officially closed.

Crack-ups occurred all over the area—many landings on wrong runways and in the fields. One plane ran into a low hill and blew up. Berg's landing without damage to the aircraft and crew, and holding the ship on the runway was a remarkable piece of flying. He handled our 24 like it was a fighter plane, and it held together. I was never so glad to touch terra firma and remain unscathed. We flew back to our base at Hethel the next day.

After two days rest, we flew our 29th mission on February 3rd. Again, we were briefed for a target at Berlin, but clouds blocked our charted route. The command pilot of the wing dropped the formations down below the clouds and took us past Hanover while encountering a lot of flak, and then on a circuitous route, we went in to bomb railroad marshalling yards at Magdeburg. We climbed back up to 25,000 feet altitude (minus 42 degrees Fahrenheit outside) and bombed the yards through a solid wall of barrage flak.

We were flying deputy lead in J+, and Lt. Bonner in "Delectable Doris" piloted the left wing ship of our lead element. After bombs away, Doris went down, and there were reports that several chutes developed from the ship. However, only the co-pilot and a waist gunner survived as told by the co-pilot in his letter in the Epilogue on page 355.

The 453rd Group followed us in to the target, and by the time they arrived the Jerry AA gunners were well warmed up and really devastated the 453rd, knocking down nine ships.

The B-17 Forts reached and bombed Berlin this day. They could get to 29,000 to 30,000 feet altitudes, and got over the clouds that stopped the B-24s at 26,000 feet.

…Salute…

One could not discuss or evaluate the successful operation of the B-24 Liberators without recognizing the great contributions of the skilled and dedicated maintenance crews assigned to our operations.

Each B-24 was assigned a "hardstand" (concrete parking area) where it was stationed, repaired and maintained. A maintenance crew, often headed up by a master sergeant mechanic-technician, was assigned to each plane and station. The maintenance chief had two assistants, usually tech or staff sergeants.

Individual plane maintenance crews worked with other crews to balance workloads. All were usually busy, and one bad mission resulting in a passel of shot-up ships might see maintenance working 24 hours straight while grabbing naps at the stations.

These men loved the ships, and respected the guys who flew in them. I've seen tears in their eyes when planes didn't make it back, and in some cases when their baby came back all bruised and battered.

They were considerate of the flyer's needs, and would try to help us in any way possible. After my first two missions in "Little Gramper Jr.", I lamented about the inadequate and poorly designed desk space at the navigator's station in the nose. A couple of days later when we flew the "Gramper" again, the chief mechanic asked me to look in the nose and let him know what I thought. He had designed and installed a dandy work desk, which could be folded out of the way when not needed. I thanked him profusely, and his work became the model for installation of better desks in all the 389th flock plus perhaps ships in other groups.

I was always amazed at the skill and ingenuity of the maintenance people. A flak-ridden fuselage would come in, and within a relatively short time it was repaired so you could hardly tell where it had been damaged. When engine or controls repairs were made, they ran the engines up and even taxied the planes while going through the preflight checklist to be sure they were operating satisfactorily before releasing them to the pilots.

Truly our mechanics were heroes to us, and worthy of our salutes.

...Wrapping It Up...

My 30th and last mission was flown on February 6th, 1945. Again we struck railroad marshalling yards at Magdeburg, and bombed from 23,800 feet altitude. Flak was plentiful, but scattered, and our Group suffered little damage. There was an unexpected shift in wind direction, and for a while we were about 25 miles off course on our trek out of Germany.

About 80 miles out from our home base all four props ran away and we left our squadron and group formations. We roared into Hethel while shooting flares with emergency colors, but Berg brought our ship around and in tight and low to make a great landing. The only damage noted was a burning haystack that had been ignited by one of our flares. You could bet that the U.S.A.F. paid a premium price for that hay whether it was marsh grass or high quality timothy.

It was time for celebration. We had completed our combat tour with 30 missions under our belts, and none of the crew had been awarded purple hearts, or recommended for psychoanalysis.

Someone had scrounged up a bottle of Scotch whiskey, and we lugged in a keg of "Mild and Bitters" beer to our barracks. We drank up for a while, but not for long.

Within two days, travel orders were cut to transfer Beno and me out of the 389th Group in preparation for our return to the States. Bergman would be delayed for a while until his promotion to captain came through, which was contingent on his completion of 30 combat missions and experience as commander of a lead crew. Earlier, Laws had been promoted from flight officer to second lieutenant. He would remain with Bergman until transfer, but I never knew if he received another promotion to first lieutenant—he certainly deserved it. I never thought to inquire of Berg as to Laws' final rank when many years later he visited me both in New York and Missouri. The enlisted crewmen did not leave Hethel until a week or more later.

I knew I would miss our crew members and actually had hoped to linger at Hethel for a while after completing our missions so I could explore the countryside a bit more leisurely, and also become better acquainted with the enlisted crewmen who had been quartered in barracks separate from my area. However, operations didn't mess around with any planned idleness. I suppose they figured us as excess baggage if we weren't available for flying. Moreover, new crews were arriving daily for the continuation of the pounding of Germany's Wehrmacht and Luftwaffe.

L to R: Copilot Laws, Bombardier Beno,
Pilot Bergman and Navigator Malone
in front of quarters
at Hethel air base in England

Author with cigar at Hethel

B-24 Liberator bomber R+,
"Delectable Doris"

"Delectable Doris"

Bombs away
from a 389th Bomb Group B-24

"Little Brother"
P-47 fighter escort

Lead Crew Commendation

On this _5TH_ day of ___JAN.___ nineteen hundred and forty five the members of the following crew, of the _389TH_ Bombardment Group, leading the _LOW LEFT SQ.,389TH GP,_ are awarded this token for their meritorious achievement in the destruction of the target at ___NEUSTADT___ , ___GERMANY___

PILOT-LT. S. E. BERGMAN	R.OP-T/SGT. H.W. JEFFREY	GUN-S/SGT. G.E. LOESER
CO-PILOT-F/O. O. LAWS	ENG-T/SGT. W.G. ROBERTSON	GUN-S/SGT.C.E. SCARBROUGH
NAV-LT. A.V. MALONE	GUN-S/SGT. T.D. HYDE	
BOMB-LT. S. BENO	GUN-S/SGT. C.L. CULLEY	

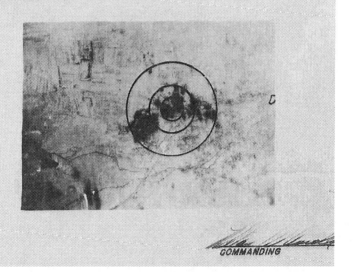

COMMANDING

B-24 Lead Crew Commendation

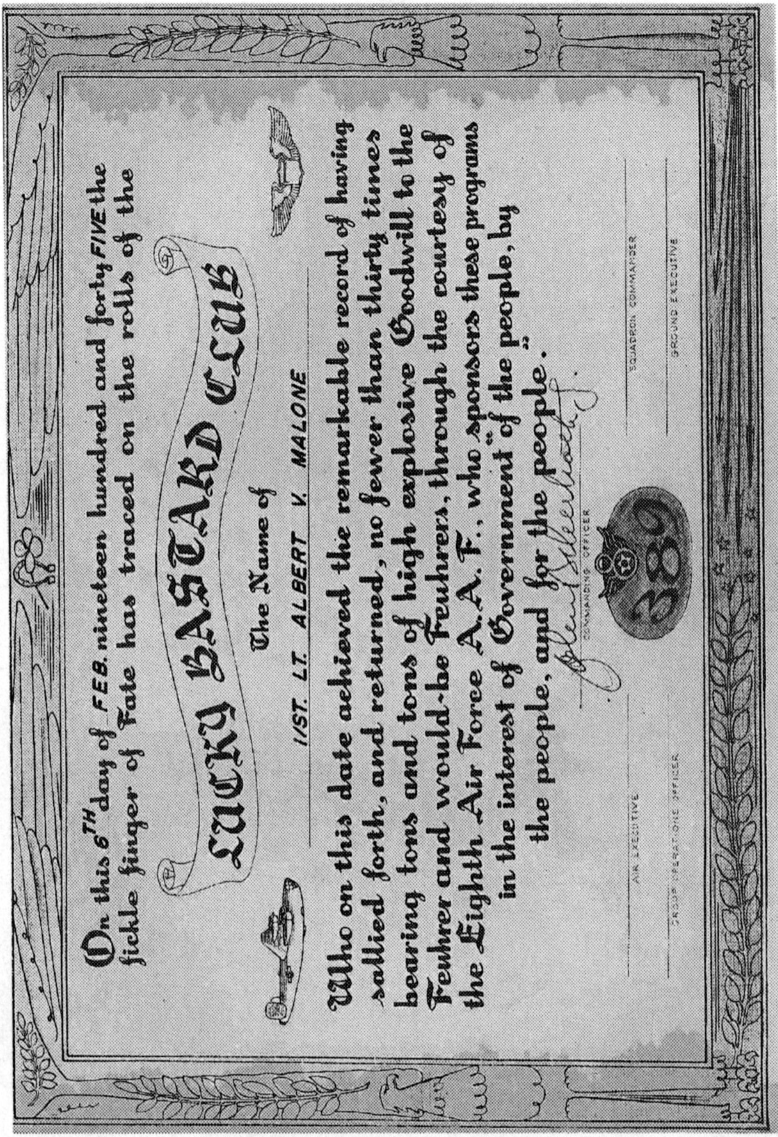
On this 6TH day of FEB. nineteen hundred and forty FIVE the fickle finger of Fate has traced on the rolls of the

LUCKY BASTARD CLUB

The Name of

1ST. LT. ALBERT V. MALONE

Who on this date achieved the remarkable record of having sallied forth, and returned, no fewer than thirty times bearing tons and tons of high explosive Goodwill to the Feuhrer and would-be Feuhrers, through the courtesy of the Eighth Air Force A.A.F., who sponsors these programs in the interest of "Government of the people, by the people, and for the people."

COMMANDING OFFICER

AIR EXECUTIVE

SQUADRON COMMANDER

GROUP OPERATIONS OFFICER

GROUND EXECUTIVE

"Lucky Bastard" citation

23/   Cheerio & Hi Ho the Ozarks

…Tatters & Salt…

More than a fortnight was required for me to become accustomed to the Limey accents. Actually, I could understand the women better than the men. You can draw your own conclusions on that. I'll never forget the frustrated and dyed-in-the-wool outlander bus driver's reaction when I asked the fare, and I couldn't get it even after his repetition. He said half penny something like ape-pen-e, and a three pence coin was "thrupence". I finally pulled a handful of English coins from my pocket and thrust them in front of the exasperated driver and he picked out two coins that looked like a half penny and a three pence, which apparently was the proper fare for the two-decker bus on that route.

A flashlight was a torch, and I enjoyed the manner in which the gals would say, "Do you 'ave a torch?" A torch was almost a necessity because of nighttime blackouts all over England.

Toiletries were especially scarce in England, and a few goodies such as soaps, lotions and cosmetics were often tickets to friendly fraternization. I liked the English gals, but never hankered to establish any lasting relationships.

A majority of the American airmen smoked, and though cigarettes were rationed, I usually was allotted more than I smoked, so I gave the excess to heavier smokers or to the English gals who liked our American brands. I sure didn't care for the English cigarettes.

When I was flying with my first crew, a small crossbred dog with some Scotch terrier ancestry showed up at my barracks, and took a liking to me. He was around a lot, and I brought food to him from the mess hall. Later, I was visiting with a navigator friend and mentioned the dog. He said the dog was a jinx, and other airmen to whom the dog had become attached had subsequently gone down on a mission. This superstition didn't really bother me, but the dog did disappear, not to return, after the mid-air collision of my first crew. Coincidental or not, the situation sort of got my attention and sometimes I still wonder.

Once while stationed at Hethel the Commandant acquiesced to throwing a big party and dance for all airmen on the base and gals whom the airmen wanted to invite. The names and addresses of the gals were to be submitted to the base intelligence department for background checks and clearance, but I thought the system might have been a wee bit loosey-goosey from the looks of some of the women. I don't think Axis Sally was in the bunch, but there very well could have been some enemy infiltrators.

Another airman and I, fortunately or not was moot, did not invite anyone, and we were sidelining the affair. About eleven p.m. we decided that it was time to check out some of our docked B-24 Liberators to see if anybody was being liberated. Every hardstand and aircraft that we scouted was occupied with creatures that emanated giggles, exclamations, little shrieks, bumps, gasps and other sounds.

Just to vent the natural evil in us we thumped on a couple of fuselages and yelled, "Major or Captain so-and-so wants to see you in the orderly room on-the-double," and then we skedaddled. Captain so-and-so just might have been in one of those planes.

During my tour with the 8th A.F., Jimmy Stewart was a Lieutenant Colonel and command pilot, and based at Second Wing headquarters. I met him once after one of our more important missions when all lead pilots, navigators and bombardiers were brought to Wing HQ for debriefing, and he had flown as Command pilot for our wing. Based on his demeanor, he could have been playing a movie part. He was calm, collected, courteous and listened attentively to what others had to say. He didn't talk a lot, but asked sensible and well directed questions. The guy impressed me that day, and he has remained as one of my favorite movie actors.

I also got to see the famous Jimmy Doolittle a couple of times when he was Commanding General of the 8th A.F. and visited our base at Hethel, but I never had the opportunity to speak to him.

The B-24s were fitted with relief tubes for taking a pee while in flight, and there were no holding tanks. So, if you were a ground pounder below a low flying B-24 and thought it was raining, better check to note if the sun was shining. If those disposal systems were not blown out with air occasionally to clear the tubes they would freeze up in the colder upper altitudes. One time when the tube in the nose of my ship froze up, I just had to go, so I peed in the well where the nose wheel was stored during flight.

The pilot steered the B-24 on the ground by throttle jockeying of engine thrust and braking of the two main landing gear wheels—the nose wheel was fixed, and could not be steered. It was absolutely essential that the nose wheel was down and locked in a straight and forward rolling position before landing, and after the pilots dropped the nose gear, the crew chief climbed down to the wheel well and visually checked to see that the wheel was down and locked in place.

The day of my pee emergency, the residue from my effluence had thawed out by landing time, and when the crew chief rushed down and stuck his head in the wheel well opening to check the nose landing gear, he got more than just air in his face from the blast emerging from the open well. He collared me after we landed, and said, "Damn you, Navigator, and don't ever piss in that nose wheel well again!" I grinned at him, and the next time we flew he handed me a can when we boarded. He was crew chief of my first crew and we got along well.

Flying wingman in B-24 formations was truly a strenuous and laborious job for the pilots, and especially for the outer elements off the lead elements. The pilot and co-pilot took turns flying to relieve stress and fatigue. They were constantly jockeying the throttles, rudders and control wheel for elevator and ailerons, and flicking their eyes between wing tip and instruments. It was grueling duty for periods of four to eight hours.

Quality navigation, too, was a laborious activity. Weighted down with cold weather type flying clothes, a backpack parachute, hooked to an oxygen supply system when above 10,000 feet altitude and standing most of the time was a prescription for fatigue. I could never write legibly with gloves on my hands, so I wrote and plotted on logs and charts with gloves off, and then put the gloves back on to prevent freezing of my fingers. When intense flak was expected, I put on a steel helmet and flak jacket, and the load almost put me on the floor.

Well, at least when we got back to our bases in England, we usually had a dry place to lay our heads, in contrast to the fox holed infantry soldier.

Stressed out navigators might be allowed to wallow in their woe for a while, but not pilots. There was a co-pilot who became "flak happy" after a few tough missions, and he was sent off for extended rest and recreation (R&R). He returned in high spirits, and fawnching to get on combat flying status again. The flight surgeon and operations demurred, but the co-pilot was adamant, and finally they relented and he was scheduled for a mission.

The rehabilitated co-pilot's ship took off without incident and everything was hunky-dory until they entered the target area and the flak began to fly. The plane was hit by shrapnel and a small piece penetrated all the way through the bottom of the plane and up through the co-pilot's seat, then penetrating his seat cushion just enough that he felt the impact—no blood was drawn. With recognition of what had happened, the co-pilot lost it and was still babbling when the aircraft landed at Hethel, and an ambulance met the plane after landing. He was shipped back to the States as soon as he could travel—what happened after that, I never heard.

One of my most shocking experiences was watching bombs dropping through our formation while on a bomb run. Another squadron had slid across and over us on their bomb run and dropped on top of us. Obviously, they were off target. One bomb struck one of our squadron planes in the middle, breaking it into two pieces, and I saw only three chutes from the pieces. For a while I was mesmerized, but later almost got sick, though I have never been airsick.

Personal effects were not overly important to me except for a knife that I had purchased in New York City while we were staging at Mitchell Field. It was a heavy, high quality knife with two blades, and one blade was a "flicker." I have not seen one like it since I lost it on a B-24 at Hethel. I couldn't pinpoint the time of loss, but it must have slipped from my pocket, and then fallen down between inner and outer paneled aluminum sheet sections in the deck area. The plane went down over Germany while being flown by another crew. I have always wondered if some kraut might have found my knife.

When aircrews were lost in combat it was assumed that they were dead or prisoners of war. If parachutes had been observed, then there was hope that they were alive, and some with the help of French partisans might make their way to Switzerland or back to liberated parts of France, Belgium or Holland. Most of those parachuting into Germany became prisoners of war, or were executed by either civilians or German soldiers.

When there was confirmation that a crew had gone down in enemy territory, possessions of the crewmen were sort of up-for-grabs. Operations and personnel administration made an effort to take possession of the downed flyer's goods before they could be plundered, but barracks mates of the unfortunate flyers often were in the vanguard and preempted headquarters.

That fellow airmen would abscond with a dead companion's possessions may appear callous and barbaric. Actually, the surviving relatives would receive only the most personal effects and a set of dress uniforms from administrative personnel. Much of the deceased or enemy interned airmen's clothing would find its way into hands of others regardless, and some items such as jackets, overcoats, boots and shoes were always in short supply, so they were in demand and the first to be grabbed.

Though an accepted part of the reality of our operations, I had qualms about the scavenging and plundering system, and could envision buzzards circling overhead, waiting for a dying airman to succumb. Nonetheless, I had no qualms about the act of wearing a dead man's clothing, and in one case accepted a shirt belonging to a fallen flyer.

Occasionally, when we returned from a particularly rough mission, a shot of whiskey was offered to us as we dragged in to the change rooms at headquarters. The beverage was usually a good quality rye or Irish whiskey, and it was a welcome jolt for me. Some guys did not participate, and I wised up fast. I would grab a couple of non-imbibers before reaching the dispenser and convince at least one of them to take a shot glass of whiskey and pass it on to me. Alcohol never had any hold on me, but a couple of belts of whiskey did relax my battered nerves, and even helped my system to accept some of the bland offerings of the mess hall and to relax for a nap.

The weather in England was miserable much of the time in winter, but never so cold as that encountered in Europe. A snow of four inches depth fell on our base during December 1944, but it melted within a day or so. The waters surrounding England mitigated temperatures while at the same time contributing to promulgation of fog and excessive cloudiness. Earlier we discussed weather's baneful effect on flying.

In Chapter 21 we wrote about the German "buzz bombs". The Germans were also advanced enough in rocket missile development to begin sending rockets with explosive charges at England in the fall and winter of 1944. Several times while flying over the coastal areas of Germany I witnessed the launching of these V-2 rockets. Their exhaust trails were distinctive and unmistakable, and displayed their climbing trajectories as they headed for England. Most of the launching sites were in heavily concreted ground bunkers near the coastal areas when the rockets were first introduced. Then as Allied bombers began pounding the reinforced bunkers with deep penetration bombs they shifted to mobile launching sites. The V-2 rockets were more effectively guided and targeted than the V-1 buzz bombs and caused more damage, but nonetheless, the English citizenry was still more frightened by the unpredictability of the buzz bomb's landing sites. The rockets could be tracked by radar so some degree of warnings was possible.

Uncle Sam Burleson was based in England with Signal Corps troops while I was with the 8th AF. My mother sent his address to me, and I visited him at his location, just southwest of London. He took me to visit some of his English civilian friends, and we were served tea and crumpets. I learned to drink tea with cream in the manner of our English friends, and it wasn't bad at all.

Uncle Sam was 39 years of age at the time, and did not have to participate in the D-Day invasion.

Jonah Adams was another Seaton native (see Chapter 13) who was in England during my stay there. He was stationed with Air Force support troops at a fighter plane base near Cambridge. We were not able to get together, but he was kind enough to obtain photographs of the U. S. military cemetery at Cambridge for me to send to the mother of the co-pilot of my first crew (see Chapter 21, "Change of Venue").

...Hurry Up and Wait...

Beno and I traveled by train from Norwich to Worley, a U.S. staging base near Liverpool where we would wait for transportation to the United States.

No duties were assigned to us at Worley and it was a restless period for three weeks. I could lounge in my bunk, close my eyes and hear the roar, rumble and prop pitch whine of thousands of 1200 horsepower Liberator engines overhead as the B-24s assembled for a mission. I thought about those still flying who might never be bored with waiting at Worley.

There was a lot of bull-shooting and card playing. I saw poker games with pots of $500 and more—big old British five-pound notes stacked high with a slew of one-pound notes. At that time the British pound was valued at $4.03 as compared to $1.56 at this writing. The U.S. Armed Forces payrolls were dispensed as cash, and in the currency of the country where the soldier was stationed.

I eschewed the high stakes poker games. Why push my luck after surviving 30 combat missions. Actually, I never figured luck had much to do with my survival. Omnipotent, omniscient and omnipresent God was in charge all the time, and demonstrated his mercy, love and grace.

The village of Worley sported two fairly decent pubs, and was within walking distance of our station. Girls were around, and most had seen a lot of G.I.s with all the rapid turnover of transient personnel.

If you got to the pubs early you might finagle some scotch whiskey from the barkeep, but their supply never lasted long. They always had warm black "stout" beer, but sometimes ran out of the warm "mild" beer. I have always wondered how the "mild" would have tasted if it had been refrigerated at 40 degrees Fahrenheit. I have not been to England since my military service so maybe I can amble over there in the future and see if I can imbibe some cold "mild" while also visiting the old "Hethel base that is not an air base anymore. However, the landowner of the former base and other local citizens have renovated and restored the base chapel and added a museum containing memorials, mementos and artifacts about the 389th Bomb Group.

The holding base at Worley was also a major mail receiving and distribution center for troops in the British Isles. The mail unit asked for volunteers to censor mail bound for the U.S. I censored for a few days until the task became too boring after reading about every type of communication you could ever imagine. Writers were various shades of comedians, preachers, statesmen, whiners, melancholy babies, philanderers, poignant penmen, military tacticians, pornographers, artists cartoonists, politicians, economists, philosophers, poets, professors, linguists and just about any other kind of character you could think of. When anyone wrote in a language other than English we would automatically whack it out. But mostly, the G.I.s were interested in their wives, kids and families, and that's what they wrote about—their loves, concerns and hopes.

Censorship was not a fun game, and though needed in wartime, its institution left me dejected from the intrusion into people's private thought and lives—a violation of the principles we were all fighting for.

We checked the bulletin boards frequently, and after what seemed an eternity (only three weeks), on March 1st, Beno and I along with a host of other repatriates from various combat operations in England and the European Theatre were listed for departure.

Meetings were called to brief us on procedures for departure and to tell us what baggage we could take and how to handle it. It was inferred that baggage checks would be made to deter the taking of contraband, but I didn't note any examination of our group's stuff at any succeeding point in our transfer. I could easily have brought back a "lost" Colt 1911 .45 caliber issue pistol, but I had been intimidated before leaving Hethel.

…Convoy & Home…

From Worley we were railed to Glasgow, Scotland, where we boarded the "Alexandra", a large combination passenger-cargo ocean-going ship that had been converted to a troopship. Apparently, the Alexandra had hauled huge loads of troops on many voyages because the tiered bunk beds were stacked five high in some sleeping quarters. Relatively, our contingent was small, and a lot of us had the bottom bunk with no one above. There was a sizeable number of airmen and ground soldiers who had been wounded, and some still under the surveillance of nurses on one deck. Most were ambulatory, but some were using walking assistance devices.

We were in dock two days before pulling anchor to join a forming convoy of about 30 ships. German U-boats were still a scourge in the North Atlantic, and U.S. destroyers escorted the convoy. After the convoy was underway for two days, the Jerry submarines located us and began testing the perimeters of the fleet. The next three or four days the U-boats waited until dark to try to penetrate the convoy because they were vulnerable to the challenges posed by torpedo aircraft patrols during daylight.

We were watching a movie one of those evenings when we heard and felt a depth charge go off. One or more U-boats had penetrated to the center of the convoy where the Alexandra was running, and the destroyers were dumping ash cans (depth charges) one after the other and near us. The explosions were so close that the ship was rocking and pitching. Then the assembly alarm was sounded—everyone was to don life jackets, and then get on the upper decks where the lifeboats were located. About that time, one depth charge exploded and jarred us so hard that the inside lights went out. Nobody panicked, but a lot of people were mighty scared, including myself. The barrage of the destroyers subsided, the electrical power was restored, and then we returned to our quarters for a restless night.

The U-boats attempted to gain torpedo positioning during the following two nights, but they were invading the convoy away from the Alexandra. However, from the Alexandra we could still hear and feel some of the destroyer's depth charges.

The Alexandra's crew did not divulge much information about the destroyer's activity, and the passengers never learned if any of the submarines were damaged or destroyed. Insofar as we could observe, our convoy did not lose any ships, but that observation was neither confirmed nor denied.

After the stalking by enemy submarines, we encountered some real rough weather for a couple of days in the mid North Atlantic, and a lot of guys became sick. I have never been air or sea sick, and other than the period of U-boat menace, it was a pleasant jaunt, and the only time I have traveled on an ocean-going vessel. I am not fond of big waters, salt or otherwise.

We traveled on the ocean for a total of eleven days, and the latter days were pleasant as we moved through relatively calm waters. Food was good, and served to us with the accouterments of a normal dining room atmosphere.

It was great to see U.S. soil again as I awakened that morning in mid March to see us already docked at Perth Amboy, New Jersey, and the ship's crew preparing for our disembarkation. We were hauled by truck over to Camp Kilmer, about ten miles west, where we were quartered for three days while records were checked and brief physicals invoked to determine if anyone needed medical attention before sending us on our way to a regional processing center. Beno's home was just fifteen miles or so away in Elizabeth, New Jersey, and he managed to get away from Kilmer a day ahead of me to check in with his wife before going to Fort Dix, N.J. for regional processing. It was the last time I would see or talk with Steve. We exchanged Christmas messages for a few years. I believe that he is alive and healthy today and Bergman did correspond with him until Berg's death in 2003.

Travel arrangements were prepared and I was transferred from Camp Kilmer to Jefferson Barracks, Missouri, in south St. Louis, the same station where I was inducted and endured basic training. My records were reviewed and updated, more physicals performed, service and travel pay provided, and then papers were issued for traveling and assignment to my next station. Substantial leave time was included with my orders. I was out of the Barracks and home to Seaton on the 27th of March. My orders directed me to report to AAF Redistribution Station No. 4, Santa Ana, California for processing and reassignment—no later than April 22, 1945. So, I would have about three weeks at home.

"The Barefoot Boy with boots on" had returned, and it was wonderful to see my folks and friends at Seaton and in the surrounding towns.

While visiting in Rolla, I stopped to talk with Herman Castleman, proprietor of Superior Chevrolet. I told him the war would soon be over, and when auto manufacturing was renewed I wanted one of his first new Chevies. He responded quickly, "You will be one of the first on my list."

My sister, Kathleen, had graduated from high school in 1943, after I had entered the AAF. She had taught at rural Swyers school in eastern Phelps County for the 1943-44 term, and at this time was the teacher at rural Hale school located about eight miles northeast of Seaton for the 1944-45 term. Dad had taught her to drive Wilbert's '35 Chevy, and she commuted from Seaton.

Kathleen's school term ended in mid-April and she mentioned that she would like to travel to see Wilbert, who was stationed at Salt Lake City, Utah. So, she and I traveled together to Salt Lake, and after visiting with Wib and his friends for three days, she returned to Seaton, and I headed down to Santa Ana, California.

We rode the choo-choo most of the way, and traveling in the springtime was nice. While in Salt Lake, we, of course, toured the Great Salty Lake, the state capitol, the Mormon Temple and other attractions. Also, we enjoyed visiting in the homes of Mormon friends of Wilbert.

…Psycho-Babble…

I reported to Santa Ana AAB on April 22, and on schedule. You might say it was a return to my navigation roots since I had received my cadet navigator classification there in 1943. Now, I would be processed and reassigned to active duty at another station.

They ran me through the rigorous AAF physical mill again, and pronounced me in shape for continued flying status. I had applied for pilot training, and I was declared physically able to participate in that activity.

Whether they thought I might be demented to apply for pilot training, or they needed guinea pigs, I didn't know, but I was subjected to a plethora of verbal and written tests, running the gamut of earthly topics and my life history.

Actually, I believe I was part and parcel of the incipiency of contemporary psychobabble. I never received results of their psychoanalysis, but it was a challenge to me, and I busted a gut endeavoring to provide answers diametrically opposite to what I thought the convoluted minds that prepared the questions expected. In any case, no one to my knowledge tried to rescind my acceptance for pilot training.

The climate was nice, avocados were plentiful and Los Angeles (LA) was a fine city—then. It was a pleasant interlude, but after two weeks, the head shrinkers and pseudo-pedagogists had tired of my irascibleness and me, and I was reassigned to San Marcos AAFB Navigation Training School at San Marcos, Texas.

Scanning the bulletin boards, I saw a personal ad by another navigator who had a car, and he was driving from Santa Ana Airbase to San Marcos AAB. He was offering a ride to one or two airmen who would share fuel expenses. It sounded good to me, and I got in touch with him and a deal was made. I figured to come out ahead on expenses, since the AAF would pay the normal rate for my transportation costs, and to boot I could view scenery from a different perspective than by rail.

It turned out I was the only passenger, and oddly I cannot remember the driver's name, but we got along okay. I do remember that he was a clean-cut and reserved sort of person, and not garrulous which was a relief to me. His car was a four door '39 Oldsmobile in good condition. We were somewhat concerned about two tires, but he took it easy, and we made the trip without any major problems.

It was a pleasant time of year to cross the desert and other arid regions of the southwest, and we took a side junket to see the Grand Canyon, which I thoroughly enjoyed. We entered and left from the south entrance of the Canyon Park. Years later, my wife and I visited the Canyon, but we approached through the Painted Desert and entered the Canyon on the north access road that I liked best. To me, it is one of the most magnificent natural places in the U.S., truly a *Grand* Canyon, and I would visit again off-season, but my wife abhors the place. We dislike the tourist mobs, and she doesn't care for the heights and considers it one big gulch.

…Ninety Eight and Out…

San Marcos is located about forty miles north-northeast from San Antonio, and about thirty miles south of Austin, Texas. My friend and I reported to the Air Base on May 10th, and I was assigned to the navigation school to be an instructor while waiting for assignment to a primary flight training station for pilots.

Things went smoothly for a couple of weeks, and I made training flights with cadets totaling twelve hours of flight time. Then there was an announcement of a separation-from-service program, based on a point system. Points were assigned for time of service, foreign and combat time and meritorious credits. If the total points added up to 98 as I recall, you were eligible for separation.

Using posted criteria, I calculated my points and came up short, but I signed up for separation anyway, since it was likely that eligibility standards would be lowered as the war wound down.

When an eligibility list was posted, my name was on it! Immediately, I had second thoughts because I still thought I wanted to try pilot training, but I knew I was not a military type, and ultimately decided to go for separation.

Separation processing began, and on the day a group of us was scheduled to depart San Marcos AB we had been lined up to have our papers checked before release for departure. As the lieutenant in charge came to me, he looked at his file and my papers, and ejaculated, "Hell's fire, you should not be getting out of here, you don't have enough points." We stared at each other for a while, and then he softly murmured, "Dammit, it's too late now, your papers are cut, go on and best of luck to you."

Indeed my papers were cut, and directed me to proceed to the separation center at Jefferson Barracks, Missouri—my old nemesis.

I arrived at St. Louis in early June, and a few days were required to get everything in order, but finally I was officially separated from the Army Air Forces as of June 18, 1945. Actually, I departed the Barracks a few days before the official date. As a commissioned officer I was required to serve in the AAF Reserves for five years after this separation date. Hence, I received a Certificate of Service rather than a discharge document.

Discharged and separated personnel were reminded at the time of their departure that they should report to their home draft boards, and show them the discharge papers. A few days after arriving in Rolla, being a good soldier to the last, I dropped in on the draft board office on Pine Street, tendered my Certificate of Service to the arrogant woman who ran the show, and told her I had served my time, and suggested she remove my name from any rosters they might have on file. Perfunctorily, she scanned my certificate and snapped, "Come back when you get your discharge." She deserved to be directed to go to hell, but I simply responded in as sharp and harsh voice as I could muster, "This is it, it's all you get, and if you don't want the information, you will not see me again, ever." She flushed, grabbed my Certificate, made some notes and handed it back without any more surly comments and didn't look at me.

I had fully intended to instigate an investigation of the Phelps County-Rolla Draft Board, but my cursory detective work indicated possible unethical involvement by people who had befriended me, so I backed off and reconciled myself to the philosophy that the draft dodgers would have to live with their consciences for a long time.

My family was glad to see me home in one piece, and surprised that I had gotten out so soon. In fact, some people were suspicious that somebody might have pulled some strings. Anyway, it was peaceful to be in the hills again, and I relaxed for a while. But I was only 21, and I had grown up rather quickly in a wide-wide world of sights and action—I began to get restless, and uncertain about how, when, where and what I should be engaged in.

I did some courtin', but she wanted to get married, and I wasn't ready to fly that type of mission yet. I did some carousin', and took to the big cities a couple of times, but shifting gears was not easy.

Wilbert's '35 Chevy was garaged at home when I separated from the AAF, and I drove it quite a lot, even drove it to the State Fair in Sedalia. Also took a neighbor and a local country-store lawyer to Jefferson City to talk with the State Attorney General.

The neighbor's son had been shot and killed by another youth, and the neighbor was not satisfied with the local county prosecuting attorney's handling of the incident. The shooter alleged that the killing was accidental, but there had been trouble between the shooter and his victim before, and many people thought differently, choosing to believe murder or at least manslaughter was involved through a planned setup and execution.

The Attorney General argued that he should not interfere with the case, but agreed he would make inquiries, and we thought he was influential because the tempo of the investigation picked up markedly after our meeting. In a short while the county prosecutor filed criminal charges, and a subsequent jury trial culminated in a first-degree manslaughter verdict. The shooter received a five to seven year sentence to the State Penitentiary. Our neighbor continued to believe his son was murdered and grieved for several years that justice was not done—his personality changed and he was never the former congenial and active person again.

On our return home from Jeff City, a flat tire developed, and I didn't have the key that unlocked the hubcap on the outside mounted spare tire carrier. We pried the cap off with tire tools and managed to get the tires and wheels exchanged.

I worried Dad quite a bit, but he didn't comment much to me. He inspected the car each morning when I had been out the night before, and from my bedroom I could hear him talking to my mother about anything suspicious.

One night a drunken soldier smashed the rear window of the Chevy with his fist at the old Atlasta roadhouse in St James. I didn't know the window was broken until I got into the car to leave and then felt an unusual breeze and more road noise as I drove along. Next morning Dad was telling Mom about the window and blood on the car. I explained what happened, but he appeared doubtful as to whether I had made full disclosure.

Another morning, I heard Dad say to Mom, "I wonder what he's been into now." I began wondering too, and understood his consternation when later I went out to look at the car. It was a two-door car and the back windows were rolled about two-thirds down (as far as they could go) and vomit stains and streaks smeared each window and sides of the car. The night had been warm and I had driven home with the windows down, so didn't smell the puke.

I had been out with two cousins (male) and we ended up at the VFW Lounge (euphemistically speaking) in Rolla, and drinking some beer. One cousin said he didn't feel well and was going to lie down in my car. An hour or so later, he returned and wanted to go home, and I took them home with him climbing into the back seat. I didn't smell anything unusual and he said nothing about tossing his cookies.

When next I saw the puking cousin, I asked him why he could not have at the least, restricted his up chucking to one window.

A horseman I never was. The horses seemed to sense my shortcomings in equestrianism while at the same time displaying considerable man sense. Dad had a two-year old gelding that had been ridden quite a bit bareback, but not broken to the saddle. With some childhood cowboy still remaining in me, I decided to saddle up "Rex." The moment

I swung into the saddle, he began to crow-hop, and then transited into bucking. I stayed with him until he stopped bucking and reared straight up, and I just cleared the saddle in time to prevent him from falling on me. We both got up, and it was deja vu all over again, except the second time Rex fell over backward, and again I just barely got off and away from him before he flopped on the ground.

I procured a solid wooden club, and started to mount Rex again with intent to hit him between the ears when he began to rear up. With my left foot in the left stirrup a bell somewhere rang—much like the emergency bell on a B-24—and I paused to think and soliloquized, "Look, you numbskull, this horse has your number and doesn't like you, and after surviving a war with your skin whole, why let pride maybe cripple you, or worse, end your temporal life." With that, I unsaddled the obstreperous booger and released him to pasture to savor his victory.

Later, when I wasn't around, Dad saddled Rex and rode him all around the countryside without any problems at all. Dad was larger and heavier than I, but most of all he was a horseman, and the horse knew. During deer hunting season a few years after, a snowstorm left 18 inches of snow on the ground at Seaton, and Dad climbed on Rex and rode him deer hunting when nothing else could move. He shot a nice buck from the saddle without any complaint from Rex. Hummm—does Missouri's current deer hunting regulations prohibit shooting from a horse?

After Japan surrendered, more veterans began coming home and I felt better. Also, I had decided I would return to MSM for matriculation in the School's fall semester.

1944 photo of Sister Kathleen and 1935 Chevy

Though I was not excited about reentering MSM, I enrolled for the 1945 fall semester. Congress had passed G.I. Educational Benefits legislation as a major part of an overall veteran's benefit package, a.k.a. as the G.I. Bill of Rights, and it was in force when I registered. Under the bill all costs for tuition, fees, prescribed course books and supplies were provided by the U.S. Government. Also, a monthly stipend for living costs was provided for each G.I. while actively engaged in a curriculum of an approved educational institution. I participated in the G.I. Bill's educational benefits program until graduation from MSM with a B.S. in Chemical Engineering in 1948.

I take this opportunity to express my many thanks to the taxpayers of the United States for this support. The G. I. Bill is probably the most important piece of legislation ever enacted by the congress of the U.S. since the Civil War. It's favorable impact on the remarkable development and growth of our country and economy since World War II is immeasurable. Without the assistance of the G.I. Bill many if not most of the G.I.s would not have gained a college education. The effects of the Bill will likely be dissected and debated by historians for many years.

I scheduled a light load of course work for my return to college academics, including a repeat of differential calculus. Lo and behold, at the end of the semester I had scored an E (excellent and highest rating) for calculus, and that from "Spike" Dennie, my calculus professor and a taskmaster—gruff, tough but fair.

I commuted from Seaton to MSM in Wib's '35 Chevy. Only a handful of World War II veterans were in attendance for the fall semester, and I didn't exactly feel at home with the younger and non-veteran students.

As the second semester rolled around, there was quite an influx of military service veterans, and I felt more at home. I also rented a room in Rolla in the residence of Mrs. and Professor Frame who was Chairman of the Electrical Engineering Department at MSM. Two more students were housed with me in upstairs rooms. One was a veteran. We got along well, the rooms were nice and the Frames were good to us.

I was still driving Wib's Chevy, though he had been discharged from the AAF and was gearing up to go back to college in the summer. The old Chevy needed considerable repair and fixin', and Wib asked me to sell it for him, and I got $275 for it. If we had waited a while we likely could have sold it for 100 bucks more because cars were in short supply and in great demand since none had been manufactured for four years. I got by without an auto by bumming rides.

Herman Castleman was true to his word, and when he received his first shipment of new Chevies from the factory, he called me and said, "I have five four-door sedans, and you can have your pick of color, as long as it is black or blue." I told him I would be right there, and on May 7, 1946, I took delivery of a new blue four-door Chevy for $1079.24. I still have the check I wrote to pay for the car. I could have turned around and sold the car for eight or nine hundred dollars above my cost—maybe more. Herman warned me not to sell the car, though I had not signed any restrictive covenant. I had paid the sticker price.

I was confident that Herman would sell me one of his first cars and had agreed to let Wib have it because I had used and abused his old Chevy so much. I kept my word too, and sold it to him for the price I paid.

I went to Herman and told him what I had done, and audaciously asked him to put me back on his waiting list. After all, Wib had bought his '35 Chevy from Herman. He frowned a while, but under the circumstances, he was not too discombobulated, and put me on his list with the warning that I might have to wait quite a while.

I completed the second semester with fair grades, and then tried to find a decent summer job locally, but had no luck, and I wasn't ready to head off to the big cities yet, so I spent the summer helping Dad and Mom with their store, garden and livestock, and visited with friends and relatives.

Wib attended MSM during the summer session, and commuted in his new car from Seaton. It was also a time to become better acquainted with a much younger brother, Gilbert, who was born on January 17, 1939.

Wib and I began the fall semester of '46 at MSM and commuted the first week while looking for a place to live in Rolla. Wib met Roy McDowell, an Armed Services Veteran from Vienna, Missouri who was also looking for an abode in Rolla, and we jointly rented a small house. Wib and I liked "Mac", and we got along well together. We also liked the house, but it was not insulated, and our heating bills were steep for three guys going to school on the G.I. Bill.

We prepared most of our meals and took turns grocery shopping. Wib swore that he could discern the difference between "Old Judge" coffee and other brands. Mac and I bought a pound of Kroger's "Spotlight" and put it in the "Old Judge" container, and Wib never suspected our deception. He refused to believe the substitution when we revealed our trickery.

Soon after school began, Herman Castleman sent word that he had a new car for me, and similar to what I wanted—a 1947 two-door coupe with back seats. It was black and contained a radio. I don't remember the exact cost, but it was priced between fourteen and fifteen hundred dollars. Again, I paid only the sticker price. In less than a year inflation had set in with some vengeance. This time Herman insisted I sign a waiver of rights to sell the car within a year to anyone other than his dealership. I didn't quibble as to the legality or constitutionality of this requirement because I wanted the car badly, and really had no intention of selling it.

About six months later, cars still were very much in short supply, and one evening while dating a gal in

Houston, Missouri, a guy drove up and offered $2300 cash for my car. At that time the car was more important than cash to me.

The 1946 fall semester passed rather uneventfully, and I was doing okay academically. I had chosen chemical engineering as my major.

The Christmas and New Year holiday seasons came and passed, and in January I began the 1947 semester. I was pretty well in the groove academically, and the weeks went by rather quickly. I observed the St.Patrick's celebration, but was not genuinely enthused with all the nonsense.

During mid evening of April 26th 1947, people in the neighborhood of Seaton heard a facsimile of a hundred freight trains and ten B-52s passing through at low altitude when a tornado struck from the southwest. I heard about the debacle on the radio early in the morning of April 27th, and rushed out to Seaton to check on family and friends.

The destruction was intense in a narrow path of 200 to 300 yards for a distance of five or six miles. If it had hit a city with such fury the destruction of life and property would have been immense. As it was, in the open country-side, two houses with out buildings were leveled in the Seaton area, and one man was killed. Damage was similar to the southwest and northeast of Seaton but no lives were lost in those areas nor anyone injured seriously.

Along the edges of the main swath, no injuries to people were noted, but there was much wind damage, with up-rooted trees, loss of roofing and appurtenances. The main force crossed Norman Creek to the east where there were high bluffs, and from a distance the view looked as if a pair of huge hair clippers had given the top of the tree-lined bluff a crew cut.

At my parent's place the house was not damaged much, but the store lost part of its porch, and a lot of trees were down and some uprooted.

Tom Harris lived about a half mile east of Seaton on the county road that ran by Seaton, and his house and outbuildings were completely destroyed. After the tornado passed, a neighbor, Marion Bell and family, heard Tom crying for help, and then found him in the debris, still alive but barely so. They came to Dad for help, and he was able to get his truck part of the way to Tom's place, but because of downed trees and debris in the road could not reach the house place. So, they carried Tom to the truck, and then to my parents' house where Tom shortly died of his injuries.

Tom had come to Seaton in 1945 and bought his house and forty acres. He lived alone and had never spoken of any relatives.

Dad was appointed administrator of Tom's small estate, and he could not locate any relatives. Financial institutions that Tom had dealt with also could not provide any information as to relatives or associates. To this day, to my knowledge, no one has ever inquired about Mr. Harris. Everyone in the Seaton area liked Tom. His age at death was estimated to be about 70—no birth or other telltale records were discovered in the residue from the storm.

Just a half-mile southwest of the Seaton store, the home and farm buildings of Walter (Bud) and Maggie Ketchum were in the center of the twister's tail, and all buildings were demolished, except for the floor and foundation of the house, which were mostly left in place. Bud and Maggie (both in their sixties at the time) were hardly scratched, but were carried on their divan by the tornado for about 100 yards away from the house. Bud was asked what he was doing during that time, and he did not even crack a grin as he replied, "Me and Maggie jist rid along and talked."

The Red Cross organization was quickly on the scene and was of great assistance to the Ketchums. They rebuilt their house at the same location and on part of the surviving foundations.

Dad had constructed an excellent combination storm, fruit and vegetable cellar when he first moved to Seaton, and Mom and he were grateful for its protection when the tornado hit. They had heard the storm advancing and just made it to the cellar with Gilbert before the twister passed through.

My parents were always concerned about windstorms and potential tornadoes when I was growing up—partly I think, because of stories they had heard about the twister that hit Hawkins Bank (named from an iron ore mine opened by a Mr. Hawkins) in 1893, and killed twenty people. Hawkins Bank was located about five miles southeast of Seaton (see Chapter 15, High School Walk), and my grandparents knew many of the people living and killed in the Bank area.

When big blows developed, my parents would herd us kids to the cellar, and grab some blankets and a flashlight as we rushed from the house. One time in my early teens, I wouldn't go, and they departed without me. It was a measure of their fear, and they figured there was always at least one fool in a family.

I was getting anxious to finish school at MSM and get a job, so I registered for the summer session. Many former G.I.s felt the same, and the University was offering many of the courses required for graduation during this session.

My mother wanted to take a major trip somewhere, and after I got my new '47 Chevy, I had promised to chauffeur her. So, in the interim we planned a trip to Niagara Falls, and between the end of spring semester and the beginning of summer classes, we struck out for the Falls. I had not visited this scenic wonder either.

We had a good trip out, drove along the lakeshore roads of Lake Erie and up to the Canadian and American Falls of the Niagara River. I have been to the Falls several times since, but still enjoyed the spectacle, even when the crowds were there and the commercialization was plentiful.

We were heading home in early evening when a knucklehead ran into my rear end while we were stopping for a line of traffic in the Erie, Pennsylvania area. Those old Chevies were built with substantial bumpers, and nothing was damaged on my car except the trunk lid was dented. The "hitter" car's front end was severely smashed, and with a busted radiator could not be driven. The driver of the hitter car was not the owner, and it took a while to get the owner to the scene. I took his address and the car's license number, and tried to get the Pennsylvania highway patrol to investigate, but a rather rude and grumpy officer whom I awakened from a nap, I think, would not do anything about the accident because there were no injuries. It was a long night.

After we returned to Rolla I had the trunk lid dent fixed, and sent the owner of the hitter car a bill for the damages. He had given me a false address, and I didn't try to trace him, but I should have sent a report to the Pennsylvania licensing bureau. He claimed that his car was not insured at the time of the accident.

The summer classes went well, and I was rooming with Chris Buterbaugh, another student, in a private home. Our landlord was a nice elderly couple who treated us well, and took an interest in our activities. Chris was studying mining engineering, and was two semesters behind me, but we got along okay. He knew a nurse at the Waynesville, Missouri hospital (about 30 miles west of Rolla), and we made a couple of trips down that way on dates. Then the Waynesville nurse lined us up with a nurse in Houston, Missouri (50 miles south of Rolla) who had girl friends. Two other classmates and I made several trips to Houston on dates—at this time the enrollment at MSM was expanding and the ratio of students to eligible single girls in Rolla was also growing.

When MSM Homecoming celebrations rolled around during the fall semester, Chris and I invited two Houston gals to go to the parties with us, and they accepted. Then our landlady invited the girls to stay with her Saturday night. I picked them up in Houston on Saturday morning and took them home Sunday afternoon. We liked the girls and had a good time, but after another date in Houston, we sort of terminated the Houston agenda.

I was carrying a substantial academic load, and I planned to complete the requirements for a B.S. degree with the ending of the fall-winter semester. Gals and gallivanting were encroaching on needed study time. Moreover, I had become interested in a couple of local girls, one of whom would become my wife in 1949.

In my academic era, 160 hours of credit were required to meet MSM standards for granting a B.S. degree in engineering. R.O.T.C. credit hours were included, and because of my active military service as a commissioned officer, I was granted 12 hours of credit as an equivalency to advanced R.O.T.C. training at MSM.

Going into my last semester I was short three hours of elective subjects, so Dr. L.E. Woodman, head of the Physics Department reviewed my military records and approved three hours credit in meteorology, based on my training and experience in aerial navigation.

I had fulfilled requirements for a B.S. degree in Chemical Engineering by the end of the semester in January 1948, and I had experienced several job interviews. I had also gone on a senior trip to visit industries in the St. Louis, Missouri area (see Chapter 12, "Dental Dents" of "Bits and Pieces").

At the invitation of the Sinclair Oil Company (now British Petroleum Company, Ltd.) I visited their refinery in Hammond, Indiana. They paid my travel expenses for the interview and offered me a job at that location. However, Midwest Research Institute in Kansas City, Missouri, was closer to Rolla, and they had offered a job to me. At that point a little gal from the Elk Prairie community had caught my fancy. So, I went to work for MRI as a Research Chemical Engineer in January 1948. Just another confirmation of "The hand that rocks the cradle rules the world."

I returned to MSM in May 1948 to attend graduation ceremonies with the spring graduating class. My mother, my Elk Prairie girlfriend, LauraBelle Benad, who would become my wife in 1949 and her girlfriend, Boots Lenox (who became my brother Wilbert's wife in 1949), watched as I received my diploma that is still around someplace in boxes we have moved from pillar to post over the years.

Academically, my trail of the slide rule had come to an end, but the slide rule would remain a companion of mine in industrial work for many years. While employed at Midwest Research Institute I saw my first computer—the McElroy Pipeline Computer, which was a maze of tubes and paraphernalia that filled a 15 x 15 foot room. Its capabilities matched what now could be handled with a scientific pocket calculator, but that is another story as the "Barefoot Boy with boots on" left his roots to enter the world of jobs, and raising a family in a sometimes hostile environment.

This check paid in full the list price for a brand new 1946 Chevrolet four-door sedan. It was the first new car delivered To Superior Chevrolet in Rolla, Missouri, after General Motors resumed production of autos following the end of World War II. The only accessory was a heater—no power steering or power brakes, no radio or any of the other contemporary accessories considered normal today.

WINDSTORM HITS HOBSON AND LAKE SPRING AREA

FOUR LAMBS

R. B. Cowan stated this week that a recent picture in The Salem Post showing a ewe with three lambs, is nothing to compared with his record this year. Cowan had a ewe which a little over three weeks ago had four lambs, all of which are doing well.

This ewe a cross between Hampshire and Shropshire is feeding three of the lambs and the fourth has been taken to Salem by Cowan's daughter who feeds it by bottle. All four of the lambs are bucks.

Cowan's farm is about 1 mile from Hobson.

Band and Glee Club Going to State Contests

Individuals Compete Friday at Columbia. Organi-
...

Seaton Man Is Killed Under Falling House

Six Injured in Winkler Vicinity. Two are Taken to Hospital.

None Seriously Hurt in Dent

Property Damage from Tornado May Run Over $50,000.

Tom Harris, 57 years old, was killed at his home near Seaton when his house collapsed in a windstorm that caused $50,000 or more damages as it swept from south of Lake Spring through the Hobson, Seaton and Winkler communities. While property damage was high, only one life was lost and injured were few.

The twisting windstorm dipped down in farms between Lake Spring and Hobson shortly after 8 o'clock Tuesday night inflicted great loss to property.

Man dies in tornado at Seaton

Epilogue

The Demise of Delectable Doris

Several veterans of the Second Air Division of the Eighth Air Force purchased copies of the first edition of this book. I was pleased to receive their most interesting comments and stories and in some cases notations of errors in the text.

I am especially grateful for a letter from John (Jack) Merrill who was the co-pilot for "Delectable Doris" on its fateful flight of February 3, 1945.

In Chapter 22 I write that "Doris" went down while flying in our element on my 29th mission. Nine chutes were reported to have emerged from the ship before and during disintegration. We didn't know what happened after that. Jack has graciously given me permission to tell his story in his words.

Dear Al,

Enjoyed 'Barefoot to Wings" cover to cover and your letter too.

Especially interesting were your comments on pages 272 and 273—your 29th mission and my 18th. I was co-pilot with the Bob Bonner crew (enclosed find picture of our crew with names).

Unable to lift the wheels for takeoff, we aborted "Miss America" and landed with 500 lb. bombs, then replaced her with "Delectable Doris" to fulfill a maximum effort mission. We crossed Holland at 17,000 feet and caught up to fill the high-high right of the last group. This was Bonner's 35th mission.

When hit by flak we lost the nose—all instruments except the altimeter were gone or inoperative.

I recovered consciousness at about 17,500 feet. We were on fire throughout the bomb bay and the ship was in a spiral. Bonner was dead and I was ripped by flak on my left side. The result was complete disintegration of "Doris". Bill Weidman, right waist gunner and I were blown clear. I pulled the o-ring of my chute and came down through three cloud layers. Barefoot and with only my flying suit and without use of my left side, I was dragged through a frozen, muddy field for half a mile before the chute collapsed.

I survived Stalag IXC and arrived in Paris on May 6th—weighed 97 lbs. from my normal of 178—still had mud in my hair from February 3, 1945.

I was flown to The U.S.A. on May 12, 1945 to Cushing General Hospital where I had bone grafts, etc. and was a patient until October 26, 1946.

Jack recovered from his wounds and was discharged with the rank of captain in 1946. Since his service he has lived a most interesting life and when he wrote in 2002 he said his wife allows him to play golf every day in his retirement. They live in New Hampshire and his word to everyone is "MAKE EVERY DAY A GOOD ONE."

B-24 Operations In Verse

While stationed at Hethel I had acquired a copy of a song that chronicled the woes of preparing for and flying missions in the B-24s and its authors were unknown to me. I lost my copy after the ending of World War II. I remembered only a few verses and that it had been sung to the tune of "Bell Bottom Trousers."

A half century later I wrote a letter to the Editor of "The Second Air Division Association Journal" asking if anyone familiar with this song would send me a copy.

Shortly after my letter was published I received the following letter:

Dear Al,

Let me introduce myself as Baldwin (Baldy) C. Avery. I scan most of the articles in the 2nd Air Division Journal quite carefully and was brought up short when I caught the words "Bell Bottom Trousers" in your letter in the last Journal. I was sure there must be a connection to a song I helped put together way back in WWII when I was a fly-boy in the 8th Air Force in England.

I was one of the three authors of the song to which you referred in your letter. It all started when Lt. Stan Neal, Lt. Johnny Constable and myself were of the original cadre in the 445th Bomb Group in England. We were all pilots in the 701st Squadron and good friends. Our song writing career began one evening after returning from a raid on Christmas Eve in 1943 to Bonnieres, France. I won't go into the particulars on the raid but the whole mission was a disaster. It may not have been Christmas Eve but it was one of those No-ball jobs. Our leader put us into a too tight a turn for controlled formation flying and many of us dropped our bombs in the channel. Our C.O., Colonel Terrill, immediately called a meeting of all participating crews and gave us a royal chewing-out and declared the raid would be considered a "sortie." (At the time it took two sorties to equal one raid.) Neal, Constable and I thought the situation called for a drink and took off for the club. By the time we got there we had composed the following to the tune of "Pony Boy."

> Sortie Boy, Sortie Boy, won't you join our sortie, boys,
> We can't fly high, we fly too loose, far across the sea.
> We stop the flak, we don't come back, we do it all for joy
> For we're the 445th Sortie Boys.

Soon after we reached the club, we had everybody singing the song. It evidently swept through the base, because the next night I just happened to be in the club again, when Colonel Terrill confronted me and said he understood I had a song to sing for him. I hemmed and hawed and said it was really nothing at all, all the time looking madly around for Neal and Constable. The colonel just looked at me and said, "Sing it." Naturally, I sang it, much to the enjoyment of all my grinning buddies standing around behind the colonel. The colonel thanked me and walked off. I figured the Group owed me something since the next day an order came out changing the mission in question to a "raid."

We evidently thought we were pretty good, because soon after that, we made up this song:

"HARD ASS LUCK"

By Lt. Neal, Lt. Constable, Lt. Avery

Early in the morning, before the break of day,
Along comes the sergeant and pulls us from the hay,
"Briefing in an hour, boys—at school room number one,
Now don't get excited, it is an easy one."
(Chorus)
Singing hard-ass luck boys, nothing I can do,
Give me your card and I'll punch a hole for you.

We stumble to the mess hall to see what we can beg
And what do you think we get, boys, good old powdered eggs.
Next comes the briefing, to answer to roll call.
Will it be Berlin or is it a No-Ball?
(Chorus)
We wander to our locker room to gather all our stuff,
They don't have our sizes, I tell you boys it's tough.

Finally, we're ready, but then we have to wait
A half an hour or more for the men who navigate.
(Chorus)

We go out to our planes to see if things are fit,
We have three turrets out and all the engines spit.
But that doesn't faze us, we want to do our bit
We'd rather have to ditch than quit on the taxi strip.
(Chorus)

Then comes the takeoff with all the Libs in line,
The zebra goes down the way exactly on time.
We make a propwash takeoff, the turbos run away,
Our RPMs fluctuate, then we hear the tower say—
(Chorus)

Then we assemble around splasher six,
Boy, what a rat race, it nearly makes us sick.
We start out on our course and everything is fine
Until we reach Beachy Head a half an hour behind.
(Chorus)

We reach the other coast and run into some flak
There should be a hole there but there's no turning back.
Then we hit the IP, we never know we're there
Because the squadron leader forgot to fire a flare.
(Chorus)

The tail gunner calls and says there's something wrong,
Both guns are jammed and his oxygen is gone,
The bombardier is fast asleep, the glass is all frost,
The radio man has fallen out, the navigator's lost.
(Chorus)

We turn into the target, the sky is really black—
We think it is a thunderhead, but it is only flak.
We swing down the target and start our journey home,
We hear the Jerries singing o'er the interphone.
(Chorus)

When we get back to the base, the sky is really dense, They
briefed us for CAVU but now it is ten-tenths .

We come in for a landing—they fire a red-red flare,
But nobody goes around because he doesn't dare.

(Chorus)

The moral of the story is plain as you can see
It's never bring your bombs back from old Germany.
S-2 doesn't like it, nor does Colonel T.,
You can't go home with twenty-five sorties.

(Chorus)

Our song-writing career did not last very long. Stan Neal went down on February 20, 1944 on a Brunswick raid (no chutes), and four days later on a raid to Gotha, Johnny Constable got it (twelve Group planes lost). I looked up one of his gunners, Sgt. Nichols, back in 1947—he was the only survivor. I guess I was the lucky one since I lasted until May 12 before ending up in one of Hitler's summer camps, Stalag Luft III. When I returned to the States in June 1945, I looked up Constable's father in NYC and had a couple of drinks with him at the Commodore Bar. Johnny was 21 years old. Yes, I know, there were a lot of guys younger than he that didn't come back. I flew 15 raids with the 445th before being transferred to a Pathfinder Squadron in the 389th.

When "Baldy" penned the foregoing letter he was living in Florida and golfing at every opportunity. In the Winter 2006 issue of the 389th Bomb Group Newsletter he writes a letter to the editor saying that he has moved to Pennsylvania, trading in the sun and sea of Florida for the changing seasons of PA, and philosophizing "Hurricanes vs. snow, it's a toss up."

We hope he will continue singing at whatever he does and many blessings to him. I am grateful for the privilege of presenting his story.

The Dishonoring of a World War II Veteran

In Chapter two I write about my grade school friend, Grover Bowen, who was killed while fighting in Italy during World War II. In 1961 a new Army Reserve Training Center in Rolla, Missouri and home to the Missouri National Guard was dedicated and named for Grover.

In 2001 Grover was dishonored by the renaming of the armory for former Governor Carnahan who had died in a plane crash while campaigning for the U.S. Senate. I have addressed two different legislative committees in the Missouri Legislature in an effort to induce action to rescind the abominable effrontery by a political cadre.

The following paper tells the story of the sordid renaming. I have distributed this letter extensively and continue to do so, using it also in campaigning prior to elections of legislative representatives.

FOREWORD

The following story, "The Dishonoring of a World War II Veteran," is one that should be told to every citizen of the United States. Missourians, especially, ought to be informed because the locale of the story is Missouri.

With a contemporary revival of patriotism and recognition of our military personnel and veterans it is time to remind people that their applause, accolades and honors should not be tenuous or temporary. Honors bestowed must not be forgotten or subjected to usurpation or abrogation.

The Dishonoring of a World War II Veteran

On November 22, 2001, just two months after the debacle of September 11, the U.S. Army Reserve Training Center that is also home to the Missouri National Guard's 1438th Engineer Company in Rolla, Missouri was renamed and dedicated posthumously to former Governor Mel Carnahan in a big ceremony with participation by a lot of people including the local VFW Post 2025. What hypocrisy…they celebrated Veterans Day while concomitantly dishonoring a brave and decorated WW II soldier who sacrificed his life for our nation. You see, the armory when new in 1961 was dedicated and named for Grover E. Bowen and he had been honored until this willful act of renaming took place.

Grover was born and raised at Seaton, Missouri, located in Phelps County and not far from Rolla. On October 15, 1944 he was killed in action in northern Italy while defending our nation during WW II. He had been awarded the Silver Star and many other commendations for heroic and meritorious services.

Our senior Missouri U.S. Senator Christopher "Kit" Bond spearheaded this act of renaming the armory. I first heard of his plans from an AP news release of December 29, 2000. Immediately, I protested vigorously to Senator Bond in a letter of December 30, 2000. Sen. Bond did not respond to me and has stonewalled me to this day. Yet in the face of objections and with full knowledge that the armory was already named meritoriously for an honored WW II veteran he proceeded with arrangements to rename the armory. Obviously, he must have had a lot of help in the implementation of this act including the Missouri Governor, the Missouri Adjutant General and the acquiescence of Senator (appointed) Jean Carnahan. They abused our trust to serve their will. The Bowen Family was not aware that Grover's name and honor had been abrogated until quite some time after the renaming shindig was over. The people responsible for the dishonoring of Grover do not deserve the honor of representing the great state of Missouri.

Senator Jean Carnahan spoke at the renaming of the armory ceremonies and quoting the "Rolla Daily News", she said, "This armory is a 'fitting' tribute to Mel," but nothing was said by Sen. Carnahan or anyone else present about how "fitting" it was to usurp Grover's name. In fact, the local media covered this event extensively and at no time were the people informed that this was a renaming and that the armory was named in honor of Bowen in 1961. The local media covered the 1961 dedication and honoring ceremonies and they knew what was going on.

Yes, Grover E. Bowen was my friend and one of my heroes. I am a veteran of WW II and flew 30 combat missions as a navigator of B-24 bombers with the Mighty Eighth Air Forces. I was one of the fortunate...I came home alive, Grover and many others did not. I seek no honors, medals or recognition from the State of Missouri. I do appeal to the citizenry of Missouri to stand with me to nominate and elect local, state and federal government representatives who will fully restore all bestowed honors to Grover in perpetuity...and as they were in 1961 and for 40 years until November 11, 2001.

Albert V. Malone

Epilogue

Bowen relatives did not know about the dishonoring of Grover until March 5, 2002. Immediately they began to survey the situation and to contact people involved. Then they launched an appeal campaign to the people of Missouri through the media. As a result, the Missouri Adjutant General's public relations officials met with the Bowen Family at the Rolla Armory and proposed to honor Grover separately naming a section of the armory after him and calling it "The Military Educational Facility." Purportedly, the AG would sponsor a dedication ceremony for this newly created entity. At this time Another sign has been installed at the South entrance that leads to the rearward portion of the armory structure, Wording on the sign reads, "Staff Sergeant Grover E. Bowen Military Educational Facility.

Four years later there has not been a dedication ceremony.

Dear readers, I believe you get the picture.

AVM

Please feel free to copy and distribute this message.

We will continue to work to restore the honor of Bowen. In any case we hope to obtain Missouri legislation that will not allow the changing of a military monument or memorial without an official public hearing by the administering agency. May this example of political chicanery also serve as a warning to other states and government entities that do not have laws governing the preservation and care of their many precious remembrances.